Soul Sex

Tantra for Two

By

Pala Copeland
and **Al Link**

NEW PAGE BOOKS
A division of The Career Press, Inc.
Franklin Lakes, NJ

SOUL SEX
EDITED BY STACEY A. FARKAS
TYPESET BY EILEEN DOW MUNSON
Cover design by Lu Rossman/Digi Dog Design
Cover and inside photographs by Bernard McCaffrey
Illustrations by Amanda Watters and Steve Copeland
Printed in the U.S.A. by Book-mart Press

To order this title, please call toll-free 1-800-CAREER-1 (NJ and Canada: 201-848-0310) to order using VISA or MasterCard, or for further information on books from Career Press.

The Career Press, Inc., 3 Tice Road, PO Box 687,
Franklin Lakes, NJ 07417
www.careerpress.com
www.newpagebooks.com

Library of Congress Cataloging-in-Publication Data

Copeland, Pala.
    Soul sex : tantra for two / by Pala Copeland and Al Link.
        p. cm.
    Includes bibliographical references and index.
    ISBN 1-56414-664-2 (pbk.)
        1. Sex instruction. 2. Sex—Religious aspects—Tantrism. 3. Man-woman relationships.
        I. Link, Al. II. Title.

HQ31 .C816 2003
613.9'6—dc21   2002041091

**To Paul Welch,
who helped us find
faith and courage.**
Your Higher Self and Essence Training made it
possible for us to write this book..

There are many others who have contributed to the creation of *Soul Sex*. We offer our heartfelt thanks to: our extraordinary photographer Bernard McCaffrey; our playful models, including Leslie Fraser-Dobson, Shawna Morrissette, Dale Seibold, Roger and Kathy McArthur, and Lee Andrews; our extremely talented illustrators Amanda Watters and Steve Copeland; our motivating literary agent Mark Ryan; the helpful professionals at New Page Books; Rich Corman for timely edits; the many wonderful people who have participated in our Workshops and have inspired us with their daring, openness, and passion; and our families whose love and support bring continual joy to our lives.

If you would like to contact Pala and Al with any comments about this book:

E-mail: 4freedoms@tantraloving.com
Internet: *www.tantra-sex.com*
Telephone: 1-819-689-5308
P.O. Box 144
Pembroke, ON
Canada K8A 6X1

Contents

Preface

Late Autumn 1987

It was the early days of our romance. In Ottawa on a clandestine lovers' weekend, we spent most of the time in our hotel room greedily exploring each other. Late Saturday night, we lay side by side breathing deeply, our sweat soaked bodies flung wide, gathering ourselves for another round of life's most joyous dance. I stretched my leg so that my toes rested on Al's instep. As my skin touched his, electric pulses raced through me, from my toes through my legs and groin, all the way up to my head and back down. On the outside, I was barely moving. My body was a lacy ribbon waving lazily on a light summer breeze. Inside, it was as if the entire lava load of an erupting volcano were surging through my veins at incredible velocity. Every fiber of my being was shot through with light, like a time-lapse photo of car headlamps beaming down a dark roadway. I closed my eyes and let the blaze run. The familiar blackness behind my eyelids became a deep blue, vast, open, and welcoming. Huge purple orbs floated by, amethyst geodes trailing light. I lay in ecstatic wonder marveling at the beauty and the glory.

When I moved my foot away from Al's, breaking the spell of our connection, the flowing stopped. When I touched him again, it recommenced. Experimenting, I touched our bodies together at different spots—finger to nipple, hip to thigh, forehead to forehead. Each joining made a bridge for the transporting energy stream. My heart opened. Love poured in with the fire. The laughter of bliss rose up from its flames. Unable to speak, I could only keen trilling "ohs" into the night. Like a kiss from God, the merging came, a melting into Al, the room, the city. I was All, and All was rapture. When daylight found us, I was still flying high on love's ardent wings.

"What was *that*? Where did it come from? Do you think we can do it again?"

"Probably. I think what we experienced was something I have heard about called Tantra," replied Al, my new lover, my seeker of enlightenment, and explorer of all things spiritual.

We set off for the nearest bookstore to find out more about this mysterious Tantra. It was the beginning of a journey that has wrought extraordinary change in our lives, brought us ecstatic pleasure and intimate connection, and freed our hearts and awakened our spirits. It is a journey that continues.

Introduction

"Make love a creation, and life becomes art."

—Al Link

We are lovers still. Day by day and minute by minute, we recreate our love. It is quite simple, but it is not always easy. We have learned what to do and how to do it with the help of teachers and books, but mostly through our own experiments. We are self-taught lovers.

For most of our lives, sex has been a driving force for both of us, as has the desire for connection with God. In our culture, these two forces do not usually go together. When we met each other and fell into an intensely passionate relationship, it satisfied our sexual desire, but not our spiritual longing. Over time, however, we discovered that our relationship itself, our conscious loving union, could become our pathway to divine connection. Modern Tantra, which combines sexuality and spirituality in a practical, down-to-earth way, provided the perfect vehicle. Now, Tantric sacred loving is what we do full time, both in living and in earning a living.

In this book we describe how we teach others and what we actually do to keep our own relationship emotionally rich, sexually passionate, and spiritually evolving. Our purpose in writing this book is to motivate couples to act together to achieve something rare in the world: passionate relationships in which to grow spiritually together into old age, creating love year after year. We want to help you realize your dreams through discovering the four freedoms of Body, Mind, Heart, and Soul.

The 4 Freedoms

The First Freedom: BODY

"Longing, desire, and need
melt from our psyches
drip sparkling life—renewal
in these suits we call our bodies."

—Al Link

Awaken your senses. See, hear, smell, taste, and feel love. Know your body as a divine temple of love, carrier of the soul, manifestation of god and goddess. Become truly at home in your body—at ease, at peace, comfortable in your skin. Allow yourself to experience physical pleasure. Feed yourself and all around you with sublime, intimate human touch. You are your body. Your body is freedom.

The Second Freedom: MIND

"Our words meet and mingle
like hummingbirds
competing for space at the
scarlet feeder."

—Al Link

There are no limits. All limits are self-imposed. Change thought from being your master to being your powerful servant, a tool of your liberation. Turn your thinking on, and turn it off, when *you* want to. You have the power over what you think. You also have the power over *how* you think about things. Connect with your higher self for guidance and direction. You are your mind. Your mind is freedom.

The Third Freedom: HEART

"Hearts made sweet by surrender
to each other."

—Al Link

Heal your broken heart. Open your healed heart. Give and receive love easily, naturally, spontaneously, and unconditionally. Discover your lover within. Love yourself. Accept yourself. Forgive yourself. Know that you are worthy of love. Acknowledge and welcome the love of others. Dare to be the great lover you are. You are your heart. Your heart is freedom.

The Fourth Freedom: SOUL

"Souls made sweet by surrender to God."

—Al Link

Your body, mind, and heart are windows to your soul. Your soul transcends space and time. It is outside of cause and effect. Your soul is complete and perfect. When you communicate with your higher self, with god and goddess, you are communicating with your soul. Your soul has your body, mind, and heart within it. Your soul is what you are. Your soul is The Soul. Your soul is freedom.

Tantra helps you explore these four freedoms and make them your reality, not just in your relationship, but in all areas of your life.

What Is Tantra?

"Tantra is where sex is transformed into love
and love is transformed into
the higher self."

—OSHO

Tantra is a Sanskrit word that can be translated to mean "weaving." A spiritual belief system that originated in ancient Hindu and Buddhist cultures of India and Tibet, Tantra views the material world as a manifestation of the Divine. Everything is accepted and connected—woven together. The apparent division between body and spirit, between matter and energy, is an illusion. By consciously uniting perceived opposites (male and female, light and dark) human beings can transcend dualism and know that all is one.

The numerous schools of Tantra employ various forms of meditation, sacred sound, breath control, secret ritual, and prayerful thought as aids to enlightenment. Some also incorporate sexual activity as a means of spiritual awakening. The union of ordinary woman and man becomes the eternal coupling of Shakti (Divine Mother) and Shiva (Immortal Spirit). When connected in sacred, ritualized sex, our human bodies—mirrors of the cosmos—rejoin the wholeness of essential reality. Thus, Tantra weaves together sex and spirit. In much of Western society, Tantra has become associated primarily with this sexual–spiritual component. Most of the religious aspects of traditional Tantric sects, their complex philosophies, rituals, and deities are not included in this modern interpretation. Tantra has become a generic term encompassing a wide range of sacred sex practices. This is how we use the term Tantra in our work and in the title of this book: as an integration of sex and spiritual growth.

British scholars and travelers returning from India first introduced Tantra to the West in the middle of the 19th century. Foremost among them was Sir Richard F. Burton (1821–1890), co-founder of the Kama Shastra Society, through which he privately published his translations of the Eastern texts *The 1,001 Arabian Nights, The Kama Sutra, Ananga Ranga,* and *The Perfumed Garden.* Given the surface prudery of the time, these works provoked a hostile response.

However, during the same century, a series of Western sacred sex practices emerged. Each of these interpretations was given a unique, and often esoteric-sounding name. Most well known is Karezza, which was conceived by Alice Bunker Stockham, an American doctor who studied Hindu Tantra yoga in India. In Karezza, the sexual elements of Tantra are applied within the framework of Christianity. More recently, Westerners who flocked to India seeking wisdom during the late 1960s and early 1970s encountered Tantra at the ashrams of gurus such as Osho. Inspired by the healing power of these sexual secrets, pioneers such as Margo Anand, Nik Douglas and Penny Slinger, David and Ellen Ramsdale, and Charles and Caroline Muir brought the message to Europe and North America.

Tantra is particular to India and Tibet, but other cultures, such as the Taoists in China and the Cheyenne in North America, also developed sacred sex traditions that encouraged the intentional cultivation of sexual energy for spiritual growth, longevity, and creativity, as well as enhanced pleasure. Now, there are varieties of Tantric sexual practice evolving all around the world. Most of them share similar points of view and comparable physical techniques. Our work is an eclectic blend of these sacred sex teachings, current Western psychological approaches to well-being and intimacy, and techniques for energy work, both ancient and modern. Our Tantra philosophy can be summarized with the following four simple, easy-to-remember principles.

4 Tantra Principles

1. **Sex is good.** This includes physical pleasure and considers sex as a moral force. Sex is good because it is what people who love each other naturally do. It is normal and healthy human behavior. Consensual sex between adults is a primary expression of love. Among our most basic biological needs, sex is essential for reproduction and the survival of the race. Beyond this, it is also a primary way to fulfill healthy human desires for physical touching, deep pleasure, and emotional intimacy.

2. **Sexual energy and spiritual energy are the same energy.** Both energies are examples of "life-force energy." There are no words for this "energy" in the English language, but in East Indian culture, its equivalent is "prana;" in Chinese culture "chi." As the sexual energy charge builds during lovemaking, we increase our access to this basic life force. Sex offers a way to cultivate and use life-force energy for other purposes: giving and receiving pleasure, physical and emotional healing, creating love, and excelling in other areas of human endeavor such as science, business, the arts, and sports.

3. **Sexuality is a legitimate spiritual path.** Tantra is a form of yoga. Yoga means union. Tantric yoga includes the union of sexuality and spirituality. Sex and spirit are not two separate aspects of our selves. On the contrary, spiritual lovemaking is one of the simplest ways for ordinary people to experience mystical connection—union with themselves, their partners, and the Divine. The arbitrary separation of body, mind, and spirit in most cultures is an intellectual, psychological, and emotional tragedy of incalculable proportions. This error of judgment has been the cause of great suffering for countless generations of people. It is now time for sexual healing that can only be possible by reuniting sexuality and spirituality.

4. **We are each responsible for our own sexual fulfillment as well as our own personal and spiritual growth.** Despite popular belief, it is not your lover's job to bring you to sexual ecstasy. No matter how attentive or skillful your lover may be, unless you allow yourself to open fully to sexual pleasure, you will not reach the heights of orgasmic bliss. Performance anxiety is one of the killers of passionate sexual intimacy. When we each take responsibility for our own sexual pleasure and our own spiritual awakening, the pressure to perform is eliminated.

Elements of Tantric Practice

"How do I love thee? Let me count the ways.
I love thee to the depth and breadth and height
My soul can reach..."

—Elizabeth Barrett Browning

Our Tantric practice works on four levels, corresponding to our "four freedoms": body/physical, mind/mental, heart/emotional, and soul/energetic.

✤ On the physical level, you learn very specific techniques for joyous and extended lovemaking.

✤ On the mental level, you learn to shift habitual attitudes to sex, overcoming negative conditioning that may have taught you that sex is bad or shameful. Part of the training is developing the ability to focus, to become totally absorbed during lovemaking.

✤ On the emotional level, you learn to trust, to let go and surrender, and to open your heart.

✤ On the energetic level, you go beyond previously perceived boundaries to connect in ways that are much more than physical.

Tantra is about openness and transformation. Like most spiritual paths, sacred sex teaches a discipline of the mind and body. It does so amid joy and letting go of the sensual aspects of living. As a celebration of life, sacred sex teaches the importance of conscious awareness, of living totally within your actions. By focusing attention on your body and your mind, you become all-around healthier:

✤ Your emotions become more stable and more real.

✤ Your mental capacity increases.

✤ Your physical health improves as you learn to honor your body as the temple of your soul.

As for your sexual life, the glories that await you are beyond your imagination. The exercises and techniques fortify your entire urogenital system; you gain muscle strength, improved circulation, and heightened sensitivity. You shift your approach to lovemaking and learn exquisite new ways to please your partner and yourself. Ordinary lovemaking has a goal: orgasm. If you both come at the same time, you have really hit the jackpot. If neither of you come at all, you may as well have spent your time elsewhere. In Tantric loving, there is no goal. There is a purpose, however, and that purpose is union. Every aspect of your Tantric loving serves that purpose. Your intention is to merge with your lover in all aspects—body, mind, heart, and soul—not just body. As you let go of the goal of orgasms, you actually begin to have more of them. Tantra is a sure-fire way to keep the purely physical experience of sex exciting, new, and fresh for even the most long-term lovers.

Many people experience occasional, spontaneous moments of blissful oneness with their partner, with nature, with the Divine, during peak sexual experiences. With practice, you can learn to consciously create this rapturous spiritual union. As you master moving the sexual energy between your two bodies, you experience altered states of consciousness leading to ecstasy. In order to create enough sexual energy to move them into euphoric states of Divine connection, practitioners of Tantra make love for long periods of time, experiencing extraordinary levels of pleasure along the way. Tantric lovemaking involves conscious breathing, muscle contraction exercises, sound, visualization, meditation, sensual massage, sexual play, creating a sacred loving space, and other rituals. Largely through ceremony and ritual, we access our deepest consciousness and the soul. This aspect of Tantra, perhaps more than any other, transforms ordinary friction sex into *energy* sex and ultimately, if love is truly present, into what we call *soul sex*. As John Ruskin expressed it, "When love and skill work together, expect a masterpiece."

Extending far beyond the bedroom, sacred sex helps you open fully to your partner in trust and love through all facets of your relationship. Your relationship itself becomes a vehicle for spiritual growth and personal awareness. As you learn to open to yourself, to your own inner lover, you naturally open to others around you. You begin to understand that surrender does not mean submission or loss of self, but rather a loving expansion into something much greater than you.

The techniques and exercises we share in this book are what we actually do. Our essential approach is neither religious nor dogmatic, but spiritual. Playfulness is woven into the fabric of our loving—laughter and lust come hand in hand to the true lovers' bed. While we cannot guarantee that what is in this book will be effective for you, it is for us and for hundreds of couples with whom we have worked. We encourage you to experiment in order to discover what works and what does not. Keep the things that do and discard the rest. You have your own inner guide who knows what is best and what is needed. Pay attention and trust yourself to find what is right for you. Part of the delight of Tantric loving is that not only will you feel immediate results, such as more pleasure and closeness with your lover, but you can also continue to learn and advance throughout years of practice. Tantra is never-ending in its potential for personal and spiritual growth.

Who Should Read This Book?

If you think that sexuality can be more than what you learned in high school, if you are interested in combining sexuality and spirituality, if you want to take your relationship to a higher, more spiritual level, if you want a relationship that satisfies through and through, if you want to graduate from falling in love to creating love, and if you want to keep on creating love as you grow old together, then this book is for you. Wanting to take your relationship to a higher level does not mean there is anything wrong with it now. On the contrary, it likely means there is something very right about it.

This is not a book on finding love or falling in love. Rather, it is a book about creating love. Because our emphasis is on Tantra in relationships, both beginners and skilled Tantric practitioners will find value here. We offer ours as a role model for a successful long-term relationship in which we are each happy, fulfilled, and spiritually awakened. We help you learn how to:

⚭ Create love together over many years.

⚭ Keep sexual passion very hot to any age.

⚭ Keep focused on your personal growth so that spiritual (even mystical) experiences are regularly available to both of you.

Here you will find an abundance of practical tools and techniques for combining sexuality and spirituality in your daily life. Reading about Tantric relationships will help to expand your knowledge and awareness, but you must actually do the exercises to really make a difference. You will notice as you read that we use the terms "he" or "she" in various instances rather than the awkward "he/she" or "(s)he." "He" and "she" are used interchangeably to refer to both men and women unless we are speaking of decidedly male or female situations.

Benefits of Relationship Tantra

As you work with this book, you will continually be encouraged to reach a higher logical level. You will be invited to be fully present in every moment, completely aware of what you are doing and fully immersed in it. For example, you will not only breathe, you will breathe intentionally in specific ways. You will not only make love, you will use Tantric lovemaking techniques in full awareness of what you are doing and what you want to create. You will learn to dress and undress deliberately, to speak consciously, to notice the mood you are in, the expression on your face, your body language, and how these things affect your lover and yourself.

If the practice of Tantric sacred loving works for you, as it has for us and for many couples, then how you experience each day can be transformed dramatically. Everything you do will gradually become more real, regaining a significance that may have gotten lost in your daily living. You will start to feel connected to your environment, to the people around you, and to your lover. You will start to feel fully alive, awake, and alert. You will be energized and motivated. Your libido will increase, perhaps sharply if you had previously been suffering from a lack of sexual desire. You may feel such strong desire for your lover that you leave work early to come home for a surprise visit of passionate lovemaking, even though you have been married for years.

You may notice that you start to hum and sing and whistle again with the sheer happiness of your being. You will start to think creatively and apply this in your art, your family, your business, and your community. You will be delighted and amazed at the moments of "Aha!" as your deeper consciousness offers up solutions to problems you have been struggling with. Your face will glow and your spirit will radiate an inner beauty that magnetically attracts the people around you. Laughter will return to your life. You will start playing and having fun. You may even allow yourself to be foolish, acting like a kid again. You will smile. You will want to get out of bed in the morning and you will want to get back into it with your lover. You will experience the pleasure and connection you have dreamed of.

Chapter 1

Relationship as Spiritual Practice

"Someday, after we have mastered the winds,
the waves, the tide and gravity, we shall harness
for God the energies of love. Then, for the
second time in the history of the world, man
will have discovered fire."

—Pierre Teilhard de Chardin

Our extraordinary sexual pleasure and intense mystical connection continued to grow as we went deeper into our Tantric practice. We progressed steadily, but unevenly, along our sacred sex path—sometimes making great strides forward, other times falling back. Although our personal vitality and individual learning capacity affected our headway, the most noticeable influence came from the state of our relationship. When we were in sync emotionally and feeling good about each other, we could often reach the heights of bliss. If issues arose between us or if one of us was preoccupied with something else, the magic would not happen.

Tantra stresses the importance of conscious awareness and intention, as well as opening your heart. As we focused on becoming more aware, we saw that our lives outside the bedroom had a huge impact on what occurred in it. We realized that if we wanted to connect totally in our Tantric sex, we had to make our relationship the best it could be—all the time. After talking it over carefully, we decided to make our relationship the most important thing in our lives. The only thing of greater importance is our individual connection with the Divine, but because our relationship is also our spiritual path, this does not create a conflict. It is through our relationship that we come to God and give love to the world. Putting our intention into practice—daily remembering and acting on our importance to each other—visibly accelerated our mastery of Tantric skills. *As you commence your own sacred loving journey, your best possible starting point rests in a relationship that is your top priority.*

When we say our relationship is the most important thing, we mean that it takes precedence over our work, our children, our family and friends, our community, and our own needs to control or to be right. This does not mean that those other things are not important to us or that we ignore them. We are not promoting *ego à deux*, wherein we become so absorbed with one another that we lose concern for anyone or anything else. On the contrary, when we give more to each other, we have more to give the world. When our relationship is strong and vital, all aspects of our lives benefit because we have more patience, stamina, and enthusiasm.

How Important Is Your Relationship?

"Time is a created thing. To say, 'I do not have time' is
like saying, 'I do not want to.'"

—Betty Elliot

Ninety-three percent of Americans say they hope to form a lasting, happy union with one person.[1] Perhaps you also long for a fulfilling relationship. If you do, what really matters is not what you say or what you think you believe, but what your *behavior* demonstrates. Many couples tell us, "Oh yes, our relationship is the most important thing," and in the next breath add, "but we cannot find time for each other in our busy lives." Careers, children, community, and individual needs may often seem overwhelming in their immediate demands for time and attention. All too frequently, the primary relationship takes second place. As we explore the aspects of life that can draw attention away from your relationships, do you recognize any of your own behaviors?

Career: There is no getting around having to pay the rent. Most of us do have to work to earn a living, and career choices are undeniably some of the most important decisions we make. However, is your career more important than your relationship?

People begin their careers wanting to be successful, to achieve advancement, and to gain recognition. Competition with others can be severe, even ruthless. Therefore, you work very hard, putting in lots of hours. Perhaps there is stress involved, and you may become anxious and worried and begin to take it out on your partner. Alternatively, maybe your creative juices are flowing, and you are so wrapped up in the process that you cannot let it go. You begin to think about your work all the time and start to bring it home with you. On the other hand, perhaps you are a small business entrepreneur in a home office, and the job never leaves.

Another possible scenario is that you may not really like your work, but you absolutely need the income. You have chosen a standard of living that requires toys—computers, DVD players, digital cameras, sport vehicles—and you have run up debts. Now you have no choice but to work even harder, and the relationship suffers.

Maybe you know people, we certainly do, who have been in this situation: Career is everything. They seem to be living to work rather than working to live, and then suddenly their lover dies or simply leaves the relationship. Only then do they realize what their priorities have been and what it has really cost them. In the face of the loss of their love, the work that was so important does not mean anything anymore—they may not even go to work. The toys they had to have now mean nothing.

Children: Children require love, attention, and guidance to grow into healthy adults, but sometimes parents can become so preoccupied with their kids that they forget about each other. They may feel guilty about leaving their children during the day for jobs and so will not take more time away from them in the evening for their mate. Alternatively, they may be so drained by looking after little ones all day that they have no energy left for their lover. Many parents spend much of their free time driving children to and from activities. Often they say, "We'll have lots of time for each other when the kids are grown up." However, by then, because of years of neglect, they have nothing left in common and drift apart or divorce. Or, because of neglect, the relationship ends while the children are still young, and one or both of the parents hardly sees the children for whom they sacrificed the relationship in the first place.

We understand how important children's needs are—we have six children ourselves—but children must not become an excuse to hide from intimacy with your mate. If you give everything to your children so nothing is left for each other, there is a high price to be paid. Although your children may benefit from all the attention you give them, on another level they will lose, for where will they learn how to create a successful, passionate, loving relationship? They will not likely find it in the movies, on television, or in the homes of their peers. Most of us grow up never having seen what it is like for a couple to be happy together over a long period of time. The only role models most of us have witnessed, are of falling in and out of love frequently or of two people staying together out of a sense of duty while living separate lives under the same roof.

It is also quite common for parents to be embarrassed about sex and to avoid showing affection and intimacy in front of their children, but if you are comfortable with your sexuality, as Tantric practice enables you to be, if you can show affection freely and talk openly about sex, you can become a marvelous relationship role model.

Community: Community action and worthy causes are other grand ways of diverting attention from your relationship. Many who are dedicated to a cause feel they are making an important contribution to the world, and their relationship will just have to fit in somewhere, when there is a spare hour or two. They act as if it were selfish to take time to build their relationship, but selfless to sacrifice it for the greater good.

Although the world desperately needs committed, caring citizens, you do not have to deny your relationship to be an active citizen. By creating a loving relationship, you can have more to give to the world, because you will be nourished, healed, and energized. The loving energy you make can be shared generously with those near to you and energetically can have a powerful effect on the quality of consciousness around the planet.

Importance of Relationship Exercise

Answer these questions to help you determine the importance of your relationship compared to other aspects of your life. Look at what your priorities really are, based on an evaluation of how you actually spend your time. You may discover that your priorities are different than you thought they were.

Most important is that you and your partner become aware of each other's priorities. Are you in agreement about how important your relationship is? Are you in agreement about how important it *should be*? Does how you spend your time accurately reflect what you say your priorities are?

- How many hours are taken for work, including travel, and work that you bring home?

- If your work is at home, whether it be caring for family or a home-based business, how many hours per day does it take?

- How many hours do you sleep?

- How many hours do you spend preparing and eating food?

- How many hours do you spend on personal care: bathing, dressing, exercising, and so on?

❧ How many hours do you spend maintaining the household: laundry, washing the car, general tidying, working in the garden, making repairs, and shopping for all the stuff you need?

❧ How many hours do you spend on personal activity: reading, watching TV, watching the moon rise, meditating or other spiritual practice, hobbies, sports, taking courses or practicing your avocation (music, painting, amateur athletics, woodworking), and so on?

❧ If you have children, how many hours do you spend with them: playing, taking them to activities, and helping with homework?

❧ How many hours do you spend on community activities: volunteering, church/religious organizations, political and social causes?

❧ How much time do you spend with friends or family in social activities, either on your own or with your mate?

❧ How many hours do you spend on your relationship with your mate? We mean time that is actively spent building your intimate connection, where the focus is totally on each other and increasing your love, such as romantic dining, making love, reading each other poetry, dancing, massage, and heartfelt talk. Exclude from this list activities that you may do together but during which you are essentially focused on yourself or people and things other than your mate, for example, watching TV or movies together; attending the kids' school play; volunteering for the same service club; talking about family issues, finances, and vacation plans; doing the yard work; and having a party with friends.

List and total all of your hours. What does this tell you about how you are spending your time and what your priorities are?

Sorting Out Your Priorities

Work

1. Now that you have added up all the hours you spend on work, are you comfortable with this use of your time? Is your spouse in agreement? If not is there time you can borrow from work to spend on your relationship?

2. How often do you cancel or postpone time you were to have with your partner because something has come up at work?

3. Have you ever had a conflict between something scheduled for work and something scheduled with your lover when you said *no* to your work and *yes* to your lover?

4. If you were offered relocation for your work, would you consider the impact this would have on your relationship as part of your decision? Does your partner have a say in this decision? Is it really an option to say *no* to the move?

5. Are you coming home from work so stressed out that you are lashing out at your partner?

6. Are you coming home from work so tired and frazzled that you just want to be alone with the TV?

7. Considering all your answers, including time devoted to work, is your work more important than your relationship? Are you and your partner in agreement that this is how it should be?

Children

1. Are you regularly using the time you spend with your children as a reason why you do not have time for each other?

2. Do you often find yourself under so much stress from your kids that you lash out at your partner?

3. Do you often find yourself so exhausted from kids that you do not have time or energy for your partner?

4. Considering all your answers, including time devoted to children, are your children more important than your relationship? Are you and your partner in agreement that this is how it should be?

Causes

1. Do you have a cause that you regularly give time to (volunteer work, political activism, and so on)?

2. Is the amount of time you spend on this cause acceptable to you? Is it acceptable to your partner?

3. Do you ever find yourself under so much stress from your commitment to a cause that you lash out at your partner?

4. Do you often find yourself so exhausted from your commitment to a cause that you do not have time or energy for your partner?

5. Considering all your answers, including time actually devoted to a cause, is this cause more important than your relationship? Are you and your partner in agreement that this is how it should be?

Social Activities and Friends

1. Is the amount of time you spend on social activities alone or together a source of tension or disagreement in your relationship?

2. Do you always say *yes* to your friends' needs or social invitations? Do you sometimes say *no* because you want time for your partner?

3. Considering your answers, including time devoted to friends and social activities, are they more important than your relationship? Are you and your partner in agreement that this is how it should be?

Avocations

Note: An avocation is something you love to do and spend a lot of time doing, but you do not get paid for doing it, that is, it is not your paid employment. You might think of it as a hobby that starts to take over your life.

1. Is there some activity that you love so much that you give a lot of your time to it?

2. Does your partner feel neglected or resentful because you spend large amounts of time doing something you love to do?

3. Do you often find yourself so tired out by this activity (or so preoccupied—even when you are not doing it) that you do not have time or energy for your partner?

4. Considering your answers, including time devoted to your avocation, is it more important than your relationship? Are you and your partner in agreement that this is how it should be?

If after doing these exercises the reality is that your relationship is a low priority, or lower than you thought or said it was, then you are presented with a choice. Your options are to change how you spend your time, finding more time for each other, or do nothing and keep things as they are. If you do want to make your relationship a higher priority, the rest of this book gives you ways to do so, through a variety of Tantric techniques and specific tools for intimate connection.

Making Time for Each Other

How can you make your relationship your first priority? You can start as simply as blocking out two to four hours to spend together as Tantric lovers each week, regardless of how busy you are. Especially because of how busy you are! We actually put this time down as a date in our daily planners, so we can fit everything else around it.

Feeding your relationship is akin to saving money. No one ever accumulated net worth by trying to save whatever money was left over after all of their spending. The only way to save money is to pay yourself first. Set aside some of your income as savings, as if it were a bill you had to pay, before you spend it on anything else. Relationships are very similar. If you think you will fit each other into time left over, there will not be any. Moreover, if you do find a few minutes now and again, you will likely be too tired and stressed out to make good use of it. So, make a two- to four-hour Tantric date with your lover now—and keep it.

Keeping Focus on Your Relationship

Even though we know absolutely that when we focus on our relationship, life goes so much smoother, we can still become entangled in the world and act as if outside issues and tasks are more important. Time and time again, we forget and have to keep reminding each other. Here are some of the methods we use to keep our attention on our relationship:

- We make a commitment to it.
- We see it as a separate entity (our relationship image is a garden, something we have to tend).
- We follow it as our spiritual practice.

Commitment

> "Somewhere in her smile she knows
> That I don't need no other lover"
> —"Something," music and lyrics by George Harrison

Commitment is perhaps the most important factor for sustaining relationships. Real commitment comes from the heart, from the core of your personal beliefs, from the depths of your being. It can support you during periods of doubt or disquiet. If you want a lasting connection, make a commitment to your mate and to the relationship itself, and formalize these commitments, either through legal/religious marriage or through a personal marriage ceremony. Celebrating your relationship with ritual and ceremony marks the event, plants it firmly in your psyche, and gives it substance and meaning.

It is not enough to make your commitment once. In a national poll conducted for *The New York Times* in March 2000, more than 1,000 adults in all 50 states were asked: "If you got married today, would you expect to stay married for the rest of your life, or not?" Eighty-six percent said yes, and only 11 percent said no.[2] Unfortunately, this hopeful aspiration is not borne out by divorce statistics—four out of 10 marriages break apart.[3] This is partly because couples assume that the marriage itself will carry their commitment for them. They can fall into a trap of automatic behavior: taking each other for granted, allowing passion to die, losing interest in sex, forgetting kindness and respect. It is essential to keep commitment alive by renewing it again and again, recreating it from a new perspective as the two of you change over time. For instance, every year we remake our vows, renewing our pledge with as much thoughtfulness and excitement as on that first day long ago.

The Power of Monogamy

"How many husbands have I had?
You mean apart from my own?"

—Zsa Zsa Gabor

"I do not sleep with happily married men."

—Britt Ekland

Monogamy goes hand in hand with the type of lifelong commitment we are describing. The idea of sharing a loving connection in all ways with more than one person may appeal to you, as it has to us, but it is almost impossible to do well in our culture. We have both been married and divorced and have experimented with a variety of what are euphemistically called "lifestyle choices," including multiple partners. Now our preference is heterosexual monogamy. Having multiple partners did not bring us real happiness or peace of mind and often ended with considerable pain for everyone involved. While we continue to cultivate intimate relationships with other people—it is a rich and rewarding part of life—intimate *sexual* relations are only between us.

If you do choose a non-monogamous relationship, in addition to navigating the emotional minefields involved, you must also come to terms with limits of your energy and time. With the several hundred couples we have worked with, even for those who say their relationship is the most important thing, one of the most challenging issues is to make time for each other. How then could you make room for another lover without taking time away from your primary relationship?

29

Energetically, if you are focusing your sexual attention on someone else, you are not sharing it with your mate. The practice of sacred sex—high-energy states of ecstasy where the boundaries disappear and you join as one—requires an extraordinary degree of trust, an open heart willing to give and receive love. This is challenging to accomplish under ideal conditions, and adding multiple sexual partners exponentially complicates the situation. It would be extremely rare that anyone could honestly say, "I am having sex with someone other than my mate, because it is good for my mate and good for our relationship."

Viewing Your Relationship as a Separate Entity

"Happiness must be cultivated.
It is like character.
It is not a thing to be safely let alone for a moment,
or it will run to weeds."

—Elizabeth Stuart Phelps

In Tantric practice, you learn the power of visualization, which you can use to help you focus on your relationship. Formulate an image of your relationship as a separate entity created by the two of you but possessing its own integrity and independence. You are both responsible for it, and you are both responsible to it. There are many images to choose from as metaphor for your relationship: a beautiful child, a thriving corporation, a flourishing garden, a wise spiritual guide.

We see our relationship as a garden. If you plant seeds in a garden, in a clear, sunny spot of tilled, rich earth, soon they will sprout in a beautiful flurry of color. You may be delighted and proud. If you simply leave it on its own, weeds will quickly grow and overrun your lovely plants. Your garden will go to ruin. Relationships are very similar to this, and just as a garden requires continual attention to reward us with its great bounty of foods for our bodies and flowers for our pleasure, so does the relationship. If you want love, ecstasy, joy, and harmony, you must cultivate them.

Many relationships start off like our garden: clean and fresh and bursting with life. When you and your mate establish an intimate connection, there is excitement, newness, passion, and great sex. Each of you is showing the other your best, and it is effortless. It feels marvelous, but soon enough you start to see each other's warts. You become aware of things in each other you do not like. Ironically, many of the things you found intriguing and attractive at the outset can soon be annoying or downright exasperating. Spontaneous becomes irresponsible. Self-confidence turns into bragging. Attention to details shifts to nit-picking. There may not be any actual difference in the way your lover is behaving, but you might see another side to the behavior or a different interpretation that did not occur to you before.

At the same time, the world begins to intrude with demands that cannot be ignored. You cannot continue to focus only on each other because, for example, you have been offered a job in another city, your paycheck runs out before the end of the month, you still do not get along with your mother, the kids are driving you crazy, you get the flu, someone crashed into your car in the parking lot, and his or her ex-spouse is calling again. In other words, the weeds spring up. This is a critical point in the relationship. Now it has to graduate to another level. You must give it the attention it needs. You have to start weeding the garden and planting more seeds, or the relationship will be lost in a tangled mess.

Paying attention is ongoing. Weeds never stop sprouting. Seeds always need replanting. There never comes a time when you can sit back and expect nothing but fruits and flowers. In addition, you constantly have to invent new ways to fight the weeds, because the old ways get stale and stop working. What was effective yesterday in keeping the world at bay will not be effective tomorrow. It can be especially dangerous when something that formerly worked stops working. It takes effort to find new solutions, but everyone wants it to be easy. You remember that your relationship was easy in the beginning and you still crave that easiness. The terrible temptation is to go out and find it with someone else, either in an affair or by ending the current relationship and beginning a new one. Sometimes the urge to run away from the effort of tending your relationship garden is overwhelming. Where do you find the motivation to persevere in making your relationship thrive in the face of obstacles and problems? An effective strategy is to begin to view your relationship as a spiritual practice.

What Is Spiritual Practice?

"Through Tantra, one's sins are burned."
—Mahasiddha Tilopa

Spiritual practice always includes a search for the deepest meaning in life. It can be a search for personal salvation or for a direct experience with the Divine. Those who have the faith would make any sacrifice to come face to face with God. When you see your relationship in this spiritual context, there is an extraordinary motivation to do whatever is needed to make it work. Our relationship is our spiritual practice and the primary form that practice takes is Tantric sacred sex. We consciously use our personal interaction to help us bring out the best in ourselves and in each other, to continually learn and grow, and to connect with God.

Something spiritual has two main characteristics: union and transcendence. Tantric sacred loving enables us to regularly experience both of these amazing states of consciousness. The exercises and activities presented in the following chapters will make it possible for you to know them as well.

Union

To unify means to bring separate parts together. It can happen on a number of different levels.

Union of the Person

> "As a man in sexual union with his beloved
> is unaware of anything outside or inside,
> so a man in union with Self
> knows nothing,
> wants nothing,
> has found his heart's fulfillment
> and is free of sorrow."
> —*Brihadaranyaka Upanishads,* IV.3.12-22

On a personal level, all the parts of yourself that may have been in conflict or even unknown are united, so that you become whole. Acknowledging all aspects of oneself puts into practice an essential tenet of Tantra: weaving together states of consciousness and being that seem to be contradictory or perhaps mutually exclusive. In bringing them together, you do not choose one or the other, and you do not really compromise. Rather, you find a new way, a way of integrating them into a larger, inclusive whole. In Pala's words, "We create new ways from two ways." In order to do this, you allow yourself to be guided by the wisdom of your heart.

Al's experience: In Al's experience, there exist parts of himself that in any rational way could not possibly go together. Some of those parts must be what Carl Jung called "Dark Shadow," such as cruelty, violence, and selfishness. Other parts are sublimely beautiful, generous, kind, loving, and selfless. Union on the level of the self brings all those parts together in such a way that he does not have to eliminate or deny the Dark Shadow elements. He does not have to be afraid of them or feel bad because they are there. On the other hand, he can incorporate all the beautiful parts without taking personal credit for the glory. As Tom Peters, popular management guru and author of *In Search of Excellence,* said, "We are simultaneously flawed and wonderful." One of Jung's important teachings is that if you can find a way to befriend the Dark Shadow, it will not come out in harmful, cruel, or antisocial ways. To be a whole person does not require that you are only good or perfect; it only requires that you be real.

Pala's experience: Pala also found acknowledging her Dark Shadow to be a special challenge. For years she was terrified of its power. If she let it out or even looked at it, she feared that it would take her over and she would become ruthless, manipulating, and controlling. Therefore, she tried to hide it, to be perfect, and most characteristically to be extremely nice. She saw herself as a great diplomat. In reality, she was a great appeaser who, by agreeing with everyone, was able to subtly maneuver people into doing what she wanted. Ironically her niceness was an ingenious form of control, the very thing she feared doing. Now she is less "nice," and more real and whole.

Union of the Lovers

The goal of Tantric sacred sex is not orgasm, but to experience union. As Emily Dickinson wrote, "The drop that wrestles in the sea, forgets her own locality, as I, towards Thee." Through the practice of Tantra, lovers commonly experience an ecstatic connection—the boundaries between them disappear, and it is as if they were one. They do not know where one body ends and the other begins. When Pala rests her hand on Al's back during intense loving it is as if she were touching her own body. As Al says, "One and one are two—these two are one."

Orgasm becomes a shared phenomenon. Through perineum massage (see Chapter 11, page 220), Pala feels the orgasmic energy building in Al's prostate. As it begins to move up through his body, this powerful force also flows into her body through her hand. When connected energetically, lovers can send orgasmic waves into and through each other from across a room.

Union With the Divine

The third level of union is connection with the Divine, merging with God/Goddess, the Creator, Cosmic Consciousness, or whatever your concept of the highest level of being—that which includes and *is* all and everything.

There are innumerable expressions of union with God in literature, art, and religious writings. Many of these expressions share similar sentiments—feelings of bliss and joy, expanded consciousness, open hearts. The language is usually poetic and mystical. Spiritual experiences are often difficult or impossible to describe concretely (hence the reluctance of the rational mind to be convinced), but everyone recognizes one when they are in it.

Sacred sex is one of the oldest, simplest, and most easily accessible forms of spiritual practice available to men and women regardless of religion, age, ethnic background, or education. It can lead to direct personal experience with the Divine. We invite God into bed with us. At first, this may seem like a blasphemous idea. However, when human beings completely surrender their egoism, when they have let go of all remnants of selfishness and control, when they are open to the life force rushing through their bodies, when they experience giving and receiving the most sublime pleasure and happiness, is this not a moment of exquisite closeness with the Creator?

> "To see a World in a Grain of Sand
> and a Heaven in a Wild Flower,
> hold Infinity in the palm of your hand
> and Eternity in an hour."
> —William Blake, *Auguries of Innocence*, ll. 1–4

Transcendence

> "You gain strength, courage, and confidence
> by every experience in which you really
> stop to look fear in the face.
> You must do the thing which you think you cannot do."
> —Eleanor Roosevelt

Transcendence, the other key aspect of spiritual experience, means going beyond perceived limits. Transcendence carries us beyond conditioned, learned behavior as well as beyond personality and narrow definitions of self. It even takes us outside space and time and beyond cause and effect.

On a *personal* level, we transcend when we act in spite of our fears, see something with new eyes, or open up to intense possibility. In practice, this translates into experiencing a different view of the self. We understand that we are much more than we thought. We can move beyond perceived physical limitations, for instance, being able to make love for hours and emerge nourished and strengthened, not drained and exhausted. During Tantric sacred loving, timelessness becomes common— five hours fly by in what seems a minute, and a minute is eternal. Sensory capacities are heightened. Sight, sound, taste, touch, and smell are sharper, more pronounced. Extrasensory perceptions such as telepathy reveal themselves. Your awareness can be somewhere other than where your body is.

Transcendence can also elicit intense emotions and feelings. Even completely ordinary things can appear extraordinarily beautiful. Hearts crack open—love comes and goes, receiving and giving in an easy, spontaneous way. There is a sense of having returned home to a state where nothing is lacking. There is no longer any need for faith, because there is a certainty, a deep inner knowing that everything is perfect the way it is. Everything is as it should be.

On the level of *relationships*, transcendence occurs when we move beyond our perceived boundaries between each other. This can occur as a mystical ecstatic experience during sacred sex. For example, we experience each other during those times of deep spiritual connection as god and goddess—Pala becomes very young, a timeless beauty, and Al metamorphoses into all sorts of fantastic creatures—some human, others animal.

Transcendence can also occur on what we might consider a more mundane level, when we challenge our assumptions about ourselves and our relationship. We can be absolutely positive that this is the "way I am," the "way you are," the "way men and women are." Then we break through those barriers to create something new. We let down our walls of emotion, ideas, and learned behaviors. In letting those walls down, it can seem as if we are going contrary to what we really are and that we will be unhappy or even diminished if we let go. When we transcend our self-imposed limits, however, we become greater than we could ever have imagined.

For instance, you might think you are not someone who is particularly sexual. You might see enjoying sex as bad or even sinful. You may fully believe there is no way you could act lustily, as in initiating sex with your lover by walking up to him in the middle of the day, unzipping his pants, and performing fellatio. Alternatively, you may feel like you are too tired to have sex or to be excited by your partner. You have reached your physical limits and you cannot go beyond them. However, if a dear friend you had not seen in 15 years suddenly appeared at your door, that tiredness would likely disappear. You would be lively, perky, and interested. You can make the same shift with your partner. That shift, the transcendence, is primarily an internal decision.

When you transcend, you choose to behave in a certain way to create what you want in your life. This requires you to change, to go beyond your limits. You do that thing you believed was bad (like mid-afternoon fellatio) or impossible (like changing sleepiness into wide-awake enthusiasm). You have an inner guide to help you differentiate conditioned feelings, which keep you stuck in old behaviors, from intuitive feelings that are based on growing forward. These intuitive actions will be seen to be right in practice, even though they might *feel* wrong when you first consider them. We are not suggesting that you throw out your sense of morality or ethics, but that you expand your moral framework beyond cultural conditioning to one based on trust in your higher self and your connection with God. Seek moral guidance from your inner guide instead of the conditioned ego. It becomes easier to listen to your higher self as you grow into your Tantric practice.

Relationship as Sacrament

Because our relationship is our spiritual practice, it can be elevated to the level of a sacrament. It is holy. At this level of relationship, you not only feel longing and sexual desire, but true fulfillment and profound gratitude. In the sacrament, your lover is worthy of worship and adoration. As Tantra teaches, treating each other like god and goddess, not only during lovemaking but also throughout each day, raises your quality of life to new heights. You seek and find the best in yourself and each other.

At first, thinking about your relationship as a sacrament, treating your lover as a god or goddess, can seem scary because you might feel you do not know how to do it or that you are incapable. It may seem corny or the stuff of fairy tales and storybooks. It may even seem blasphemous— "Am I placing my lover before God?" In reality, you and your lover are within God, part of all and everything. When you make your relationship the most important thing, revering it as a sacrament, it is natural, and possibly inevitable to share generosity and love, and to experience union and transcendence.

> "I hear and behold God in every object,
> yet understand God not
> in the least,
> Nor do I understand who there can be
> more wonderful than
> myself."
> —Walt Whitman, *Song of Myself*, 48–50

Chapter 2

Creating Love

"For one human being to love another; that is
perhaps the most difficult of all our tasks, the
ultimate, the last test and proof, the work for
which all other work is but preparation."

—Rainer Maria Rilke

"Let's fall in love,
Why shouldn't we fall in love?
Our hearts are made of it
Let's take a chance
Why be afraid of it?"

—"Let's Fall In Love," 1933
Words by Ted Koehler, music by Harold Arlen

Modern Western society adores falling in love. Songs—from hard-driving hip hop to crooners' ballads—extol its pleasures and passions; movies and plays entice us with its mystery; magazines and books give us advice on when, where, and how to do it; and advertising of all sorts uses the extraordinary appeal of falling in love to sell us everything from coffee to cars. Because falling in love is something that happens *to* you, it is ephemeral. It only lasts for a short time, then it stops happening to you. Unless you graduate to creating love, you experience the disappointment and disillusionment of falling out of love. We all know what is at the bottom of any fall—pain. As author Marilyn Peterson says, "You do not die of a broken heart, you only wish you did." Nevertheless, falling in love feels so wonderful that we can become addicted to it, rolling from one relationship to the next looking for that feeling again and again.

Although there are numerous examples of falling in love, over and over again, models of exciting, fulfilling long-term love are exceedingly rare. Models exist for stormy long-term, and companionable long-term, and emotionally dead long-term but not hot *and* stable long-term. Therefore, we are designing our own version of lusty, lasting love and hope to inspire you to do the same.

Graduating from falling in love to creating love requires desire, awareness, and effort. You must yearn to bring about a profound connection with another human being. You must be cognizant of those beliefs and behaviors that undermine you and those that assist you in your quest. In addition, you must be willing to take action, repeatedly, to support your dream.

Recognizing Relationship Fallacies

"You got to find somebody who likes the same stuff.
Like if you like sports, she should
like it that you like sports, and
she should keep the chips and dip coming."

—Alan, age 10

"No person really decides before they grow up
who they are going to marry.
God decides it all way before,
and you get to find out later
who you are stuck with."

—Kirsten, age 10

When you set out to learn about creating love, you will discover and confront a whole range of relationship fallacies and negative models that influence your beliefs about what is possible. Dismal examples abound from high profile, highly esteemed role models, such as political and business leaders, and film and sports celebrities. For example, according to *The New York Times,* former U.S. President Bill Clinton will receive an advance of more than $10 million from publisher Alfred A. Knopf Inc., for the rights to publish his memoirs—an amount believed to be the largest ever for a nonfiction book. "In agreeing to pay the extraordinary advance, Knopf is betting that Mr. Clinton will continue to be regarded as one of the fascinating personalities of the second half of the 20th century, captivating readers both in the United States and abroad."[1] Not a small part of Mr. Clinton's attraction is the fact that he was caught having an affair during his term of office and survived the political fallout. Whether intended or not, this sends a strong message to the world about marriage, commitment, and fidelity. It is not harmless that Mr. Clinton has become a powerful relationship role model, reinforcing fallacies about what relationships can and should be.

Here are some common relationship fallacies. Which ones form part of your personal arsenal, sabotaging your capacity to realize the fulfilling love you want?

❧ Because falling in and out of love is something that happens to you, you cannot do anything about it. You are not responsible for helping love to continue.

❧ Passion dies over time. Although you may have a loving relationship, the intensity will wane and it will become boring sexually.

❧ If you do have a passionate relationship—one that is hot and sexy—it will not be stable. The passion will spill over into all aspects of your relationship and you will have lots of fights. Such a stormy relationship will not last.

❧ Infidelity is inevitable—monogamy is just too monotonous in the long term.

❧ Wives and mothers should not look or act too sexy. Men have affairs for the satisfying sex they cannot have with the mother of their children.

❧ As men and women age, they lose interest in and capacity for sex.

❧ A true mate is someone who completes you, brings you what you want in life, fulfilling all your needs. You are two halves who only become whole together.

❧ If your mate really loves you, then he or she will know what you want.

❧ There are clearly defined roles for men and women in relationship, for example responsibility for housework, childcare, making money, and initiating sex. Although these roles are often assumed rather than openly discussed, they are strictly followed.

❧ Parents should hide their sexuality from their children.

We have done our own fair share of succumbing to relationship fallacies. Al was convinced that the delight of our relationship was too good to last. Based on his previous experiences, he feared it would sooner or later become boring or unstable. He did not believe, for example, that we could continue to have magical candlelit dinners with stimulating conversation that led to fevered lovemaking. At some point that magic would fade. But, when he shifted from assuming that the *circumstances* generated his enchantment to knowing that his *intention* and *active participation* did, that constricting belief disappeared. Wining and dining and loving each other remains a favorite and wonder-filled pastime.

Pala fell into the "I have found the one to complete me" trap, the myth of love described in Plato's *Symposium,* wherein original man was split in two by an angry and vengeful god and so is always searching for his other half—"human nature was originally one and we were a whole, and the desire and pursuit of the whole is called love."[2] She found in Al a wonderful lover, a provoking intellect, a thoughtful nature, and a spirit for growth. She believed these attributes of his would satisfy her needs—because he was a good lover, they would have great sex; because he had a challenging mind, she would be creative in her thinking; because he wanted to continually learn, her intellect would expand. It was a short step to making him responsible for the quality of their sex, the liveliness of their discussions, and the creativity of their learning. Now she understands that what makes a whole relationship is two whole people, each responsible for contributing all they can, individually, to grow together.

Carefully examine your own ingrained assumptions about relationships and how they affect your hopes and your actions. Recognizing your self-limiting beliefs is a first step toward changing them.

The Sexy, Spiritual, Long-term Relationship Model

"The sex was so good that even the neighbors had a cigarette."

—Unknown

"Sex is one of the nine reasons for reincarnation... The other eight are unimportant."

—Henry Miller

"A divine force shall flow through tissue and cell
And take the charge of breath and speech and act
And all the thoughts shall be a glow of suns
And every feeling a celestial thrill."
—Savitri (XI.I.710), by Sri Aurobindo,
Sri Aurobindo Ashram Publications Trust

So, you have decided you want to make a really great relationship and you have begun to recognize some of your assumptions that can block you from having one. Now, how do you know what that great relationship would look like if there are not any positive models to emulate? You make it up. You dare to imagine your heart's dreams. If, like many people, you find it difficult to clarify the details of what you want, you can work backwards. Identify what you do not want or what has not worked and translate that into the opposite to devise your ideal relationship picture. It is a strategy we have used at various times to develop our version of a sexy, passionate, and spiritual long-term relationship.

For instance, neither of us likes to be taken for granted, something that commonly happens even in good relationships. Complacency says to you, "Oh this is good, this is secure, this is a sure thing," and you start giving your attention and time elsewhere. In our evolving picture of a spiritual relationship then, this is not allowed to happen. You both understand that there are countless disruptions that could end your relationship, no matter how good it is now. So you pay attention to each other regularly.

Passion's disappearance is a common expectation over long-term union, especially as lovers move into middle age and beyond. In a hot and stable relationship, sexuality continues to be a vital force for nourishment and stimulation. Sexual expression is actively explored and cultivated, and encouraged to evolve over time.

In a conventional relationship, partners may not talk freely about their feelings or their needs and wants. They may be reluctant to reveal what is really going on, keeping secrets, perhaps deceiving or even lying to each other. Secrets and deceptions build powerful barriers to intimacy. In a spiritual relationship, lovers are willing to be vulnerable, to take risks. You reveal thoughts that may be scary, and ideas that you think the other person will not want to hear, but you tell them anyway because it is your truth. You share your insecurities as well as your triumphs. You let each other know what you like and do not like sexually. You talk about your fears and your desires. You recognize the human longing for touch and show each other affection, even in public—in spite of social conditioning that makes people embarrassed by open displays of affection, such as holding hands when you are walking down the street. As Johnny Mathis sings, "I feel like I'm clinging to a cloud, I can't understand, I get misty just holding your hand."

It is irritating and fruitless that partners frequently want to change each other, to fix what they consider are their mate's problems, or make their lover more like themselves. In a long-term committed relationship that is both lusty and spiritual, lovers have a deep respect for each other and a willingness to allow each other to be different. They endeavor to make those differences complementary rather than to change one another. It is not a blind love, pretending that the other is perfect, but it is unconditional—unreservedly loving despite your partner's flaws. This gives you each the freedom to be yourself, liberated from acting only to please your partner, or from pretending to be other than you really are. You can be comfortable in your own skin, because at least one other human being has accepted you fully.

Unconditional love does not, however, mean that your partner cannot help you discover ways to improve. Although your partner gives unconditional love despite your imperfections, this gift does not absolve you from doing your inner work. Instead, it gives you a secure platform from which to grow. In ordinary relationships without a spiritual dimension, people may keenly hold on to their "stuff," which keeps them from growing emotionally, psychologically, and spiritually. In the spiritual relationship, when your hot buttons are pushed, you welcome it as an opportunity to grow and to heal, even though this may be uncomfortable or painful. You are both willing to do your inner work so that you become fit for relationship.

The passionate and lusty spiritual relationship reinforces this urge to grow by focusing on the best in each of you. It is too easy and too common to be critical of yourself and your partner—to hide your glory, to dwell on your weaknesses and faults. Instead, you treat each other like god and goddess, you concentrate on the characteristics and behaviors that you most appreciate and enjoy, and encourage those to come out by reinforcing them with your attention. It is not expectation because expectation implies judgment or disappointment if it is not met. Rather, it is hope, belief and awareness that you have each made a commitment to bring out your higher self and you are willing to accept help along the way.

As you can see, starting from what we did not want helped us generate a picture of what we do want. In this case:

* Complacency and being taken for granted evolved into paying attention to each other regularly.

* Waning passion evolved into ongoing sexual vitality.

* Reticence and secretiveness evolved into open, vulnerable communication.

* Needing to change or fix the other evolved into loving unconditionally.

⚜ Staying stuck in old behaviors evolved into willingness to grow and learn.

⚜ Criticism evolved into encouragement.

Attention, vital sexuality, open communication, unconditional love, willingness to learn, and encouragement to do so then became elements of our model for an enduring, passionate relationship.

Qualities of Relationship vs. Characteristics of Partners

"In this world,
Where many, many play at love,
And hardly any stay at love,
I'm glad there is you…"
—"I'm Glad There Is You," music and lyrics
by Paul Madeira and Jimmy Dorsey

When asked to picture an ideal relationship, people often create a picture that focuses on the particular *characteristics* they would like in a partner. For instance: "I want a mate who makes me laugh, is a great lover, has lots of money," and so forth. This approach to developing relationships is limiting and puts the onus of responsibility for success on the other person. It can set you up for failure.

You can, however, shift your perspective just a little and consider an ideal relationship in terms of *qualities* of the relationship itself. In Chapter 1 we advised you to treat your relationship as if it was a third entity that you were responsible to and responsible for. Framing your relationship in terms of qualities of the relationship, rather than characteristics of each other, is one way to accomplish this. For example, change "I want a mate who makes me laugh" to "I want a relationship that is lots of fun"; "a mate who is a great lover" to "a relationship that is sexually satisfying"; and "a mate who has lots of money" to "a relationship that is financially secure." This approach gives you as much power and responsibility for creating success as it does your partner.

It is crucial that you understand the difference—one is about developing something *with* your lover; the other is expecting your partner to possess certain traits that will make things happen *for* you. Partners bring their *characteristics* with them into the relationship, whereas partners co-create *qualities* of the relationship. The essence of qualities is that they are inseparable from the relationship itself. They are an expression of how the two of you relate to and with each other.

Examples of relationship qualities are:

☩ Honest, open communication from the heart.

☩ Passionate sexuality.

☩ Making the relationship the most important thing.

☩ Hot monogamy.

Once you determine what qualities are most important to you in your relationship, then what matters is the match of those qualities between you and your partner. By concentrating on qualities you both want, you can take action to manifest them in your life together, indefinitely into old age.

Creating a Relationship Vision

"What they undertook to do they brought to pass.
All things hang like a drop of dew
upon a blade of grass."

—W. B. Yeats

"Wine-colored days warmed by the sun
Deep velvet nights when we are one."

—"Speak Softly Love," music and lyrics
by N. Rota and L. Kusik

In this exercise, together you develop a vision of what you want your relationship to be.

Step 1: Individual Desires

Working individually, think about and then list what you would like in your relationship. Use clear, simple, specific statements. Be sure to identify qualities of relationship rather than characteristics of partners, as explained previously. Describe what *you* would truly like. Know you are worthy to have it and dare to believe. Do not allow yourself to be limited by assumptions such as, "Oh, that is not possible" or "She would never agree to that" or "I should want this." Also, do not list what you think your lover wants; he's making his own list.

As a starting point for your list, consider what you would like in the following:

❧ Sexuality.

❧ Commitment, fidelity, relationships with other people of the opposite sex.

44

- Communication: sharing, talking about, revealing feelings.
- Time allocations with each other, children, family and friends, career, community.
- Finances.
- Home life: practicalities (location, ownership), and ambience (tidy/messy, orderly/casual, quiet/busy).
- Decision-making, authority, power.
- Children.
- Fun, play, leisure activities, vacation.
- Personal and spiritual growth.
- Health: diet, exercise, smoking, alcohol.
- Other topics that are important to you.

Here is a range of sample statements to assist you in developing your own ideas.

Sexuality

- For me, sex must be more than a physical release; I want to explore its spiritual aspects.
- I would like our sex life to be wildly adventurous with new techniques and fantasies, and I want lots of it.
- I want our sex life to be a free and equal partnership, with both partners deciding jointly to make love, no pressures from either one to perform.
- Intercourse and explicit sex is secondary to me; affectionate touching is more important.

Personal and Spiritual Growth

- I want the freedom to continually explore avenues for awakening, whether it is on my own or with my partner.
- My faith, my religious practice, is essential to my way of life, and I want my family to be part of it.
- I want spiritual growth to be something we pursue as a couple.
- Spiritual growth simply develops from our experiences in life. I do not want to make it a focal point.

Home Life

- I want our home to be a quiet, tidy oasis where I can recuperate from the world.

- I want our home to be a lively center, where friends and family are frequent guests.

- Home for me is wherever I hang my hat. I do not want to be tied down to one place very long. I need the freedom to get up and go if we want to.

- I want to set down roots in a stable, secure environment. I need a house that belongs to us.

When you have made your list, prioritize it. Elements that are most important to you go at the top.

Step 2: Your Shared Picture

In this step you work together to align your individual desires into a shared vision for your relationship.

- After you have completed your individual lists, share what each of you has written and discuss what you discover.

- Look for items that *match*—qualities that are similar on both lists. If necessary, refine them a little more before you add them to a third list, the one that will become your shared vision.

- Notice the qualities that only appear on one list. Can you or your lover agree to add that quality to your common list so that it becomes part of your joint vision?

- If you can't or if there are other very obvious differences in approach (for example, one wants lots of sex and the other only a little; one wants to spend all your free time together but the other wants more time for separate social activities; one ranks your relationship as the top priority and the other ranks it lower on the list) have a frank discussion, including reasons underlying your choices, and see how you can reach a common ground. Techniques such as the *Heart Talk* (Chapter 5, page 97) will help.

- This is the place for complete honesty. You must know where you are as a couple on these important matters. Pretending will only result in difficulties down the line.

  ᴓ Work together on your shared list until you are both comfortable with the qualities you have chosen.

  ᴓ The more precise you can be, the better, but remember, there is room for flexibility. Like your relationship itself, this vision of it will evolve over time. It is not cast in stone.

Step 3: A Symbolic Rendering

When you have finished your joint list, together create a visual image that represents the kind of relationship you both want. You can draw a picture with pen, pencil, crayons, paints, or you can make a collage out of magazine clippings and photographs. The image can be realistic or symbolic—like a mandala. Keep this image where you can both see it every day and consciously look at it, even if for only 30 seconds. Its powerful message will work within you.

Working With Creative Tension

This process was created by Robert Fritz[3] author of *The Path of Least Resistance* and is adapted here to help you create the kind of relationship you want. It is effective for achieving almost any desired outcome, not just successful relationships. In this exercise, you work with two levels of consciousness, the Chooser consciousness and the Doer consciousness.

Your Chooser and Your Doer

Your Chooser is the aware part of your consciousness—it knows that it knows. In other words, when you wake up in the morning, you immediately know who you are, what your name is, where you are, what you are to do this day, and so on. When you look in your closet you know you prefer the green shirt, not the blue one; that you want poached eggs for breakfast, not scrambled; that you must be at work by 8 a.m., and so forth. Your Chooser has preferences, likes and dislikes, desires and wants, and is perfectly designed to make choices based on those preferences.

Your Doer also knows, but your ordinary consciousness is not aware of what it knows—your Doer is subconscious, or below rational awareness. For example, your Doer knows how to digest your food, heal a wound, protect you from disease caused by germs, and make you happy or sad, a success or a failure. Because your Doer operates at a very basic level of language, it only recognizes the subject of your thoughts, not qualifiers or negatives such as "no" or "not" or "do not want." It assumes that you want what your Chooser is focusing on. A perfect servant, your Doer never questions your Chooser's judgment, but always says yes to *whatever* is the subject of your attention, and immediately goes to work to get it for you. For example, if you say to yourself, "I do not want the flu that everyone else has," you may think you are choosing not to have the flu, but in fact, your Doer zooms in on the subject matter of your thought—the flu—and says, "Flu, right, I will get that for you." In this way, many people get what they do not want simply by paying attention to it. For instance, instead of saying, "I want to be healthy" they say, "I do not want to be sick." Instead of, "I want to maintain my erection as long as I like," they say, "I do not want to ejaculate quickly." Instead of, "I want a relationship based in trust and fidelity," they say, "I do not want a man who runs around on me." Remember this critical point: For your Doer, attention equals choice! So, always focus on what you *do* want, framing your thoughts in the positive.

Creative Tension Exercise

In the creative tension process, to achieve a particular outcome you must know where you are starting from (what Robert Fritz calls "current reality"), and where you want to get to (what he refers to as "vision"). It is the same principle as orientation with a map. Knowing where you are now and what your future destination is enables you to decide in which direction to move or what the next step on your journey should be. For example, if you want to get to Kalamazoo, you will take a different route depending if you are starting from New York City or Toronto. Likewise, if you are in Phoenix, the direction you take will differ if your destination is Chicago or San Jose.

Your *current reality*, your starting point, contains three categories of information:

1. Facts.

2. Feelings.

3. Beliefs and assumptions.

You must be honest about this information without overstating, understating, or distorting it. Strong negative feelings (fear, guilt, shame) about your present situation may tempt you to pretend that your current reality is different than it really is, but distorting your current reality is equivalent to plotting a course from New York City to Kalamazoo, even though you are really starting from Toronto. Your chances of arriving at your chosen destination are small. You will get somewhere, but not likely where you want to go.

The *facts* of current reality are the details that any objective observer of the situation could notice and agree upon. For example, "We have been married 10 years. We have sex three times a month. We follow a routine pattern in our lovemaking."

The *feelings* about your situation include all the positive and negative emotions that the facts bring up for you. For example, "I am worried about our sex life. I love my mate so much. I long to have a more exciting sexual connection, but I am afraid to talk to my partner about it."

Your *beliefs and assumptions* about your situation may or may not be objectively accurate, but because you believe them, they are true for you and you will usually act as if they are accurate. For example, "It is normal for people to lose passion. Even though we love each other, there is nothing we can do about it."

In this exercise you will work with both your individual current reality and the relationship vision you jointly created. When you hold both your current reality and your vision in your Chooser consciousness at the same time, tension arises. Fritz named it *creative tension*. This is not tension that leads to stress or illness, but rather a tension that activates your Doer to help you create the results that matter to you. For most people, their beliefs and assumptions are the most powerful influences affecting their behavior. When you compare your current reality with your vision, you create a structure within your consciousness that becomes more powerful than beliefs and assumptions, more powerful than emotional discomfort, and more powerful than conditioned behavior, because all of these become part of your current reality. They are only a small part of a larger structure that becomes senior to all the things included within it.

With creative tension, you will feel energized and motivated to take action to support yourself in moving closer to your desired outcome. You will become hyper-alert to opportunities as your Doer finds them for you. Here is a simple example of how this consciousness works. When you buy a new type of car, you notice other cars like yours. Before you got one, however, you may not have noticed those vehicles at all. So much information comes into your span of attention that you must filter what is relevant and irrelevant so you will not be overwhelmed. Your filters are your choices. When you have made a choice that something matters to you, that you want it, you will start to notice everything relevant to that choice. Then you must act on the opportunities that present themselves—you must support your choice. This can be tricky, because if moving toward your vision brings up strong negative emotions, you may be tempted instead to take actions that make you feel better even if those actions move you away from your vision.

Making your vision a reality requires that you learn new things, change old behaviors, abandon old beliefs, and contradict conditioning from early childhood. If you act to avoid the emotional discomfort these changes bring, then your Doer will conclude from your behavior that you do not want what you said you wanted and will not help you get it. However, if you act in spite of your fears, you will be amazed at what you receive. Al used this process to call forth our relationship. After two divorces, he did not believe long-lasting, passionate, and reliable commitment was possible, but he wanted it very badly. Despite oppressive doubts, he persevered in his creative tension practice. We found each other and the relationship we continue to grow far exceeds his bravest hopes.

Here are the steps to create the relationship that you want using current reality and vision to generate creative tension:

Step 1: Your Relationship Vision

1. Close your eyes and in your imagination recall the image you created for your relationship.

2. Create the picture thinking in the present tense, as if it were already a reality.

3. You can use any of the five basic senses—sight, hearing, touch, smell, and taste—to create your picture. If it is a visual image, add color, make it a moving picture, and see the image up close in the front center of your attention. If there is sound, adjust the sound to be at a volume, speed, and tempo that you find pleasing, exciting, and motivating.

4. Your image must be clear enough so that you will recognize it when you get it.

5. Do not choose to have your partner act in a specific way. Make sure you use *qualities* of the relationship, not *characteristics* or specific behaviors of a partner.

6. Do not limit yourself to what you already know how to get.

7. Do not limit yourself to what you believe you can get.

8. Do not concern yourself with how you will get what you want. The process for how to get what you want will be created along the way.

Step 2: Your Current Reality

1. Set aside the vision of what you want. Tuck it away in the back of your mind for later.

2. Switch to a picture of your actual situation now—a picture of your current reality that relates to the vision you have. Although your relationship vision was developed by both of you, your current reality is uniquely yours. You and your mate have different perspectives and feelings.

3. Your description of current reality must be objective, as if a disinterested third party is describing it.

4. State the facts accurately, honestly, and without distortion. Do not overstate or understate the situation. Do not exaggerate. Tell the truth. Include both positive and negative aspects.

5. State your beliefs and assumptions about the situation. Include both positive and negative aspects.

6. Describe your feelings about the situation. Include both positive and negative feelings.

Step 3: Creative Tension

1. Sit comfortably in a relaxed, meditative position.

2. Bring into your mind both pictures: the vision of what you want and the picture of your current reality.

3. Hold both pictures in your mind at the same time, or flip back and forth between them. Take several minutes to do this.

4. Finish by focusing only on the vision of what you want and say to yourself, "I choose to have…" and complete the sentence by naming the vision you have for your relationship.

5. Now, slowly come back to the room. Open your eyes when you are ready.

Practice the creative tension process daily. Act on the opportunities that present themselves to help you move closer to your vision.

Lovers' Ways

As you focus on creating love, your imagination will invent all sorts of wonderful ideas to spur you on. Here are some others you can add to your repertoire.

Romance

> "Romance is the glamour which turns the dust of
> everyday life into a golden haze."
>
> —Amanda Cross

Everyone loves to be romanced, men as well as women. If you think traditional romantic practices are too clichéd or worn out, think again. They are tradition because they work—they've stood the test of time. Therefore:

- Buy your mate (male or female) a bouquet of flowers or a single glorious bloom.

- Send a mushy card or write a love letter, just for fun.

- Put erotic or affectionate notes in briefcases, lunch bags, lingerie drawers, jacket pockets.

- Leave a sexy message on the bathroom mirror.

- Remember important occasions—birthdays, wedding anniversaries, first dates—and celebrate them.

- At a party, send your lover a special look across the crowded room.

- Tell your man you admire him—he is your hero.

- Tell your woman you adore her—she is your goddess.

Daily Looks of Love

> "When you love somebody,
> your eyelashes go up and down
> and little stars come out of you."
>
> —Karen, age 7

Every day, take a full minute to gaze deeply into each other's eyes. Just one minute works wonders, but of course you can look longer if you like. Without speaking, send and receive unconditional love, only with your eyes. You can both send love, or you can take turns being the sender and the receiver. This simple practice connects you energetically and emotionally. The results are cumulative and exponential, a daily strengthening and renewing of your love and your commitment.

Eye-gazing, a universal feature of Tantric lovemaking, may be intimidating at first, because your eyes are the "windows to your soul." You make yourself vulnerable when you allow someone to really look inside.

But, the joy that arises when you open yourself and then are accepted is so superbly sweet. You may find yourself weeping in happiness—we often do.

Daily Looks of Love

Showing Affection

Openly show affection when you are at home with your family. Allow your children, your parents, and your friends to see you touch, hug, and kiss. When you are out in public hold hands, hug, kiss, and touch each other. We are not advocating exhibitionistic displays of explicit sex, but a genuine disclosure of your sensual appreciation of each other. In whatever way is most comfortable for you, let your children know that you make love, that you thoroughly enjoy it, and that making love is normal, healthy, and beautiful. Allow for the possibility that they may hear you making love sometimes. Talk openly with your children about love and sex as soon as they show an interest, no matter what age they may be.

If you find this difficult to do, stop and ask yourself what that tells you about your subconscious beliefs and assumptions about sexuality and affection. If sex is good, why hide it? Compare how you think about sex with how you think about arguing in front of your children and other people.

Lovers' Time

We have already suggested that you set aside a two- to four-hour block of time each week for Tantra loving. You can also use some of that time or make other dates for non-sexual loving. The essential ingredient is *love*. During your lovers' time, the two of you are the only event. You focus on:

- ⚜ Nourishing, strengthening, and enlivening your relationship.

- ⚜ Reaffirming how absolutely fabulous your mate is.

Besides weekly dates, aim for overnights or weekends away every few months, especially if you have children. They'll appreciate you more when you return and your escape to romance will recharge your parenting batteries.

Embracing Effort

> "Love doesn't just sit there like a stone;
> it has to be made, like bread,
> remade all the time, made new."
>
> —Ursula K. LeGuin

Creating love is something you learn to do. Long-term, sustainable, unconditional love does not just happen to you. In fact, learning how to create unconditional love would be part of the curriculum if you were studying for a Ph.D. in the art of loving. Earning a Ph.D. in anything takes a lot of effort—focused, continuous effort. Maybe you are not tough enough for love? Perhaps you do not want to take the time to learn? But if you choose not to, you will likely miss out on what may be the only way to make a relationship last in the long run, through all of life's ups and downs, rewards and disappointments. You may forego growing old in passionate love with your soul mate. Everyone has what it takes, but not everyone will choose to use what they have. Will you? As Guatama Buddha said in the Dhammapada, "You yourself must make the effort: Buddhas do but point the Way."

Such talk of effort might intimidate you, but it is helpful to start a journey having some sense of what you are in store for. Remember our garden metaphor? If you do not continually care for the garden (weeding, replanting, watering), you will not harvest any food. Going for gold in the Olympics is different than playing a game in the neighborhood park—different preparation, motivation, and commitment are required. Climbing Mount Everest is not your usual afternoon hike. Tantric sacred loving is not just a roll in the hay. Tantra is a different way of loving that offers the possibility of raising your lovemaking to an art, your relationship to a sacrament, and your partner to a god or goddess. However, before artistic creation comes skill. Skill requires learning, patience, and practice—lots of repetitions. Fortunately, with Tantra, the practice necessary in order to learn the skill is itself lots of fun! "The wise man, therefore, does not force the pace too much at the beginning but, like an experienced mountain climber, gives himself time to grow acclimatized at every stage of the ascent before rising to the next unconquered pinnacle."[4]

Chapter 3

Celebrating the Differences

"Sometimes I wonder if men and women really suit each other. Perhaps they should live next door, and just visit now and then."

—Katharine Hepburn

"You like potato and I like potaeto,
You like tomato and I like tomaeto;
Potato, potaeto, tomato, tomaeto!
Let's call the whole thing off!"

—"Let's Call the Whole Thing Off," music and lyrics by George and Ira Gershwin

"Love is grand; divorce is a hundred grand."

—Unknown

Early on in our relationship, we made a pact to celebrate our differences. After all, opposites attract, right? What originally drew Pala to Al, aside from his deliberate sexuality, was his articulate intellect with its focused, methodical thought processes. It's at a 180-degree angle from the way she moves through life, and it intrigued her from the outset. However we have both been through enough relationships to know that what starts out as intriguing often ends up as annoying, exasperating, or threatening.

You know, in the first blush of love, John's slow moving approach to life is revered as mellow and laid back and taking time to smell the roses. Sooner or later, he's just another lazy guy. Or a new lover's eyes may see Barbara's need for order and security as competency, efficiency, and astounding preparedness. With just a little shift in perception she's just another controlling woman.

We do not want to do that with each other. We want to build on what we have started, not tear it down, thus our bond to celebrate our differences. This means that whatever drives us nuts about each other, we attempt to use as a way to learn something about ourselves. This is one of the most important ways that we consciously use our relationship as a spiritual practice. It is *not* always easy. In fact we do occasionally just lose it and throw a petulant tantrum. Who wants to keep working on your own stuff all the time? It is easier and more fun to try and fix other people. For the most part though, we keep to our bargain. Our relationship gets stronger because we do. And we each learn to look at the world through bigger eyes.

Higher Logical Level—The Observer/Witness Consciousness

"Out beyond ideas of wrongdoing and rightdoing,
there is a field. I will meet you there.
When the soul lies down in that grass,
the world is too full to talk about.
Ideas, language, even the phrase *each other*
doesn't make any sense."

—Rumi[1]

In Chapter 1, we suggested that a good place to begin your Tantric journey would be to make your relationship the most important thing in your life. In that chapter, we explored some of the things people make higher priorities than their relationship, for example, children, careers, and community projects. In addition to these external distractions your own ego and its baggage can pull you away from a relationship focus. While disagreements are normal in the healthiest relationship, how you handle them can continue that health or lead to relationship terminal illness. Common illness-inducing behaviors in disagreements are:

1. Conditioned responses in which you act as if the current situation were a different one from your past.

2. Protecting your self-identity through winning and always being right—even when you are wrong.

Conditioned Response

"All marriages are happy. It's trying to live together
afterwards that causes all the problems."
—Shelley Winters

During disagreements, strong feelings may arise that subconsciously remind you of a previous experience. Without being aware of it, you begin to react in the present as if you were in that past situation. Perhaps you have heard of Pavlov's famous experiments with dogs. Each time he gave the dogs food, Pavlov rang a bell. When the food appeared, the dogs salivated. Eventually the dogs salivated when they heard the bell even though no food was presented. This is a conditioned response—one thing is associated with another and a certain behavior occurs. Every time that condition is matched closely enough, the same response happens automatically without thought or conscious intention.

Sometimes conditioned response is a good and useful thing—for instance when Pala looks at Al a certain way, he knows she's thinking sexy thoughts about him. He becomes turned on and excited about going on to making love. However, if a current situation reminds you of some negative past experience and you automatically respond now as if you were still in the past, it is not useful at all—in fact, it is detrimental. For instance, Cecile's first husband, a possessive, jealous man, strenuously objected any time she went anywhere at all without him. Now she's married to Luc, who trusts her implicitly, and she knows it. However, when she wants to go away for the weekend with her women friends and he wants her to go with him to his business conference instead, her conditioned response is triggered and she reverts to Marriage Number One. Rather than discussing their differences calmly, she immediately becomes defensive and angry, snarling, "Can't you ever let me out of your sight? Don't you trust me to be on my own without you always around?"

Always Being Right

"If a man speaks in the woods, and there is no woman to
hear him, is he still wrong?"
—Unknown

Being in relationship can be overwhelming. It can seem difficult to maintain your individuality. Your sense of self, who you are, and what you stand for may be threatened when your mate has a decidedly different opinion or exhibits behavior very different from yours. An unconscious desire to maintain your self-identity urges you to make the other person agree with your point of view—conflict results. When you are in a conflict situation with negative feelings running high, you may want to win, to be in control, to protect yourself, to punish the other person, and so on. At that moment, winning can become an all-consuming desire. You may say or do completely irrational things that cause long-term damage to your relationship.

Later, when you have cooled down and gained some emotional and psychological distance, you can see that the little thing (or even the big thing) you were fighting about was not really that important. At the time however, you acted as if it were the *only* thing that mattered. Or you may realize that your response was just a conditioned reaction that was completely inappropriate to what was really going on. How can you remember at these times that your relationship is the most important thing? We use a process we call *jumping to a higher logical level*.

Although the higher logical level process is easy to understand, like many simple things, it is not necessarily easy to do. Jumping to a higher logical level is a matter of gaining emotional distance from the source of your internal disturbance so that you can give it a name. Then you are no longer caught in it because some part of your awareness is witnessing events as they unfold. Calling on your internal observer is part of the Tantric path of becoming aware, of learning to use your mind as a tool for your spirit rather than allowing it to be your master. Once your witness, or observer, is turned on, you move out of the realm of powerlessness into the realm of freedom, where you have choices and options.

When you are feeling powerless, you have no choice—you are stuck. You carry an emotional weight of fear and inadequacy. It seems as though events just happen to you and everything is arbitrary. You have no way to influence outcomes. Behaviors tend to be automatic, conditioned responses. However, when you jump to a higher logical level, activating your observer consciousness, you do have choices. You can choose *what* to think about and *how* to think about it. You have the options of focusing your attention on something other than what you were caught in, and you can change how you were thinking about what you were caught in.

For example, if you notice yourself worrying about money, you could instead stop, listen to the sounds that you hear, the aromas you smell, the sights you see, and so on. Paying attention to your senses will always bring you back into the moment, out of the never-ending labyrinth of your mind. Or you can decide that instead of thinking about money right now, you will think about the rendezvous later this evening with your mate. Or you can decide to repeat an affirmation over and over to yourself, such as, "I can learn to create abundance in all areas of my life. I can learn to easily attract all the money that I need and want."

Jumping to a higher logical level is a meta-strategy, a strategy that enables you to manage other strategies in your life. It is generally useful in any situation where 1) the contents of the process are less important than the nature of the thought process itself, and 2) the thought process exhibits increasingly negative side effects and fewer tangible benefits. For example, what I worry about is less important than that I am engaged in the process of worrying. Why I am hyperactive is less important than that I am hyperactive. What I am procrastinating over is less important than that I am procrastinating. What I lose my temper over is less important than that I am losing my temper.

Jumping to a higher logical level does not mean you pretend that you do not have any problems or ignore your responsibilities of relationship, parenting, finance, employment, health, and so on. This is not an avoidance strategy. Rather it helps you handle your difficulties in appropriate ways at appropriate times.

Jumping to a Higher Logical Level in Relationship

"Let's stop hurting each other. You go first."

—The Poet Alta

For us, our relationship is more important than our own needs to control or be right, but we often see things very differently. When we disagree, both of us can become so caught up in insisting upon and defending our positions that we overheat. We have learned how to cool things down using the higher logical level technique. In previous relationships, we argued with our spouses in ways that were hurtful. Now when we find ourselves becoming irrational, we stop and say something like: "We are arguing in a way that is disrespectful. Is fighting what we really want to do? Are our positions so important that we want to say and do things that could hurt each other and damage our relationship?" This is a crucial step. This is naming the thought process, and by doing so we gain emotional distance enabling us to step off a runaway emotional roller-coaster.

By jumping to a higher logical level we move into the realm of freedom and choice. We are no longer puppets moving on the strings of conditioned behavior from our past. Fully present in the moment, we can usually find some mutually agreeable solution. Jumping to a higher logical level helps us remember our commitment to our relationship. We transcend our issues of control and unite again on our spiritual path.

61

Jumping to a Higher Logical Level Exercise

1. In any negative state of consciousness accompanied by bad feelings and emotions, stop for a moment and NAME the process you are engaged in. For example, if you were worrying about money, shift from actually figuring out why you were worrying about money, or trying to figure out how to get more money, and instead ask yourself if this is what you really want and need to do right now:

> "I am worrying again. It happens to be about money. Is this what I want to do? No. I have real issues about money. I can and will take action to solve my money problems later at a time that is more appropriate. There is nothing to be done about that now. Worrying about money right now is a waste of time and energy and just makes me feel bad."

2. Switch your conscious attention to something that you do want to be doing right now. Pay attention to sensory information: What do you see, hear, taste, or smell? What sensations do you feel? Replace your thinking with something that you do want to think about. Remember that you have power over not only *what* you think about, but also *how* you think about your thoughts. In addition, change your behavior and start to do something you want to do. This is freedom.

Your Lover as a Mirror for Yourself

"Success in a marriage is more than finding the right person. It's becoming the right person."

—Unknown

It is easy to blame difficulties or stresses in relationship on the short-comings or oversights of your partner. By slightly altering your assessment of the situation from "my partner as source of the problem" to "my partner as a mirror of my own foibles," you can move forward both personally and as a couple.

For instance, if Pala is feeling that the romance in our relationship is dwindling, she might rake Al up and down for his inattention and expect him to spice the mix up. Or she can take an honest look at what *her* contribution has been to the hearts and flowers part of our life. Is she acting lovingly? Is she regularly giving him hugs and sweet kisses for no particular reason? Is she sending him sexy e-mails or erotic poems? Is she inviting him to a special rendezvous? If the answers are no, then it is a good sign that she needs to take action to create the romance she wants.

Looking to yourself first to understand your part in a situation does not mean that you always have to make all the contributions. This is a practice for both partners and sometimes your lover may be slacking off. If Pala were to answer yes to all her questions, then it would be time to approach Al with her concerns, perhaps using a technique like the *Heart Talk* (Chapter 5, page 97).

Next time you want to haul your lover over the coals, stop and ask yourself, "What is this reflecting about me?" "Am I doing all I can to create the outcome I want?" Then consider specific behaviors.

Examples:

1. You feel that you have no time together. It seems as though your partner is always working late, going out with friends, focusing on the kids' events. Before you start complaining, look carefully at what you spend your time doing. Do you set aside time for the two of you? Are you expecting your sweetheart to fit into your schedule? Is there something you can do to reduce your lover's activity load?

2. You feel that your lovemaking is too hurried. Somehow your lover always heads right for the "good stuff" and it is over before you know it. What are you doing to prolong your lovemaking? Are you taking the initiative to introduce new practices or techniques? Have you made suggestions about altering the time, place, or circumstances of your sexual connection?

Your Lover as a Mirror Exercise

1. Identify the issue with your partner that is upsetting you.

2. Turn on your observer consciousness and ask:

   a. "What is this reflecting about me?"

   b. "Am I doing all I can to make the situation the best it can be?"

3. Depending on your answer:

   a. Make your contributions to better the situation.

   b. Talk to your partner about your concerns in a loving way, for example, use a *Heart Talk* (Chapter 5, page 97).

Calling Each Other on "Stuff"

"The easiest kind of relationship for me is with
ten thousand people.
The hardest is with one."

—Joan Baez

Al says, "I get in ornery, crappy moods, and there is no logical, rational reason for it. If Pala is in the same room, she gets a sour look or a harsh, disrespectful tone of voice." Pala says, "Usually he is not even aware of it!" Because we both want to be as aware in every moment as we can be, we have given each other permission to bring it to the other's attention if either of us is being unpleasant without any apparent reason. When we call each other on a negative energy mood, we do *not* say, "Do not speak to me in that tone of voice, you jerk!" even though that may be our first thought. Rather, we reveal the hurt or concern beneath the irritation, like this: "The way you are looking at me makes me feel very uncomfortable, even frightened," or "The tone of your voice is harsh. I feel you are judging me, dismissing me, rejecting me, or attacking me. Is that your intention? Is there anything that I have done or said? Is there an issue we need to work on right now?"

We both want to make our relationship work, and want to be in a positive energy space as much of the time that we are together as possible. When Al asks Pala about a negative emotional state in a non-confrontational way, she has the option of becoming aware of the space she's in and can choose to come out into a more loving, calmer space. Making the choice to move into the positive requires desire, self-discipline, and a sense of humor. It is not always a rapid transition. As Al admits: "Sometimes I am so deep in my "stuff" that I feel justified in feeling bad and want to stay there! In such a situation, I go away from Pala so that my mood will not be inflicted on her. Then, because I am not getting any attention for it, and there is no one to fight with, I can usually see my folly and return quite quickly to a better state of mind."

When either of you notices the other is arbitrarily in a bad mood, do not ignore it as if this ill humor does not matter. Bring to your partner's attention the effect that her sullenness is having on you. It is important to show your own vulnerability by sharing how you are affected emotionally. For example: "When you speak to me with that tone of voice, it makes me feel very insecure and afraid that I have done something wrong." If all you reveal is that her moodiness makes you angry and want to fight, there is a good chance that is where you will end up. If you find out there is indeed a particular reason for her upset, then you have the opportunity to resolve it immediately rather than letting it fester away, poisoning your relationship.

Calling Each Other on "Stuff" Exercise

1. Agree to allow each other to bring negative moods to your attention.

2. When the situation arises, call attention to the behavior with kindness, revealing your feelings.

3. Make a choice based on awareness.

Chapter 4

Sex and Spirit: Reuniting Heaven and Earth

"Those who realize true wisdom, rapt within
this clear awareness, see me as the universe's
origin, imperishable. All their words and all
their actions issue from the depths of worship;
held in my embrace, they know me as a woman
knows her lover."

—*The Bhagavad Gita*

"There are two kinds of love. Our love. God's
love. But God makes both kinds of them."

—Jenny, age 4

As children, we were both intensely passionate about God. Raised
as a Roman Catholic, Al found a spiritual home in the church, devoutly
performing the duties of altar boy and praying to be a priest some day.
Every Sunday, with her parents and siblings, Pala absorbed the Christian
message at St. Columba's Anglican Church. There, in adolescent
fervor, inspired by her mother's faith and the promise in God's words,
she ached to become a missionary, to spread salvation around the globe.

At the same time, we were feeling the effects of another need as
powerful as our spiritual longing—the inherent sexuality of our bodies.
From the moment of his earliest memories Al had been enamored of
girls, taking every respectful opportunity he could to kiss and caress
them. Pala was compelled by the sensual pleasure of touch—as a young
girl through the mystery and excitement of playing doctor with other
neighborhood children, then in her early teens by discovering the exquisite
euphoria of masturbation.

Throughout our youths and into adulthood we each explored the intriguing byways of these two elemental forces—spirit and sex. But they were always quite distinct aspects of life, or so we were told and so we believed, at least on the rational plane. Yet somewhere deep in the knowing center of our selves was the awareness that in fact they are united, for early in our life together we encountered a profound spiritual fulfillment conceived through loving, liberated sex. Likewise we experienced the astonishing pleasures of a sexuality elevated by spiritual awareness.

Although we now live a reality of integrated sex and spirit, most others, particularly in the Western world, do not. Yes, there are eloquent arguments for separating the two, but primarily they are based on fear, not free will. The power of sex has overwhelmed humanity since our earliest days. The raw aching need it provokes, the vulnerability and loss of control it demands, the mystical heights it propels us to, not to mention its undeniable connection to survival of the human race, create such turmoil that societies from ancient Egypt to modern America feel obliged to contain it.

Sex in History

"Do not seek to follow in the footsteps of the men of old,
seek what they sought."

—Basho, Zen Poet

"When authorities warn you of the sinfulness of sex,
there is an important lesson to be learned.
Don't have sex with the authorities."

—Matt Groening

Degrees of sexual license have varied from culture to culture across the centuries, but for the most part, unwritten societal mores and officially prescribed regulations regarding sexual conduct have been oppressive to say the least. Just about every sexual practice, from simple touch between men and women to choice of sexual partner, from all manner of foreplay to particular styles of intercourse, have been banned at one time or another. Punishments for perceived sexual transgressions range from mild ostracism to imprisonment and physical mutilation to death. Women particularly have borne, and in most cultures continue to bear, the brunt of sex-repressing beliefs. The ancient Hebrews stoned women to death for adultery. Early Romans could kill their wandering women as well. Later they were simply obliged to divorce them, as were husbands in classical Greece. Europeans kept their women from straying by the use of chastity belts, which first appeared there during the 12th century and became quite popular during the 1400s and 1500s. Even in today's so-called civilized times sexual horrors, purportedly in the name of decency, are rampant. Amongst the most pervasive of these is female genital mutilation. According to Amnesty International, approximately 135 million girls and women have been subjected to this barbaric practice that ranges from clitoridectomy—removal of all or part of the clitoris—to infibulation. The most brutal form of mutilation, infibulation includes clitoridectomy, removal of the inner vaginal lips, and fastening the outer lips together to form a barrier over the vagina. Excuses for female genital mutilation run from maintaining cultural tradition to enhancing a girl's femininity, from ensuring fidelity to guaranteeing cleanliness.[1]

Secular approaches to sex are inextricably linked with a culture's prevailing religious beliefs. Religious thinkers have long pondered the role sexual urges play in relation to humanity's spiritual life, and most have determined that the one is a definite obstacle to the other. Few, primarily Taoists and Tantricas, have entertained the idea that sex can be an actual gateway for spiritual awakening. Some religions, including Judaism, Islam, and modern Hinduism, consider sex a distraction from spiritual attainment but tolerate it, within strict confines, as a necessary and even pleasurable duty to be performed as part of a reverent lay person's life. Others, most notably Christianity, denounced sex, not just as a diversion to rise above, but as a truly damning pastime.

Christianity, more than any other force, has profoundly influenced Western society's relationship to sex. Its intensely anti-sex viewpoint has less basis in the actual scriptures than it does in the personal struggles of a handful of early churchmen. As Anais Nin says, "We do not see things as they are. We see them as we are." During the 4th and 5th centuries, Fathers of the Church such as St. Augustine and St. Jerome, repentant of their formerly active sex lives but still tormented by desire, decided that sex, because of its uncontrollable power, was wicked. St. Augustine, the same St. Augustine who prayed, "Lord give me chastity...but not yet," reinterpreted Adam and Eve's fall from grace in the garden of Eden, changing it from an act of simple disobedience to disobedience fueled by lust. Through his arguments, sex evolved from a troublesome distraction away from the godly path into a sin that infected all of humanity.[2]

Although the majority of Christian religions dramatically redefined their position on sex during the latter part of the 20th century, the oppressive weight of 1,600 years equating sex with sin confines our culture's current perceptions. Even as sex is now more openly displayed, more freely accessible, and almost obsessively examined, on a grand societal scale it remains at heart soul-less—separate, fleeting, and essentially physical. While sex may be an expression of genuine love, it is just as often a means to gain power, a bargaining tool for self-worth, a routine tension release, or a hedonistic escape. Sex may feel good, but for many deep down it is still bad, as is most pleasure.

Even though the pursuit of pleasure is part of the American dream—an unassailable right—it is a guilt-ridden hunt, filtered through the notion that what comes from the body or pleases the body is against the soul. People are caught between choosing one or the other—diving headlong into hedonism—where only pleasure is important and all else falls by the wayside—or denying themselves pleasure to save the spirit. It is understandable that in order to explain why there is such suffering in the world religion needed a scapegoat and was able to easily find one in the arbitrary willfulness of the flesh. The body was seen as unruly, shameful, and unworthy, so of course it should suffer. The way to salvation therefore is to focus on your spiritual side, sublimating or rising above physical wants so that you can escape the prison and pain of life. Many have come to spiritual peace and awakening through just such a path. But there is also another route, albeit not often traveled, that allows for a different perspective.

Pleasure as Healer

"Men are admitted into Heaven not because they have curbed and govern'd their passions or have no passions, but because they have cultivated their understandings."

—William Blake

This path asserts that our task here on this worldly plane is to manifest the soul through the body, to bring out the Divine by truly uniting our physical and spiritual selves. You set your soul free by celebrating your body, not by denying it. Pleasure then becomes a universal, uplifting and healing experience that brings you closer to each other and to God, not an individual craving that sets you apart and drives you deeper into selfishness. Indeed, in this view it is the absence of pleasure that brings about suffering. For instance, developmental neuropsychologist James W. Prescott advanced the theory that deprivation of bodily pleasure has a direct impact on the amount of warfare and interpersonal violence. "The reciprocal relationship between pleasure and violence is such that one inhibits the other; when physical pleasure is high, physical violence is low. When violence is high, pleasure is low. This basic premise...provides us with the tools necessary to fashion a world of peaceful, affectionate, cooperative individuals."[3] Sacred sexuality is one of those tools. By reuniting these two most powerful motivators—spirit and sex—we can heal the damage their separation has caused.

A reframing of sexual and spiritual life is gaining momentum in our society through books, conferences, and workshops that challenge outdated and unworkable attitudes and seek to formulate new ones. They provide a stimulus, and make it more acceptable, for individuals to examine their own assumptions and to take action for change in their own lives. In Appendix A, we offer a list of reference materials you can use in your quest. You are encouraged to look at all your relationships and consider how to best live them out. If, for example, you want to strengthen your relationship between your spirit and your body you may choose, as we have, to connect them through your sexuality.

Sex and Spirit as One

"We and God have business with each other,
and in opening ourselves
to God's influence
our deepest destiny is fulfilled."

—William James

As with learning to create love, making the decision to unite sex and spirit is your first step. Because awareness goes a long way toward helping you change, the second step is examining your beliefs and conditioned behaviors. What messages have you absorbed over the course of your lifetime, from your family, your friends, your schooling, and your church, that tell you sex and God do not belong together? As you examine the concepts that have shaped you, consider which of these you want to retain and which you need to let go of for your growth and happiness.

We are not suggesting that you give up on your existing religious affiliation, but that you examine it and determine how you can incorporate spiritual sexuality into it. Couples from a wide range of faiths—for example, Bahai, Baptist, Buddhist, Hindu, Jewish, Methodist, Mormon, Roman Catholic, Wiccan—have attended our workshops and found that sacred sex strengthened their religious practice. At the end of this chapter you will find a Sexual Beliefs Questionnaire that will help give you some insight into your current assumptions about sex and spirit.

Next, begin putting your desire into action. If you want to connect sex and spirit, the most straightforward path is to bring your spiritual life into the bedroom—there are many exercises in this book to help you do just that. You can also draw on your own creativity—the creativity you use for solving business challenges, mediating family squabbles, and juggling hectic schedules—to integrate your sexual, spiritual, and romantic relationship.

For example, in traditional Tantric practice, lovers learn to see themselves as the god and goddess Shiva and Shakti. They leave their daily selves behind and become manifestations of the gods. This form may suit you well. On the other hand, Shiva and Shakti may not have a personal meaning for you, but if your spiritual perception is that god or goddess or Creator is *within* you, you can employ a similar mental picture to let that divinity out. You can focus on expanding that essence of the Divine within so that it encompasses you entirely—you and your lover become All. Speak aloud your intention as you join in passion together: "We are divine, we are one, we are All in our love." Moreover, show appreciation for the connection you share: "Thank you for this bliss."

If your perception is that God, Goddess, or Creator is *external*—separate from you—you can envision your sexual longing as a mirror of your spiritual longing. Your loving connection with your partner is seen as an expression of your desire to connect with God. It is a prayer for union. Give voice to it as such at the peak of your abandon, "Oh God, come into us." Or you may see your lovemaking as worship, a way to show your love of God and to give thanks. "Dearest Goddess, we humbly thank you for our bodies and through our passion show our gratitude." At first speaking aloud about reverence, holiness, and divinity while you are in the fever of loving may be difficult. It can bring up all sorts of feelings—embarrassment, shame, guilt, astonishment—as it did for us. However, persevere; your uneasiness will pass as you begin to truly live the joyous union of sex and spirit.

Perhaps you do not have a particular faith, or you may not consider yourself a spiritual person. Often, people who do not see themselves as being particularly spiritual, but who practice Tantra for an improved sex life and more intimate relationship, find that with Tantric loving a spiritual awakening happens spontaneously. The practices you will explore, of breathing, being in the moment, mindfulness, opening your heart, surrender and letting go, moving sexual energy, and the experiences these practices bring (altered states of consciousness), lead to a connection that is more than physical. It leads out from the self in union and transcendence, to the partner, to the Divine, so a spiritual sensibility is awakened. You become a sexually spiritual person.

Sexual Beliefs Questionnaire

These statements about sexuality are intended to help you become aware of your own (and your partner's) beliefs, assumptions, and attitudes about sex. The purpose is not to categorize you, judge you, or make you feel either good or bad. This is an exercise in sexual self-awareness. If you already have a sex-positive consciousness, you are fortunate indeed. That will make it much easier for you to progress rapidly in the use of Tantra as a spiritual practice. If you discover that you are carrying the weight of a sex-negative consciousness, you are presented with a challenge and an opportunity. Your challenge is discovering how to let go of your negative conditioning. Remember, recognition is a step on the road toward change. Your opportunity is to mature spiritually as a whole human being, to celebrate life in a body that is the holy temple of your soul. In this maturity, you can learn to give and receive love sexually, to surrender to your lover, to experience your birthright of bliss. Certainly, human beings have a remarkable capacity for growth.

Sex-Positive Statements

> "His voice was as intimate as the
> rustle of sheets."
>
> —Dorothy Parker

1. Sex is good, healthy, and normal.
   Agree ☐ Strongly Agree ☐ Disagree ☐ Strongly Disagree ☐
   Do not Know or Not Applicable ☐

2. Sex is important or essential in my life.
   Agree ☐ Strongly Agree ☐ Disagree ☐ Strongly Disagree ☐
   Do not Know or Not Applicable ☐

3. Sex is a source of pleasure and meaning in my life.
   Agree ☐ Strongly Agree ☐ Disagree ☐ Strongly Disagree ☐
   Do not Know or Not Applicable ☐

4. It is good to talk frankly about sex with children, at whatever age they show interest.
   Agree ☐ Strongly Agree ☐ Disagree ☐ Strongly Disagree ☐
   Do not Know or Not Applicable ☐

5. Male and female naked bodies are beautiful.
   Agree ☐ Strongly Agree ☐ Disagree ☐ Strongly Disagree ☐
   Do not Know or Not Applicable ☐

6. Women can be just as sexual as men.
   Agree ☐ Strongly Agree ☐ Disagree ☐ Strongly Disagree ☐
   Do not Know or Not Applicable ☐

7. Sex can continue happily well into old age.
   Agree ☐ Strongly Agree ☐ Disagree ☐ Strongly Disagree ☐
   Do not Know or Not Applicable ☐

8. Sex can be a meditation.

   Agree ☐   Strongly Agree ☐   Disagree ☐   Strongly Disagree ☐
   Do not Know or Not Applicable ☐

9. Sex can be a spiritual practice.

   Agree ☐   Strongly Agree ☐   Disagree ☐   Strongly Disagree ☐
   Do not Know or Not Applicable ☐

10. Sex can be sacred and holy.

   Agree ☐   Strongly Agree ☐   Disagree ☐   Strongly Disagree ☐
   Do not Know or Not Applicable ☐

11. Through sex, it is possible to have a mystical or religious experience.

   Agree ☐   Strongly Agree ☐   Disagree ☐   Strongly Disagree ☐
   Do not Know or Not Applicable ☐

12. Masturbation is normal and healthy.

   Agree ☐   Strongly Agree ☐   Disagree ☐   Strongly Disagree ☐
   Do not Know or Not Applicable ☐

13. Anal sex is normal and healthy.

   Agree ☐   Strongly Agree ☐   Disagree ☐   Strongly Disagree ☐
   Do not Know or Not Applicable ☐

14. It does not matter what a person's sexual orientation is.

   Agree ☐   Strongly Agree ☐   Disagree ☐   Strongly Disagree ☐
   Do not Know or Not Applicable ☐

15. We openly show affection by hugging, kissing, and touching when
    we are around our children.

   Agree ☐   Strongly Agree ☐   Disagree ☐   Strongly Disagree ☐
   Do not Know or Not Applicable ☐

16. Our sex life continues to evolve.

   Agree ☐   Strongly Agree ☐   Disagree ☐   Strongly Disagree ☐
   Do not Know or Not Applicable ☐

17. I have fun with sex.

   Agree ☐   Strongly Agree ☐   Disagree ☐   Strongly Disagree ☐
   Do not Know or Not Applicable ☐

18. I can be creative in sex.

   Agree ☐   Strongly Agree ☐   Disagree ☐   Strongly Disagree ☐
   Do not Know or Not Applicable ☐

19. I am confident with myself as a lover.

   Agree ☐   Strongly Agree ☐   Disagree ☐   Strongly Disagree ☐
   Do not Know or Not Applicable ☐

20. I have sex frequently.

Agree ☐   Strongly Agree ☐   Disagree ☐   Strongly Disagree ☐
Do not Know or Not Applicable ☐

21. I love to try new sexual techniques and do so often.

Agree ☐   Strongly Agree ☐   Disagree ☐   Strongly Disagree ☐
Do not Know or Not Applicable ☐

22. We experiment with different locations for sex.

Agree ☐   Strongly Agree ☐   Disagree ☐   Strongly Disagree ☐
Do not Know or Not Applicable ☐

23. We have tried using a variety of sex toys.

Agree ☐   Strongly Agree ☐   Disagree ☐   Strongly Disagree ☐
Do not Know or Not Applicable ☐

24. We sometimes watch erotic or sex instruction videos together.

Agree ☐   Strongly Agree ☐   Disagree ☐   Strongly Disagree ☐
Do not Know or Not Applicable ☐

25. I have read at least one sex-instruction book since high school.

Agree ☐   Strongly Agree ☐   Disagree ☐   Strongly Disagree ☐
Do not Know or Not Applicable ☐

26. I have taken at least one workshop or course on sexuality since high school.

Agree ☐   Strongly Agree ☐   Disagree ☐   Strongly Disagree ☐
Do not Know or Not Applicable ☐

27. The idea of extending lovemaking for hours is appealing.

Agree ☐   Strongly Agree ☐   Disagree ☐   Strongly Disagree ☐
Do not Know or Not Applicable ☐

28. I try to come to our lovemaking well rested, calm, and relaxed.

Agree ☐   Strongly Agree ☐   Disagree ☐   Strongly Disagree ☐
Do not Know or Not Applicable ☐

29. I open my heart to my partner during lovemaking.

Agree ☐   Strongly Agree ☐   Disagree ☐   Strongly Disagree ☐
Do not Know or Not Applicable ☐

30. Sex is a way that I join with my partner on much more than a physical level.

Agree ☐   Strongly Agree ☐   Disagree ☐   Strongly Disagree ☐
Do not Know or Not Applicable ☐

31. I sometimes laugh or cry with joy during or after sex.

Agree ☐   Strongly Agree ☐   Disagree ☐   Strongly Disagree ☐
Do not Know or Not Applicable ☐

32. I regularly communicate with my partner about what I like and dislike sexually.

    Agree ☐   Strongly Agree ☐   Disagree ☐   Strongly Disagree ☐
    Do not Know or Not Applicable ☐

33. One of the things that turns me on is when my partner is really excited.

    Agree ☐   Strongly Agree ☐   Disagree ☐   Strongly Disagree ☐
    Do not Know or Not Applicable ☐

34. I pay wonderful attention to my partner's responses when we make love.

    Agree ☐   Strongly Agree ☐   Disagree ☐   Strongly Disagree ☐
    Do not Know or Not Applicable ☐

35. Our lovemaking includes much more than intercourse.

    Agree ☐   Strongly Agree ☐   Disagree ☐   Strongly Disagree ☐
    Do not Know or Not Applicable ☐

36. Our lovemaking sometimes lasts more than one hour.

    Agree ☐   Strongly Agree ☐   Disagree ☐   Strongly Disagree ☐
    Do not Know or Not Applicable ☐

37. We share being active and passive partners—givers and receivers of pleasure and initiators of sex.

    Agree ☐   Strongly Agree ☐   Disagree ☐   Strongly Disagree ☐
    Do not Know or Not Applicable ☐

38. I do not usually touch my partner's genitals until she is very highly aroused and well lubricated.

    Agree ☐   Strongly Agree ☐   Disagree ☐   Strongly Disagree ☐
    Do not Know or Not Applicable ☐

39. I usually wait until she has come close to or has had an orgasm before vaginal penetration.

    Agree ☐   Strongly Agree ☐   Disagree ☐   Strongly Disagree ☐
    Do not Know or Not Applicable ☐

40. Masturbation is a good way for me to learn about what I like sexually.

    Agree ☐   Strongly Agree ☐   Disagree ☐   Strongly Disagree ☐
    Do not Know or Not Applicable ☐

41. I masturbate for my lover.

    Agree ☐   Strongly Agree ☐   Disagree ☐   Strongly Disagree ☐
    Do not Know or Not Applicable ☐

42. It turns me on to see my lover masturbate.

    Agree ☐   Strongly Agree ☐   Disagree ☐   Strongly Disagree ☐
    Do not Know or Not Applicable ☐

43. I reach orgasm quite easily through masturbation.

 Agree ☐ Strongly Agree ☐ Disagree ☐ Strongly Disagree ☐
 Do not Know or Not Applicable ☐

44. I regularly experience orgasm during lovemaking with my partner.

 Agree ☐ Strongly Agree ☐ Disagree ☐ Strongly Disagree ☐
 Do not Know or Not Applicable ☐

45. I experience different types of orgasm.

 Agree ☐ Strongly Agree ☐ Disagree ☐ Strongly Disagree ☐
 Do not Know or Not Applicable ☐

46. I make lots of sound during sex.

 Agree ☐ Strongly Agree ☐ Disagree ☐ Strongly Disagree ☐
 Do not Know or Not Applicable ☐

47. I enjoy giving oral sex.

 Agree ☐ Strongly Agree ☐ Disagree ☐ Strongly Disagree ☐
 Do not Know or Not Applicable ☐

48. I enjoy receiving oral sex.

 Agree ☐ Strongly Agree ☐ Disagree ☐ Strongly Disagree ☐
 Do not Know or Not Applicable ☐

49. We have experimented with anal sex.

 Agree ☐ Strongly Agree ☐ Disagree ☐ Strongly Disagree ☐
 Do not Know or Not Applicable ☐

50. Anal sex can be very pleasurable.

 Agree ☐ Strongly Agree ☐ Disagree ☐ Strongly Disagree ☐
 Do not Know or Not Applicable ☐

51. We frequently open our eyes during lovemaking, and look into each other's eyes.

 Agree ☐ Strongly Agree ☐ Disagree ☐ Strongly Disagree ☐
 Do not Know or Not Applicable ☐

52. We sometimes harmonize our breathing during sex.

 Agree ☐ Strongly Agree ☐ Disagree ☐ Strongly Disagree ☐
 Do not Know or Not Applicable ☐

53. We have learned to stay relaxed at peaks of sexual arousal.

 Agree ☐ Strongly Agree ☐ Disagree ☐ Strongly Disagree ☐
 Do not Know or Not Applicable ☐

54. I sometimes choose not to have an orgasm in order to build my sexual energy charge to a higher level.

 Agree ☐ Strongly Agree ☐ Disagree ☐ Strongly Disagree ☐
 Do not Know or Not Applicable ☐

55. I can separate orgasm from ejaculation and can have an orgasm without ejaculating.

Agree ☐   Strongly Agree ☐   Disagree ☐   Strongly Disagree ☐
Do not Know or Not Applicable ☐

56. I give my lover a prostate massage.

Agree ☐   Strongly Agree ☐   Disagree ☐   Strongly Disagree ☐
Do not Know or Not Applicable ☐

57. We sometimes use acupressure points to help sexual energy to move.

Agree ☐   Strongly Agree ☐   Disagree ☐   Strongly Disagree ☐
Do not Know or Not Applicable ☐

58. We sometimes end lovemaking while we still have desire.

Agree ☐   Strongly Agree ☐   Disagree ☐   Strongly Disagree ☐
Do not Know or Not Applicable ☐

The more of these statements you agree to, the more sex-positive are your attitudes, beliefs, and assumptions about sex. If you agree with many or most of these statements, you are probably comfortable being in a body and with your sexuality. You are well informed and have considerable knowledge and skill of sexual technique and style. Your sexuality is likely integrated within the context of your relationship and your entire life. Sex for you is fun, healthy, normal, and possibly even sacred. You are able to give and receive pleasure, surrendering to your lover, and letting go of the need to be in control during lovemaking.

Sex-Negative Statements

"Sex is a bad thing because it rumples the clothes."

—Jacqueline Kennedy Onassis

Almost everyone will answer *yes* to some of these negative statements. This should not be of concern to you assuming you answered yes to many more of the sex-positive statements. The opportunity is for you to become aware of any strong sex-negative bias. There are 74 questions in three categories that follow. If you agree with more than 20 of these questions, this indicates a strong sex-negative bias. You may also want to look at the specific questions that you agree with and see if that provides you with useful information about your sexuality, indicating specific areas to work on.

You will have to decide what your answers mean by looking inside of yourself. Once you are aware of a powerful sex-negative bias, you can take steps to change it—if you want to. This book offers many ways for you to transform a sex-negative bias into a joyous celebration of spiritual sexuality. If you feel it would be helpful, you may wish to seek assistance through sexual counseling or therapy.[4]

Current Sexual Experience:
Negative Attitudes, Beliefs, and Assumptions

1. Sex is bad, abnormal, unhealthy, dangerous, dirty, or a sin.

    Agree ☐   Strongly Agree ☐   Disagree ☐   Strongly Disagree ☐
    Do not Know or Not Applicable ☐

2. Sex outside of marriage is a sin.

    Agree ☐   Strongly Agree ☐   Disagree ☐   Strongly Disagree ☐
    Do not Know or Not Applicable ☐

3. Sex without love is bad; only sex with love is acceptable.

    Agree ☐   Strongly Agree ☐   Disagree ☐   Strongly Disagree ☐
    Do not Know or Not Applicable ☐

4. Sex is acceptable only in order to have children.

    Agree ☐   Strongly Agree ☐   Disagree ☐   Strongly Disagree ☐
    Do not Know or Not Applicable ☐

5. It is okay for men to like sex, but not for women to like sex.

    Agree ☐   Strongly Agree ☐   Disagree ☐   Strongly Disagree ☐
    Do not Know or Not Applicable ☐

6. Men cannot control themselves when it comes to sex.

    Agree ☐   Strongly Agree ☐   Disagree ☐   Strongly Disagree ☐
    Do not Know or Not Applicable ☐

7. It is the woman's responsibility to avoid provoking men's interest in
    sex. If a woman looks, talks, or acts sexy, she is just asking for it.

    Agree ☐   Strongly Agree ☐   Disagree ☐   Strongly Disagree ☐
    Do not Know or Not Applicable ☐

8. Good girls do not show interest in sex.

    Agree ☐   Strongly Agree ☐   Disagree ☐   Strongly Disagree ☐
    Do not Know or Not Applicable ☐

9. Mothers should not act, talk, dress, dance, or be sexy.

    Agree ☐   Strongly Agree ☐   Disagree ☐   Strongly Disagree ☐
    Do not Know or Not Applicable ☐

10. Women should not initiate sex; only men should initiate sex.

    Agree ☐   Strongly Agree ☐   Disagree ☐   Strongly Disagree ☐
    Do not Know or Not Applicable ☐

11. Sex is just a physical thing.

    Agree ☐   Strongly Agree ☐   Disagree ☐   Strongly Disagree ☐
    Do not Know or Not Applicable ☐

12. Truly spiritual people are not very interested in sex; if they do have sexual interest they sublimate it.

Agree ☐   Strongly Agree ☐   Disagree ☐   Strongly Disagree ☐
Do not Know or Not Applicable ☐

13. Homosexuality is bad or a sin.

Agree ☐   Strongly Agree ☐   Disagree ☐   Strongly Disagree ☐
Do not Know or Not Applicable ☐

14. Anal sex is bad or is a sin.

Agree ☐   Strongly Agree ☐   Disagree ☐   Strongly Disagree ☐
Do not Know or Not Applicable ☐

15. Masturbation is bad or a sin.

Agree ☐   Strongly Agree ☐   Disagree ☐   Strongly Disagree ☐
Do not Know or Not Applicable ☐

16. Masturbation is second best to "real" sex.

Agree ☐   Strongly Agree ☐   Disagree ☐   Strongly Disagree ☐
Do not Know or Not Applicable ☐

17. Sex toys are only for people who do not know how to do it right.

Agree ☐   Strongly Agree ☐   Disagree ☐   Strongly Disagree ☐
Do not Know or Not Applicable ☐

18. A woman should never use a vibrator.

Agree ☐   Strongly Agree ☐   Disagree ☐   Strongly Disagree ☐
Do not Know or Not Applicable ☐

19. Sex is a duty.

Agree ☐   Strongly Agree ☐   Disagree ☐   Strongly Disagree ☐
Do not Know or Not Applicable ☐

20. I am uncomfortable touching, hugging, and kissing in front of my children, parents, family, and friends.

Agree ☐   Strongly Agree ☐   Disagree ☐   Strongly Disagree ☐
Do not Know or Not Applicable ☐

21. I do not like my body.

Agree ☐   Strongly Agree ☐   Disagree ☐   Strongly Disagree ☐
Do not Know or Not Applicable ☐

22. I worry about what my lover thinks about my body.

Agree ☐   Strongly Agree ☐   Disagree ☐   Strongly Disagree ☐
Do not Know or Not Applicable ☐

23. I feel threatened, afraid, insecure, or inadequate if my lover wants sex frequently.

    Agree ☐   Strongly Agree ☐   Disagree ☐   Strongly Disagree ☐
    Do not Know or Not Applicable ☐

24. I am embarrassed to make sounds during sex.

    Agree ☐   Strongly Agree ☐   Disagree ☐   Strongly Disagree ☐
    Do not Know or Not Applicable ☐

25. I use sex to bargain for what I want.

    Agree ☐   Strongly Agree ☐   Disagree ☐   Strongly Disagree ☐
    Do not Know or Not Applicable ☐

26. I withhold sex to show disapproval or to punish my lover.

    Agree ☐   Strongly Agree ☐   Disagree ☐   Strongly Disagree ☐
    Do not Know or Not Applicable ☐

27. The idea of extending lovemaking for hours turns me off.

    Agree ☐   Strongly Agree ☐   Disagree ☐   Strongly Disagree ☐
    Do not Know or Not Applicable ☐

28. I would be embarrassed to invite God into my bedroom while I am having sex.

    Agree ☐   Strongly Agree ☐   Disagree ☐   Strongly Disagree ☐
    Do not Know or Not Applicable ☐

The more of these statements you agree with, the more repressed is your sexuality. You probably do not enjoy sex and are likely to avoid it if possible. During sex, you may feel shame, guilt, and fear. For you sex is purely physical, lacking any spiritual dimension. You may use sex manipulatively to get what you want or as a weapon to be in control.

Sexual History:
Negative Sexual Experiences From Your Past

1. Sex was rarely openly discussed in my family.

    Agree ☐   Strongly Agree ☐   Disagree ☐   Strongly Disagree ☐
    Do not Know or Not Applicable ☐

2. One or both of my parents taught me that sex was bad or a sin.

    Agree ☐   Strongly Agree ☐   Disagree ☐   Strongly Disagree ☐
    Do not Know or Not Applicable ☐

3. There was little or no physical affection in my family.

    Agree ☐   Strongly Agree ☐   Disagree ☐   Strongly Disagree ☐
    Do not Know or Not Applicable ☐

4. According to my religion or the religion I was raised with, sex is bad or is a sin, except within marriage, and then is primarily for procreation.
    Agree ☐   Strongly Agree ☐   Disagree ☐   Strongly Disagree ☐
    Do not Know or Not Applicable ☐

5. I received little no or sex education in school.
    Agree ☐   Strongly Agree ☐   Disagree ☐   Strongly Disagree ☐
    Do not Know or Not Applicable ☐

6. Sex education in school left me with the impression that sex was bad, dangerous, dirty, or a sin.
    Agree ☐   Strongly Agree ☐   Disagree ☐   Strongly Disagree ☐
    Do not Know or Not Applicable ☐

7. Sex education in grade school or high school left me with the impression that sex was okay for males, but not okay for females.
    Agree ☐   Strongly Agree ☐   Disagree ☐   Strongly Disagree ☐
    Do not Know or Not Applicable ☐

8. Men's naked bodies are ugly or shameful.
    Agree ☐   Strongly Agree ☐   Disagree ☐   Strongly Disagree ☐
    Do not Know or Not Applicable ☐

9. Women's naked bodies are ugly or shameful.
    Agree ☐   Strongly Agree ☐   Disagree ☐   Strongly Disagree ☐
    Do not Know or Not Applicable ☐

10. The longer we can delay having children learn about sex, the better.
    Agree ☐   Strongly Agree ☐   Disagree ☐   Strongly Disagree ☐
    Do not Know or Not Applicable ☐

11. The idea that my children would hear the sounds I make during sex is unacceptable.
    Agree ☐   Strongly Agree ☐   Disagree ☐   Strongly Disagree ☐
    Do not Know or Not Applicable ☐

12. I feel shame or guilt when I think about or have sex.
    Agree ☐   Strongly Agree ☐   Disagree ☐   Strongly Disagree ☐
    Do not Know or Not Applicable ☐

13. I become afraid when I think about or have sex.
    Agree ☐   Strongly Agree ☐   Disagree ☐   Strongly Disagree ☐
    Do not Know or Not Applicable ☐

14. I sometimes cry with sadness during or after sex.
    Agree ☐   Strongly Agree ☐   Disagree ☐   Strongly Disagree ☐
    Do not Know or Not Applicable ☐

16. I can remember at least one experience of sexual abuse, sexual trauma, or being forced to have sex against my will.

Agree ☐   Strongly Agree ☐   Disagree ☐   Strongly Disagree ☐
Do not Know or Not Applicable ☐

The more of these statements you agree with, the more likely you are to carry a burden of sex-negative conditioning from home, school, and/or church. There was probably little discussion of sexuality at home, and the message you received from school and church was that sex was to be avoided. You may have experienced sexual abuse or sexual trauma. You may avoid sex, or paradoxically you could be promiscuous.

Sexual Knowledge and Skill

1. Our lovemaking typically lasts less than 30 minutes.

Agree ☐   Strongly Agree ☐   Disagree ☐   Strongly Disagree ☐
Do not Know or Not Applicable ☐

2. Our sex usually begins and ends at the genitals; there is little or no foreplay.

Agree ☐   Strongly Agree ☐   Disagree ☐   Strongly Disagree ☐
Do not Know or Not Applicable ☐

3. Our sex has become routine or boring.

Agree ☐   Strongly Agree ☐   Disagree ☐   Strongly Disagree ☐
Do not Know or Not Applicable ☐

4. Our sex has become primarily a release of tension.

Agree ☐   Strongly Agree ☐   Disagree ☐   Strongly Disagree ☐
Do not Know or Not Applicable ☐

5. Sex is not complete without intercourse.

Agree ☐   Strongly Agree ☐   Disagree ☐   Strongly Disagree ☐
Do not Know or Not Applicable ☐

6. Having an orgasm is the goal of sex.

Agree ☐   Strongly Agree ☐   Disagree ☐   Strongly Disagree ☐
Do not Know or Not Applicable ☐

7. Ejaculation is usually involuntary for me.

Agree ☐   Strongly Agree ☐   Disagree ☐   Strongly Disagree ☐
Do not Know or Not Applicable ☐

8. Our sex typically ends abruptly with the man's ejaculation. We rarely cuddle after that. We usually go to sleep or get up to do something else.

Agree ☐   Strongly Agree ☐   Disagree ☐   Strongly Disagree ☐
Do not Know or Not Applicable ☐

9. I sometimes fake orgasms.

Agree ☐   Strongly Agree ☐   Disagree ☐   Strongly Disagree ☐
Do not Know or Not Applicable ☐

10. We almost always have our eyes closed during lovemaking.

Agree ☐   Strongly Agree ☐   Disagree ☐   Strongly Disagree ☐
Do not Know or Not Applicable ☐

11. I do not tell my lover what I like and do not like.

Agree ☐   Strongly Agree ☐   Disagree ☐   Strongly Disagree ☐
Do not Know or Not Applicable ☐

12. My lover should know what I want.

Agree ☐   Strongly Agree ☐   Disagree ☐   Strongly Disagree ☐
Do not Know or Not Applicable ☐

13. I do not know how to turn my partner on.

Agree ☐   Strongly Agree ☐   Disagree ☐   Strongly Disagree ☐
Do not Know or Not Applicable ☐

14. I would like to learn more about sex techniques but I am afraid to admit it.

Agree ☐   Strongly Agree ☐   Disagree ☐   Strongly Disagree ☐
Do not Know or Not Applicable ☐

15. I learned what I need to know about sexual anatomy and sexual techniques in grade school or high school.

Agree ☐   Strongly Agree ☐   Disagree ☐   Strongly Disagree ☐
Do not Know or Not Applicable ☐

16. Sex should just come naturally; planning for it or learning about makes it artificial.

Agree ☐   Strongly Agree ☐   Disagree ☐   Strongly Disagree ☐
Do not Know or Not Applicable ☐

17. Sex should happen in the bedroom, in bed.

Agree ☐   Strongly Agree ☐   Disagree ☐   Strongly Disagree ☐
Do not Know or Not Applicable ☐

18. We rarely experiment with different positions during intercourse; usually it is "man on top."

Agree ☐   Strongly Agree ☐   Disagree ☐   Strongly Disagree ☐
Do not Know or Not Applicable ☐

19. I do not know how to touch my partner sexually.

Agree ☐   Strongly Agree ☐   Disagree ☐   Strongly Disagree ☐
Do not Know or Not Applicable ☐

20. I do not know where the G-spot is.
    Agree ☐   Strongly Agree ☐   Disagree ☐   Strongly Disagree ☐
    Do not Know or Not Applicable ☐

21. I do not know what the prostate does.
    Agree ☐   Strongly Agree ☐   Disagree ☐   Strongly Disagree ☐
    Do not Know or Not Applicable ☐

22. I do not know where the prostate is.
    Agree ☐   Strongly Agree ☐   Disagree ☐   Strongly Disagree ☐
    Do not Know or Not Applicable ☐

23. Delaying ejaculation is dangerous for a man's sexual health.
    Agree ☐   Strongly Agree ☐   Disagree ☐   Strongly Disagree ☐
    Do not Know or Not Applicable ☐

24. The only reasons a man loses his erection are because he has
    ejaculated or because he is suffering from erectile dysfunction.
    Agree ☐   Strongly Agree ☐   Disagree ☐   Strongly Disagree ☐
    Do not Know or Not Applicable ☐

25. Sex after menopause rapidly drops off.
    Agree ☐   Strongly Agree ☐   Disagree ☐   Strongly Disagree ☐
    Do not Know or Not Applicable ☐

26. People are not interested in sex after age 60.
    Agree ☐   Strongly Agree ☐   Disagree ☐   Strongly Disagree ☐
    Do not Know or Not Applicable ☐

27. People are not capable of sex after age 90.
    Agree ☐   Strongly Agree ☐   Disagree ☐   Strongly Disagree ☐
    Do not Know or Not Applicable ☐

28. Only really beautiful, young people have fabulous sex lives.
    Agree ☐   Strongly Agree ☐   Disagree ☐   Strongly Disagree ☐
    Do not Know or Not Applicable ☐

29. I cannot imagine why anyone would want to extend lovemaking for
    hours.
    Agree ☐   Strongly Agree ☐   Disagree ☐   Strongly Disagree ☐
    Do not Know or Not Applicable ☐

30. Tantra is just a cult.
    Agree ☐   Strongly Agree ☐   Disagree ☐   Strongly Disagree ☐
    Do not Know or Not Applicable ☐

31. Tantra is just disguised hedonism.
    Agree ☐   Strongly Agree ☐   Disagree ☐   Strongly Disagree ☐
    Do not Know or Not Applicable ☐

The more of these statements you agree with, the less satisfying your experience with sex likely is. You need more knowledge and skill to create a consistently fulfilling sex life. You entertain some common misconceptions about sex. You may not think sex is bad, but it may well be a duty or obligation, or a simple stress or tension release, rather than a source of pleasure or a spiritual practice. If you are a woman, you may have difficulty having orgasm. If you are a man, you may have performance anxiety and feelings of inadequacy about pleasing your partner. You may ejaculate prematurely.

Sharing Your Answers With Your Lover

We highly recommend that you share your answers with each other. Have a very honest discussion about your beliefs, attitudes, and assumptions about sex. Then make decisions about how you wish to move forward in your desire to create a joyous sexuality as part of your life together. One option is to work systematically with the techniques presented in this book to raise your lovemaking to an art.

> "You fill my eager heart with
> Such desire,
> Every kiss you give
> Sets my soul on fire.
> I give myself in sweet surrender,
> My one and only love."
> —"My One And Only Love," music and lyrics by
> Guy Wood and Robert Mellin

Chapter 5

Mastery and Surrender in the Art of Love

"Life is either a daring adventure or nothing at all. Security is mostly a superstition. It does not exist in nature."

—Helen Keller

"Those who restrain desire, do so because theirs is weak enough to be restrained."

—William Blake

"I regret to say that we of the FBI are powerless to act in cases of oral-genital intimacy, unless it has in some way obstructed interstate commerce."

—J. Edgar Hoover

Control

People love to be in control; it makes them feel safe and secure. Very few are attracted to what may be perceived as its opposite—being *out of control*. Being out of control can be scary, frustrating, even terrifying, and so people expend much time and energy trying to keep themselves, each other, and their environment under control. They develop many strategies, from the subtle to the overt to help feel they are in command, for example, keeping belongings and furnishings in precise order; maintaining strict schedules for waking, sleeping, and eating; making love in the one right place at the one right time in the one right position; or insisting on trying to win an argument whether their point is valid or not. Control can also be a subtle dance of manipulation appearing in the guise of helpless need, or alternatively, as solicitous concern for others—making certain everything runs smoothly and all are happy; taking responsibility for everyone's well-being, so that ultimately everything is under control.

We see the opposite of control not as out of control, but rather as surrender or letting go. Being in control is simply an illusion; when it comes right down to it, no one has absolute control over anything. You do however have a choice—you can choose to try and make things happen precisely as you want them to (and get frustrated when they do not turn out that way), or you can let go, surrendering to the ebb and flow of life.

Surrender

"He who bends to himself a joy
Doth the winged life destroy,
But he who kisses the joy as it flies
Lives in Eternity's sunrise."

—William Blake

Surrender is essential for creating love and for spiritual union. Perhaps you are afraid of surrender because you equate surrender with submission, but the two are very different. Submission exists in the context of power in relationships; it implies domination. Someone submits when they are overpowered or overwhelmed, but surrender is not submission, nor is it passivity, losing, or being inferior. Surrender is an active process of conscious, courageous choice, because although you are not submitting, you do have to give something up. Your ego knows and fears this. Your ego likes things as they are. If some change is required, it wants to take credit—to feel the pride of accomplishment and success. But in the spiritual quest, you give up this self-importance. You give up the claim "I did it on my own, my way."

The fear of surrendering can be so strong that you may feel as if you will be diminished, even annihilated—*you* will disappear. The actuality is very different. Instead of diminishing you, surrender makes you bigger, expanding and connecting you to something so much greater than your ego could ever have imagined.

If surrender is not giving up, giving in, or being dominated, what is it? It is:

* Trusting that there is a larger life process that you are part of and can be in alignment with.

* Showing vulnerability, admitting when you do not know what to do and when you feel fear and insecurity.

* Making choices and taking risks—acting in spite of your fear and insecurity.

* Letting go of attachment to the results of your choices.

* Suspending judgment when things do not go the way you want them to.

* Being open to surprises—allowing that there may be more possibilities than you thought or could have imagined, and that these may be better, not worse, than what you wanted.

As you begin to explore the meaning of surrender, in terms of actual behavior, you will come to a critical distinction. On the one hand, there are those things in your life that you make happen, that you take from life, or that you achieve with willpower and as the result of acquired talent. There are others that come to you as gifts from out of the mystery, the Universe, or from God, wonderful surprises, beyond anything you could have imagined, better than you could have planned or even hoped for.

> "Once in awhile,
> right in the middle of an ordinary life,
> love gives us a fairy tale."
>
> —Unknown

Spiritual gifts often come to you after great effort during which you apply your intellect, knowledge, and skill, but these spiritual gifts are not the *result* of your effort. For example, the rooster crows just before the sun rises, but certainly, we all know that the rooster does not cause the sun to rise. As Joan Baez says, "It seems to me that those songs that have been any good, I have nothing much to do with the writing of them. The words have just crawled down my sleeve and come out on the page."

Spiritual Surrender: Work and Play

Al and Pala approach their surrender to spiritual awakening from two different viewpoints. Perhaps this is a reflection of the yin and yang—the archetypal feminine and masculine forces of receptivity and action. Nevertheless, Al and Pala end up at the same spot: together.

Al's Perspective

Al began from a place of hard work for spiritual awareness—aiming for enlightenment through willpower and discipline. His unsuccessful struggles led him to understand that you cannot make enlightenment happen just because you do certain things or avoid doing certain things. On the other hand, even though some individuals historically have experienced enlightenment without any effort at all—Moses, Saul on the road to Damascus—this is such a rare occurrence that for the vast majority of people, if they wish to evolve spiritually, some effort seems to be required. This is one of many spiritual paradoxes that confound the rational mind. St. John Chrysostom says: "A man's readiness and commitment are not enough if he does not enjoy help from above as well; equally help from above is no benefit to us unless there is also commitment and readiness on our part...Thus I entreat you neither to entrust everything to God and then fall asleep, nor to think, when you are striving diligently, that you will achieve everything by your own efforts."[1]

Al says, "All methods of practical spiritual work have the same end: To prepare you to let God in. My sense of what is required is to make a choice to evolve spiritually, to cultivate a deep burning desire to know God. You choose to have this connection with the Divine, and then you select some spiritual path or practice, which determines the specific form your effort will take. For example, Tantra, Zen, yoga, meditation, and religions such as Christianity all require particular physical and mental disciplines. The danger lies in developing a cause and effect relationship or goal orientation to your practice, expecting 'If I do well with this spiritual practice, then I will get the result I want. If I do it just right, I will become enlightened.' This is really a way for your ego self to try to control your higher self. Instead, you continue your practice, but at some point you 'give up.' You give up your expectation, not your intention or desire. 'Giving up' means that you understand there is no direct connection between any effort you make and whether or not you will have an ecstatic experience. At the point where you give up or surrender, it is likely that the form of your disciplined spiritual practice will continue pretty much unchanged, but your relationship to that practice will change. Instead of it being something that you are doing with the expectation of a result, it becomes an expression of who you are. It becomes an expression of your spirit rather than a search for it. Your spiritual practice becomes a form of worship or prayer rather than an expectation of reward." As Don Juan Matis says, "Choose a path and follow it with heart."

Pala's Perspective

> "Ain't it just like a human,
> here comes that rainbow again."
> —Johnny Cash

Pala approaches spiritual surrender from the perspective of play, moving through life in a joyous celebration, opening her eyes and her heart as she goes. Play, for her, does not equal hedonism. It is not about laying back and slacking off. She puts in lots of effort and she pays lots of attention. But her effort is not a striving to make the glory appear; rather her effort is to open herself so it can come out.

She says, "I consider myself a spiritual experiencer, paying attention to my experiences and learning from them. I am a soul and a body discovering how to live in harmony together. By observation I have come to know when I am acting in a way that supports this, a way that is spiritual—meaning that I am connected, at home regardless of where I am or whom I am with. Through observation, I have found particular actions and attitudes that enable or assist me to be in that state of connection. For instance: trusting my inner self to guide me; cultivating joy in every moment; welcoming the ever-changing flow of life; and doing it all in ways that are truly light-hearted, so as not to take life so intensely seriously. My approach is to live a life that is reverently, lovingly, playfully, sensually aware—what will be will be. I do not struggle to recreate that connection and I do not predict that it will always happen. When I occasionally do fall into a mode of 'get that goal,' it is artificial, so I end up just wanting, not being.

"For instance, when we began our Tantric loving practice, I observed that if we made love for about four hours, I would experience deep bliss, a heart-stopping, mind-blowing euphoric connection with All. I ached for more and so began to focus on making it happen—making love to get the 'spiritual' result I wanted. I forgot that I had reached that place of extraordinary union because I allowed myself to go so completely and unreservedly into every moment of our loving, expecting nothing, holding nothing back. I left my playful, heart-opening, sensual surrender behind and with it went the bliss it had brought me to in the first place!"

Letting Go of Results

"When one door of happiness closes, another opens;
but often we look so long at the closed door
that we do not see the one
which has opened for us."

—Helen Keller

Surrendering means you maintain your intention and you dive in whole-heartedly, but you let go of any expectation that things will turn out the way you planned or expected.

More than 25 years ago, spiritual teacher George Bullied (then director of Twin Valleys Community, with the Emissaries of Divine Light) said to Al in a personal conversation, "The world has lots of spiritual *seekers*. What we need now are more spiritual *finders*." Al says, "I found the statement perplexing because he spoke in a special way suggesting that being a spiritual finder was a decision or an intention rather than an accomplishment, but at the time I was full of my ego self trying to make enlightenment happen with effort. Whether that was what he really meant I do not know, because I have not spoken to him since, but I have made the decision to be a spiritual finder, and I keep making the decision over again each time I get lost. I now believe that he was referring to something as simple as *being continuously in the moment without concern for the results of my actions*."

When you let go of the attachment to end results, you disconnect from the typical emotional overreaction that occurs when things do not turn out as expected. You do not have to worry about the precise outcome beforehand. You do not have to be angry or depressed if it does not turn out your way. You cannot fake this detachment, but you can be aware of your emotions (for example worry, fear, anger.) When you feel negative emotions rising, you can use emotional release techniques to help let them go. It is easier to detach from expectations when you do not suppress or deny your emotions, but instead let them out in constructive ways, like letting off the steam in a boiler. (See Exercise 2: *Emotional Release* exercise on page 100.)

When you let go of attachment to a particular outcome, you allow yourself to be open to the surprise of something other than what you wanted. You acknowledge that what is coming could be better than you had imagined, rather than uselessly indulging yourself in the fear that it will be worse. Certain positive effects appear in your life quickly when you let go of all concern for a particular outcome. For example, your stress level from worry drops off sharply, you can make better decisions, and you act more efficiently when you can stay emotionally calm, even when things do not seem to be going your way.

A simple example of this occurred during one of our trips to Tobago. We had booked a room in a small remote beach resort. The transaction was conducted via telephone before leaving Canada. They did not accept advance credit card payment and did not supply us with any written confirmation. They did not even give us a reservation confirmation number. The man we talked to reassured us it would be fine. Al was skeptical, having traveled in a number of developing countries, but there was nothing else to be done. Sure enough, when we arrived late in the day to claim our room, there was no reservation for us; the place was full and we were turned away. Al was furious and threatened to report the manager to the Tobago Ministry of Tourism. Pala, trying to calm Al's anger, suggested, "Relax, let it go, there's nothing to be done about this, something else wonderful will turn up for us."

There were no other guesthouses available, night was rapidly approaching, and we were more than two hours over steep and winding roads from another town. Just then, a local man who had overheard us suggested a possible solution. He knew of a bed and breakfast that was still under construction. He volunteered to show us the way, in the off chance they might be able to accommodate our stay. They could. The place was marvelous. We had the completely private use of a huge deck overlooking the ocean. There were no stores to buy food, but the proprietor supplied us with a delicious meal. We had one of our most memorable nights in Tobago, listening to the pounding surf, the romantic jazz of Lester Young, and making love all night long on that fabulous deck under the stars.

When you surrender and let go of any expectations about what the results of your actions will be, you will come to understand that even when things seem to go badly, in the longer perspective, these seeming setbacks lead to larger outcomes that are extraordinary and filled with unanticipated delight.

Instead of losing some imaginary freedom, this way of living offers you true freedom. You can do anything you want, but of course, as an aware human being, you will not do just anything at all. On the contrary, you will consistently act in ways that are seemingly "right" as you move to higher levels of self-actualization. You will know the meaning of abundance and share it freely with others. Your optimism and comfort in yourself will radiate. People will feel good to be around you.

You cannot fake surrender; you cannot pretend to give up expectation. You must simply jump into the abyss.

Letting Go in Relationship

> "I wanted a perfect ending. Now I've learned,
> the hard way, that some poems do not rhyme,
> and some stories don't have a
> clear beginning, middle, and end.
> Life is about not knowing, having to change,
> taking the moment and making the best of it without
> knowing what's going to happen next."
>
> —Gilda Radner

What causes the relationSHIP to sink is the accumulated weight of unresolved "stuff." In relationships, letting go means to reveal the emotional truth of what is going on inside you. (See Exercise 1: *Heart Talk* exercise on page 97.) Vulnerable emotions are usually the fear and insecurity that lie below anger. In this you are taking a risk—the other person could reject, judge, or take advantage of you. It means revealing your limitations and weaknesses, which may be as simple as admitting you don't know how to do something or you don't have the solution to a problem.

Revealing emotional vulnerabilities in a loving relationship will deliver immediate benefits in your life.

- ⚘ You give your partner permission to take off the mask of infallibility and perfection.

- ⚘ Your lover will be much more inclined to show you affection if you are vulnerable. Unbending strength is unapproachable, while being vulnerable is an invitation to intimacy. We are not talking about whining and complaining, or false modesty, but being true about your limitations and your capabilities. Revealing your vulnerabilities is not a strategy to seduce someone, but an honest, open attempt at real intimacy.

Letting Go in Sexuality

> "With my body and soul
> I want you more than you'll ever know
> So we'll just let it go
> Don't be afraid to lose control"
>
> —"(I've Had) The Time of My Life," music
> and lyrics by Donald Markowitz,
> John De Nicola, and Frankie Previte

In sexuality, letting go means communicating to your partner about the things you like and do not like to have done to you or to do to your partner. (See the exercises in "Discovering and Asking For What You

Want," starting on page 103.) You can talk about it. You can use sounds, demonstrate, read books, or watch instructional videos to help communicate your likes and dislikes. Sometimes you also take the risk of trying new things that push your envelope, for example taking a Tantra workshop.

Letting Go Energetically

> "Why is it when we talk to God we're said to be praying, but when God talks to us we're schizophrenic?"
>
> —Lily Tomlin

> "Love the moment, and the energy of that moment will spread beyond all boundaries."
>
> —Sister Corita Kent

Energetically, letting go means that as you begin to experience new sensations through your Tantric lovemaking, such as seeing colors, hearing sounds, feeling tingling through your body, or going into altered states of consciousness—where time stops and you seem really huge and connected to everything, that you do not stop and think about it or pull back in fear to your safe zone, but allow yourself to stay open to these new experiences, trusting that you are safe in a cocoon of love.

Letting go energetically also means letting go of expectations of what you are supposed to experience. Early in our Tantric practice, Al had expectations based on things he'd read, and things he'd learned, for example through the Catholic religion, about what a mystical experience was supposed to be like. If his mystical experience was not like that, then he concluded he had not had one. One of the things Tantra teaches both for sensual, sexual experience as well as for spiritual and energetic experience is to forget about what someone else said happened or what you think is supposed to happen, and instead to become an observer of what really occurs. Trust your higher self that what you are experiencing is real and that it is good.

Men and Ejaculation Response

One of the skills men learn in Tantric lovemaking is mastery of the ejaculation response—ejaculation becomes voluntary. A common mistake, one that Al made, is to assume that controlling the ejaculation response is the most important key in Tantric mastery. By keeping all the sexual energy inside, he believed he would quickly build it to such high levels that it would rush up through his body, open his crown chakra, and he'd have enlightenment—perhaps within two weeks! He used willpower and sheer physical strength to stop ejaculation, using control as a strategy. All that happened was that he got a very sore prostate, and was miserable. He quickly learned that control would not work. He instead had to surrender and let go. By letting go of control, he was able to encourage the energy to move away from his genitals, up through his body, rather than out of the end of his penis. He did achieve a degree of mastery with techniques for circulating this hot sexual energy, but that was less important than making the shift in consciousness away from controlling ejaculation to surrendering to the natural flow of energy through his body.

Women and Distracting Thoughts

It is common for women to become distracted by thoughts that come in and grab their attention during lovemaking. One thought leads to another and before you know it, you're not present in the lovemaking anymore. You might assume you should try to stop thinking, to control your thoughts. This doesn't work—the harder you try to control thoughts, to stop thinking, the more thoughts you have, because you are focused on thinking. Instead, surrender to what is going on in your body and allow yourself to let go into the pleasure. This is a skill similar to reading a book and becoming so absorbed in it that you don't hear what is going on around you.

Opening Your Heart

> "Change from the mind to the heart,
> from thinking to feeling,
> from logic to love."
>
> —OSHO

Tantra is about 90 percent learning to open your heart and only 10 percent applying special lovemaking techniques. It is about being emotionally open, taking risks to show your vulnerability, daring to love and be loved. For a woman, focusing on the love she feels for her partner is a great assist to letting go into pleasure and relaxing into her body. For a man, opening his heart helps to delay ejaculation. You are not trying to perform, but by allowing yourself to be emotionally vulnerable, the energy pours out through your heart into your lover and the urge to ejaculate does not arise as quickly. Focusing on the heart chakra for both men and women helps move your hot sexual energy up from your genitals through your body.

Exercises

Heart Talk

"Listening, not imitation, may be the sincerest
form of flattery."

—Dr. Joyce Brothers

We believe that ecstasy in lovemaking is your birthright and that it should be a common experience for lovers, but it is rare. One of the reasons it is rare is that relationship "stuff" gets in the way. People have so much stuff accumulated that they do not allow themselves to become vulnerable to their lover. You become angry, upset, and frustrated with each other and withdraw, barricading your hearts inside your emotional armor for protection and security, blocking your energetic flow and the spontaneous experience of ecstasy. The Heart Talk is a way to dismantle the barricades that keep your hearts closed, a way to take off your emotional armor. That is why we call it a Heart Talk—it helps you open your heart. It is superb for any issue with a heavy emotional load attached to it—one that brings up strong feelings you may have difficulty coping with.

The Heart Talk is remarkably effective and incredibly powerful, but only if you honor the process. This is one place where you must follow the instructions to the letter if you want it to work. **Do not vary the process at all.** If your lover asks for a Heart Talk, do not agree unless you commit to honoring its structure.

A Heart Talk is *not* a two-way conversation. One person talks. The other listens. You listen with patience and respect. You listen without judgment. You listen without taking responsibility for what or how the speaker is feeling. You listen without giving advice. You listen without showing approval, anger, or any other reaction. **You just listen.** The only time the listener can say anything is if you have not *heard* what the speaker is saying or if you do not *understand* what the speaker has said. **The listener does not respond until 24 hours later.**

Listening is harder than you might think. As listener, you will feel an overwhelming urge to do one of three things:

1. You will want to make the talker feel better by offering condolences, comforting hugs, or verbal reassurances that it really isn't so bad and that everything will be all right.

2. You will want to defend yourself if you feel misunderstood or unfairly judged.

3. You will want to offer a quick solution—to jump in and fix the problem.

But as listener, you can do none of these things. The listener can only listen.

The difference that effective listening can make is remarkable. We have heard people comment after a Heart Talk, "I can't believe you did not tell me this before." The talker has replied, "I've told you dozens of times!" When you really listen, you will understand, perhaps for the very first time what is really going on. Deep listening, such as you will do in a Heart Talk, coupled with the 24 hour waiting period, can lead to the solving of problems and the healing of wounds that have existed for many years. We have seen couples clear up issues in a five-minute Heart Talk that they had been struggling with for 10, 20, or 30 years!

In almost every relationship, one person or the other is verbally dominant—quicker with words, more articulate, more aggressive, and able to steer the conversation in a particular direction. This can be intimidating and confusing for someone who is not so quick with words. You can become easily sidetracked and may never really get a chance to express clearly what you want to say. Furthermore, what you are feeling inside is not always obvious. You may not always know what you are feeling or what it means.

The Heart Talk creates a level playing field. Because the listener can only listen, the person talking will not be interrupted, will not have to worry about the reaction of the listener, and will not have to contend with the response, defense, or counter-attacks from the listener, because there will not be any. You will eventually find the right words to explain what is going on inside as you talk about your emotions honestly and openly. You make yourself vulnerable to your partner by stating how you really feel. You take responsibility for your feelings and actions, even if the feelings may be precipitated by something your partner has said or done. You use "I" statements to explain what is happening with you. This helps to clarify feelings and ideas for you as well as your partner, and may be all that is required for healing to take place.

Sometimes the talker will want an immediate response. If so, do not ask for a Heart Talk. If you undertake a Heart Talk and do not honor the process, this invaluable tool will be forever lost to you and that would be most unfortunate.

When you have an issue for a Heart Talk, do not assume that your lover will respond and react in a certain way. You will likely be wrong. Your assumptions about your partner often have more to do with your own fears and suppositions than they do with your partner's reality.

Usually you would not follow one Heart Talk with another Heart Talk 24 hours later. That is possible but is not common. More likely there will be a normal talking dialogue to work on the issue if that seems appropriate. Alternatively, as listener you may have understood the message so clearly, and realized your part in it, that you markedly change your behavior. Whatever your method, a response of some type is necessary.

Pala absolutely loves the Heart Talk even though she finds it one of the most difficult things to do. She loves it because, with it, she can reveal her vulnerabilities—that is also why it's so difficult. She hates to show her self-perceived weaknesses and fears, wants to be strong and perfect. Through the Heart Talk process, she has come to understand that revealing her vulnerabilities actually makes her stronger. This understanding has not made the actual asking for and doing a Heart Talk any easier, but she acts on it anyway, despite her anxiety. Heart Talks help her surrender.

Heart Talk Steps

1. Ask specifically for a "Heart Talk." Your partner knows what the rules are, and by consenting to a Heart Talk, agrees to follow the rules.

2. Begin by sitting with each other for a moment or two, just connecting. Take a deep breath. Relax your body. You can hold hands, look in each other's eyes, or match your breathing.

3. The person who has requested the Heart Talk then speaks without interruption for as long as they need. Usually Heart Talks do not last a long time because there are no interruptions! A long Heart Talk would be 15 minutes.

4. This is not a license to "dump" on the listener. This is about identifying and taking responsibility for how you feel. Use "I" sentences, such as "I become very sad and frightened when I think you are ignoring me." Do not use "you" sentences, such as, "You make me sad by ignoring me all the time." If all the talker reveals is anger, not much will happen, but if the talker can reveal the deeper emotions of fear and insecurity, the results of a Heart Talk can be astonishing. If the talker is only dumping on, blaming, or haranguing the listener, it is not a Heart Talk and the listener can end it.

99

5. No response is allowed for 24 hours. This is essential for the process to work. Tremendous healing can take place during that time.

6. After the Heart Talk, it is a good idea to do some emotional release to change the energy, which may be supercharged with emotion. (See Exercise 2: *Emotional Release* that follows.)

7. After the 24 hour period, the listener gives a response—it may be a discussion, a change in behavior, or an acknowledgement that he has heard what has been said but cannot quite respond yet as he needs a little more time. The response will differ from situation to situation.

Heart Talk Example

Pala is feeling that Al has been ignoring her for a few weeks, so she asks Al for a Heart Talk. Al agrees.

This is what she DOES NOT say:

"I feel like you've been ignoring me. You haven't been affectionate; you've been preoccupied with writing and business. You get surly when I approach you. You haven't bought me flowers or told me I'm wonderful. You haven't taken me out to dinner. You're being a selfish, boorish jerk, and I'm sick and tired of it. You better get your act together, buster, or you don't even want to think about what's going to happen, you twit!"

This is what she DOES say:

"I feel like you've been ignoring me. When that happens, when you are preoccupied with other things and are not affectionate with me, I become insecure. I start to worry that you have found something or someone else more interesting. It brings up my fears of desirability because I'm aging. I don't want to make you feel guilty telling you this, I know you care, but I'm feeling sad and lonely…."

In a Heart Talk you describe your feelings, and many more of them may come up as you are talking or as you are listening. What do you do with them? After your Heart Talk, you let those feelings out with conscious emotional release.

Emotional Release

Al says, "I do not know about you, but I have within me stuff that is irrational, primitive, violent, stupid, and scary. I have within me hurt that I have no idea where it came from. I have within me anger, fear, insecurity, frustration, and a whole lot more. I suspect you do also. What can we do with this? How can we let it out, release it, and let it go in a way that heals without hurting anyone else?" The answer: conscious, constructive emotional release.

Moving your body and making lots of sound are the simple keys to emotional release. Some of our favorite techniques include yelling, screaming, crying, beating the floor with whackers, laughing, and wild dancing. A Styrofoam pool noodle cut in half will give you a four-foot beater with which to hit the floor (not each other). In a space where you can be very active, put on a blindfold, turn on some loud music, and let go with all you have for a few minutes or a few hours. You can do this alone or together. This is not a process of thought, but a way to get out of your rational mind, into your body, and the feelings locked deep inside, allowing those feelings to come out in a way that no one gets hurt.

Do emotional release deliberately, on a regular basis, daily or weekly, as a way to regularly blow off the steam that is building up inside your pressure cooker. One dimension of this process is the purging of a whole bunch of emotional energy—which can make you physically or mentally ill if you suppress it. Another dimension of the process is that purging of this "yucky" stuff makes room for light and love to come in. Pala always asks for clarity and light as she is whacking and hollering.

After doing emotional release for just a few minutes, turn off the loud music. Stand up and remain completely quiet and still. Allow your attention to scan your entire body to become aware of how you feel. Al says, "I find that I am usually flooded with intense emotion, expanded awareness of the presence of love—sometimes to the point of weeping with joy—my perceptions are cleansed and senses amplified so that everything around me appears sparkling and beautiful. I become completely calm and peaceful."

Conscious emotional release is a wonderful practice for children. It helps them learn to be free with their feelings while not becoming taken over by them. If you are in a place where you cannot make a lot of noise pounding the floor and yelling, use laughter and wild dancing without sound. Screaming in your car with the windows rolled up works great, too.

Life Reflection Exercise

"If you can meet with Triumph and Disaster
And treat those two impostors just the same…"
—*If*, Rudyard Kipling

This exercise helps you learn to become detached from the results of your actions. In this way, you can more easily stay completely immersed in the moment, fully enjoying each step along the path you are on. This can dramatically increase the effectiveness of your actions (that is, you get consistently better results), the clarity of your thought improves, making decisions is greatly simplified, worry and distress are reduced or eliminated.

Step 1: Look back over your life and pick out three examples of success, accomplishment, or achievement (times when you got what you wanted), and three examples of failure, defeat, disappointment, loss, or tragedy (times when you did not get what you wanted).

Step 2: Reflect on your successes. How have they contributed to the formation of your character? How have they helped to mold the person you have become? How have they helped you to grow and develop as a human being? How have they helped you to increase your capacity to give and receive friendship, intimacy, and love? How have they helped you to develop qualities such as generosity, kindness, compassion, humility, selflessness, creativity, honesty, and expanded awareness and wisdom? How have they contributed to the quality of your life? How have they helped to make your life a good life? How have they helped prepare you to discover and follow your life's work—your bliss? How have they helped you have faith in something greater than yourself?

Step 3: Reflect on your failures. How have they contributed to the formation of your character? How have they helped to mold the person you have become? How have they helped you to grow and develop as a human being? How have they helped you to increase your capacity to give and receive friendship, intimacy, and love? How have they helped you to develop qualities such as generosity, kindness, compassion, humility, selflessness, creativity, honesty, and expanded awareness and wisdom? How have they contributed to the quality of your life? How have they helped to make your life a good life? How have they helped to prepare you to discover and follow your life's work—your bliss? How have they helped you to have faith in something greater than yourself?

Step 4: Compare your reflections on success and those on failure. Was there any great difference between how these things have contributed to the quality of your life today? Were you surprised to discover that not getting what you wanted often helped you to grow and develop in ways that were ultimately positive, however painful they may have been when they were happening? Did you discover that, in hindsight, failures have been equally valuable to successes in making your life what it is today? Could you conclude that in this context, success and failure are equal? Can this help you to let go of attachment to results of your actions? According the Christian mystic John Climacus, "I find myself amazed by the way in which inward joy and gladness mingle with what we call mourning and grief, like honey in a comb."[2]

Discovering and Asking for What You Want in Bed

"And sometimes when we touch,
The honesty's too much."

—"Sometimes When We Touch," music and lyrics by
Dan Hill and Barry Mann

It may be difficult to ask for what you want in bed if you do not know what that is. Furthermore, you may not have any language to use to ask for what you want. Here are some simple exercises to help you discover what you like and do not like, and to create a common language that you can use to communicate with each other what those things are.

Anatomical Mapping

"If sex is such a natural phenomenon, how come there
are so many books on how to do it?"

—Bette Midler

Anatomical Mapping of your lover's genitals is a way to create a common language for telling each other what you like and do not like in lovemaking. The active partner explains to the receiving partner what she is doing as she does it. Here are some examples:

- "I am touching your clitoris on the left side, with a very light pressure and a soft up/down motion."

- "I am very slowly rotating my index finger around the edges of your anus, and I am using a bit of silicone lubricant."

- "I am running my fingers up and down the inside of your thigh with a feather-light touch."

ᕲ "I am putting my first two fingers inside your yoni, turning them up toward the ceiling and touching your G-spot about two inches inside, through the upper vaginal wall."

ᕲ "I am firmly stroking your penis—pulling gently and twisting a little at the end."

With a number of repetitions of this process, you will each come to know what you like and what your partner likes. Try setting aside special lovemaking time, where you are only doing this, not trying to go on to have orgasms. You can spend hours learning about yourself and each other in this delightful way.

Ask and Ye Shall Receive

"...and then I asked him with my eyes to ask again yes and
then he asked me would I yes to say yes my mountain
flower and first I put my arms around him yes and drew
him down to me so he could feel my breasts
all perfume yes and his heart was going like mad and yes I
said yes I will Yes."

—James Joyce, from Molly Bloom's soliloquy in *Ulysses*

Once you have acquired the terminology for describing your lovemaking, you can use it to let your lover know exactly what you want. If you ask for what you want, without making it mandatory for the giver, you make yourself vulnerable. She could refuse, he could become offended, she could judge you, and so on. If you ask for what you want and it is really a command for your lover to perform as expected, this would be another form of control, and is not what we are suggesting.

Masturbating While Your Lover Watches

"...millions of the females in the United States, and a
larger number of the males, have had their self-
assurance, their social efficiency, and sometimes their
sexual adjustments in marriage needlessly damaged—not
by their masturbation, but by the conflict between their
practice and the moral codes."

—Alfred Kinsey

In the practice of sacred sex, masturbation, or self-pleasuring, is not only a beautiful and loving act, it is also a key for learning. You can learn about your own body, and if you watch your lover masturbate, you can learn about her body. Masturbating while your lover watches is one way to teach him about how you like to be touched, but it is also an excellent way to learn about letting go. This is a particularly effective way for women to discover surrender and allow vulnerability.

Experiment with the masturbation ceremonies for men (Chapter 8, page 171) and women (Chapter 9, page 187).

Anal Penetration for Men

"There are only two guidelines in good sex:
'Don't do anything you don't really enjoy' and
'Find out your partner's needs and don't balk at them if
you can help it'."

—Alex Comfort

Almost everyone holds tension, including sexual tension, around their anus, but this is particularly true for men. Heterosexual men are typically comfortable being the ones who penetrate, but the strongest man can quake with insecurity and even terror at the thought of being penetrated. For a heterosexual male to allow himself to be anally penetrated takes some serious surrender to his lover. When your lover is penetrating your anus, you are completely vulnerable to her and at her mercy. Anal sex is not the only way to learn surrender of course, but it is one of the best ways for heterosexual males.

If you are new to anal sex, there are some simple techniques to learn to make the experience the source of great erotic pleasure. Women may also love anal attention. (See *Anal Massage* in Chapter 11, page 221.) We also recommend some excellent videos that can help you quickly learn the sensual art of anal massage, externally and internally, in Appendix A.

"Therefore, one who desires Buddhahood
Should practice what is to be practiced.
To renounce the sense objects
Is to torture oneself by asceticism—do not do it!
When you see form, look!
Similarly, listen to sounds,
Inhale scents,
Taste delicious flavors,
Feel textures.
Use the objects of the five senses—
You will quickly attain supreme Buddhahood."

—*Candamaharosana*, Tantra Text

Chapter 6

Be Here Now

"Many thousand kisses have we strewn along
our way,
each fresh as the first,
more powerful than the last."

—Pala Copeland

Although we have made love at least 2,000 times in our years to-gether, our lovemaking is fresh and immediate, because each time we make love we are fully in the moment. With 100 percent of our senses zeroed in on exactly what is going on at that moment, we are able to see and feel everything anew. By learning to *be here now,* you too can have a dynamic and vital connection with your lover, not just during sex, but also in all your activities, and you can extend that zest over a lifetime together. It's likely that you have already experienced being wholly in the moment, for example, when you were enraptured by music, or the setting sun, or immersed in dancing, running, creating, or lovemaking. In such moments, time and space seem to disappear. Your senses are hyper-alert. Your heart is at peace. All is right and complete. As the poet Margaret Sherwood says, "In great moments life seems neither right nor wrong, but something greater: it seems inevitable."

Although you would like more of these experiences, you may be-lieve that you have little or nothing to do with creating them, that they are occurrences completely outside your realm of influence. Yet being here now is a state of consciousness. It is only marginally related to the circumstances of a situation, and in no way dependent on them. You can learn to be in the *now moment* at any time or place, under any set of circumstances, positive or negative.

Being in the moment—totally immersed in your actions—is a simple concept; one you would think should also be simple to do. Unfortunately, for most adults it is not. Children do it, moving effortlessly from one total experience to another, but by the time you are grown, you have learned to bring into most situations the unnecessary baggage of previous incidents, present responsibilities, and future pursuits. Your mind pokes its interfering nose in when it need not, luring you into thoughts of the future, or of the past, or into analysis of your current actions so that you miss what is actually happening.

Getting There vs. Being Here

"Generally people spend their lives in activity and rarely,
if ever, take time out for contemplation, or to simply be
in their own presence, unaffected by outside
distractions. Perhaps we are not human beings but
human doings."

—Deepak Chopra

Because so much of human behavior is goal-oriented, people's attention is usually engaged in *doing*, with each action taken primarily to lead somewhere else. Actions then lose their intrinsic meaning—their only importance is to move you closer to your goal. But when you are truly *being*, you are not concerned with reaching somewhere else—you are already there.

For instance, a goal orientation in lovemaking makes orgasm the focus. When you are *doing it* rather than *being it* there is an arbitrary separation between orgasm and "all the other stuff." The other stuff, although pleasurable, is second best, for unless you reach climax, what's the point? All other lovemaking activities are simply the sensual means to reach an orgasmic end. With this perspective, you deny yourself the potential of bliss that waits in every touch and caress. Tantric lovemaking, however, teaches you to realize that potential, because being and doing become one. The separation between the person doing the act and the act itself disappears—the dancer becomes the dance, meditation becomes contemplation, and lovers experience disappearance of all boundaries.

Tantric lovemaking is our favorite way to enter into the contemplative state, because, not only is it a spiritual practice, it is also a source of great pleasure. We do not make love only because we yearn for spiritual awakening; we make love in order to "make love." Nor do we make love just to experience the thrill of orgasm—every moment of our sexual union is an end in itself, and by immersing ourselves in each moment, we experience connection with the Divine.

The Curse of Memory

Memory can rob you of being in the moment. Memory is quick to fill in the blanks, completing your thought, or your sensory impression, before the whole has been received and integrated into your experience. You remember the last time you saw something and you see it as you remember it, rather than as it is *now*. You do the same with all the senses—smelling what you have always smelled, hearing what you have heard before. You do not walk up the stairs *now*, you walk up the same stairs you have walked up countless times, without any awareness of what you are doing. You touch your lover's body from memory. It is not real skin, it is the skin you remember having touched hundreds of times before.

Running on memory is like running on empty. There is just not enough juice in memory to sustain excitement, motivation, and passion. You want something new; you want *variety*. If you touch new skin, if you see a different body, you pay attention in a way that makes you aware that you are alive. After all, as the saying goes, "Variety is the spice of life." But you do not need to find variety and newness outside. Variety does not just come from what you see, but rather how you see it. If you really pay attention, you can train yourself to take in information through your senses as if for the very first time. Once you learn to consciously stay in the moment, then no matter how many times you have touched, tasted, smelled, or seen your lover's skin, it will be unique and new.

> "Love, ageless and evergreen
> Seldom seen by two
> You and I will make each night the first
> Everyday a beginning"
> —"Evergreen," music and lyrics by Barbra Streisand
> and P. Williams

Learning to Be Here Now

"Life is not a matter of milestones but of moments."
—Rose Fitzgerald Kennedy

We try to bring into the rest of our lives the capacity for being in the moment that we have found in Tantric lovemaking. We want to be truly present always. Sometimes it seems hopeless. At others, when we are in the rhythm, the beauty of *being* tells us that everything is possible.

There are simple tools—techniques common in meditative practices the world over—that we use as we are learning to be here now. You already have the equipment you need; all that is necessary is to put it into action. You can:

- Train your mind to focus—make it your servant, not your master.

- Get out of your head by going in to your senses.

- Utilize the extraordinary power of breath.

Mental Awareness and Focus

Stop! Are You in the Moment Now?

What do you do while you are jogging, washing dishes, making love, and so on? If your answer is anything other than jogging, washing dishes, or making love, you are not in the moment.

Try this exercise three times a day. When you are engaged in a particular activity, such as writing a report, playing catch with the kids, washing your car, weeding the garden, chopping wood, eating food, or hugging your mate, stop and ask yourself "What am I doing?" For example, while you are hugging your lover, ask, "Am I doing anything in addition to hugging?" You may find that you are worrying, dreaming, or thinking about something else, talking about unrelated events, rushing to get out the door, and so on. If so, then you are likely missing out on the full sensual pleasure of your two bodies touching. You may miss the deep emotional connection that happens when you focus on opening to another, and you will not receive all the energetic nourishment that hug could give you. As you practice pausing and asking, you will begin to recognize when you are really immersed in your activity and when you are distracted by other thoughts or actions.

Time and Space

This delightfully simple yet power-packed exercise is from Ram Dass' remarkable book *Be Here Now*[1].

Part 1: Ask yourself: Where am I?

Answer: Here.

Ask yourself: What time is it?

Answer: Now.

Say it until you can hear it.

Part 2: Remind yourself during the day (at least three times)—with Post-it notes or agenda items or programmable wristwatches—to stop and ask yourself the same questions and give yourself the same answers. "Where am I?" "Here." "What time is it?" "Now." You will begin to understand that no matter where you are in the world, you are always *here*. No matter what the clock says, it is always *now*. Life goes on, but you are *here* and *now* in the eternal present.

Seeing for the Very First Time

One trap of memory is that you can end up making love to your recollection of your partner's body rather than to your living, breathing lover. If you've made love many times before, you can assume that you know your partner's body perfectly—you know exactly the feel of her breasts or his buttocks, you are completely familiar with his scent. With Tantric lovemaking, even though you have touched that breast hundreds of times and think that you know it perfectly, you touch it, lick it, or suck it "as if" for the first time.

Trick your mind into paying attention by pretending there will be a test later during which you'll be blindfolded and presented with a number of different breasts. From amongst them you will have to identify your lover's. How would you pay attention to that breast in order to identify it blindfolded? You would smell, taste, and touch very consciously, with highly focused attention—that is what experiencing as if for the very first time means. You won't need to employ this tactic after you have trained your mind to the attention habit.

Death as Advisor

"Love is the emblem of eternity;
it confounds all notions of time;
effaces all memory of beginning, all fear of an end."
—Madame de Stael

Your mind will pay close attention to what is happening if it believes this is the last time you will be experiencing something. Use death as your advisor. Remind yourself that nothing is constant, you never know how much time you, or anyone else, has in this world. You may be kissing your lover for years to come, or the kiss you share this morning may be your last. This is not a fear tactic, but a way to help you transform a habit of inattention into the practice of mindfulness.

111

Thought Backtracking

This exercise helps you catch yourself when your mind wants to wander off on an irrelevant train of thought. After repeating it a number of times, you will catch yourself quickly. Eventually the wandering happens less and less frequently and you will remain in the now moment more and more.

Focus your attention on any chosen object, for example, a plant in a pot. Try to pay attention only to the plant. At some point, you will notice that you are thinking about something completely unrelated to the plant. Stop as soon as you have become aware of your wandering thoughts and attempt to follow your thoughts back to their origin—the plant. For example while looking at the plant, you might have noticed the rich green color of the leaves. This led you to the thought that the color of the leaves would look great in the upstairs bedroom you are planning to repaint. There is a sale coming up at the carpet store and you could get a new carpet to go with the paint, but you're not sure your mate will agree to spend that much on the room. You wonder how much is left on the credit card or should you wait on the carpet, because you know you really need to get the brakes replaced on the car…. At this point, you realize your mind has been wandering. Stop and recall each thought back to the start from replacing the brakes, to waiting on the carpet, to how much is left on the credit card, to your mate agreeing to spend that much money, to getting a carpet to match the green paint, to the sale at the carpet store, to painting the upstairs bedroom green, to the lovely green color of the leaves of the plant.

Try to separate yourself from your thoughts and emotions by staying objective and impersonal in relation to them. This draws on your "witness" consciousness, a part of you that can watch what you are thinking and feeling without need to judge or act. Imagine your mind is a movie screen and your thoughts are scenes passing by. They come, they go, and no action is required.

Sensory Awakening

Perception Without Naming

"Thinkers, listen, tell me what you know of that is not
inside the soul? Take a pitcher full of water and set it
down on the water—now it has water inside and
water outside. We mustn't give it a name, lest silly people
start talking again about the body and the soul."

—Kabir

Paying attention to sensory information helps you learn to be fully present. In this practice, you simply experience sensory phenomena, you do not analyze or even name what you are experiencing. Naming can set in motion a train of thought that pulls you out of the moment. For example, if Pala, who loves to smell things, sniffs Al's neck and gets a whiff of his musky cologne, she savors it through her nostrils, enjoying the pleasure she receives from this aroma—a big "mmmm." She does not sniff it and then think, "Mmmm—Jovan Musk, I love that smell. It smells so good on Al. I wonder if my brother would like it too. I could get him some for Christmas. Maybe I should get it at the duty-free store when we go across the border to visit Al's Dad. When will we be going? I better call him."

Another example is listening to a bird's song. You may simply enjoy the lovely lilt of its call. Alternatively, you may hear it and start thinking, "Oh what a lovely sound. That sounds like a mourning dove. Isn't it great that there are mourning doves nearby. I wonder if I can make a house for them so they will stay around? What kind of house would I make? Maybe the library has a book on birdhouses."

Do the following sensory attention meditation three times a day. It is based on a one-minute meditation developed by Osho, a 20th century enlightened master from India.

- Stop whatever you are doing and become still.

- For one minute, pay attention to your senses: sight, smell, touch, taste, and hearing.

- Notice what is coming to you through your senses—simply smell the smell, hear the sound, and so on, without naming anything.

Enliven Your Senses

This exercise helps to revive and stimulate senses other than sight. It is akin to Margo Anand's "Sensory Awakening Ritual,"[2] one of many outstanding exercises that have inspired us from her comprehensive books on sacred sexuality.

1. Gather items to help stimulate the senses of sound, touch, smell, and taste. Gather at least nine items for each sense. For example:
   - Sound: chimes, drum, Tibetan singing bowl, whistle, music box, bell, rattle, metronome, pot lid and wooden spoon, recorded bird song, stiff fabric that rustles as you crinkle it in your hands, gong, flute, and so on.

ᴕ Touch: feathers, silk, fur, warm oil, ice cubes, misting water bottle, powder, pumice stone, wooden massage roller, cotton balls, rough fabric (canvas, twill, homespun wool), leather, fleece, and others. Gather items to pass softly over your lover's skin, bare arms, neck, face, and so on.

ᴕ Smell: essential oils, perfume, men's cologne, jars of spices, baby powder, fish sauce, coffee, aromatic flowers, and the like.

ᴕ Taste: fruits (fresh or dried), chocolate, nuts, hot sauce, raw vegetables, liqueurs, crackers, cheeses, olives, pickles, and so on. These you will feed to your lover with your fingers and/or pass some tasty bits from your mouth to hers.

2. Seat your lover in a comfortable chair and blindfold her.

3. Help her to relax by breathing slowly and deeply together.

4. Whisper softly into her ear something like this: "With your permission, I am going to take you on a journey of sensory awakening. As I present you with each new item, allow yourself to experience it fully without trying to name or identify it."

5. Begin with the sense of sound. Make each sound for approximately 30 seconds. Take a 30-second break between sounds.

6. Proceed to touch, then smell, and finally taste. Take a 30-second break between each sensory item in your repertoire.

7. Go *very* slowly. Allow your partner plenty of time to experience each delightful sense. Be playful, loving, and respectful.

8. Do this for each other on different days. If you want to take turns on the same day, use different items for each sense. This is also a marvelous exercise to do at a party.

Loving Body Discovery

Take a loving visual, tactile tour of your mate's body. Create a sensual ambience for your body discovery. Make sure the room is warm.

Lighting should be bright enough to see clearly but soft and caressing to your skin, for example candles or a red light bulb. Play music that relaxes you and makes you feel sensual.

Begin by asking your lover's permission: "My beloved (or your name for your lover), I come to you with love, desire, and the utmost respect. May I please explore your wonderful body?" Your lover responds: "Yes, I welcome you with love and trust." You can make up your own words to show respect, love, trust, and care. Sometimes, the receiving partner may be shy or uncomfortable having a particular body segment thoroughly explored. If this is the case, it is important to be open and honest. Tell each other how you feel, and respect your limitations.

Begin from a distance with a slow, soft caressing look from head to toe and back again. As you are looking, tell your lover what pleases you about her. Remember most of us are not accustomed to being gazed at all over, especially with love and adoration and desire. Your partner may be feeling uncomfortable—ask her to breathe deeply, to relax any tension in her body, and to try to feel the vital energy coming from your eyes into her body.

Move closer and mix your looking with touches. Go slowly. Begin with her hands, lifting them, caressing her palm, stroking it lightly then gently sucking each finger. Work your way up her arms, feathering lightly with your fingers, repeating the path with a sniffing, tickling nose, repeat again with pouty nibbling lips and darting, slippery tongue. As you explore, keep letting your lover know how much you are enjoying your tour—tell her with words, sounds, facial gestures. Look into each other's eyes frequently and feel the connection between the two of you deepening.

From arms, move up to her head, neck, ears, then eyes, face, mouth, chin, and back down to her neck. Take your time. Feel her skin beneath your hands, smell the unique scent of each part of her, listen to her breath and to any sounds she may make in response to your touch. Switch from her head to her feet. Play with them as you did with her hands. Then proceed up her legs. Take your time. Be playful. Focus all your attention on your lover and allow your heart to open.

When you reach the tops of her legs, roll her on to her stomach and explore her back with your hands, then your nose, then your mouth, and combinations of all three, from the base of her neck all the way down to her feet.

Once again, roll her on to her back and starting at the hollow of her neck work your way down her torso in waves using your hands, nose, and mouth. Pause at breasts and belly or other spots on her torso that give both of you pleasure. Finally, turn your attention to her vagina. This

Loving Body Discovery

is the seat of creation, the wellspring of life. Explore her gently with nose, mouth, and fingers. Your purpose is to heighten awareness for both of you, not to turn her on (although this may happen). Do not use habitual touches that you know will bring her to orgasm. If either, or both, of you become sexually excited, relax and *be* with the excitement. This is an opportunity to feel the body electric—to raise and keep the energy high without going over the edge to release. If your charge is too intense, try deep, slow breathing and *grounding* (Chapter 7, page 127). You may be surprised to find that the loving body discovery can also be more relaxing and affectionate than sexually stimulating. Whatever happens is right.

Finish with a complete hug—head to toe for two minutes. Feel your hearts beating. Match your breathing rhythm. In love and respect, thank each other, and then switch partners.

Remember, the Loving Body Discovery is not a massage, nor is it done with the intention of arousing your lover sexually, nor is it leading up to intercourse or an orgasmic climax. Separate the Loving Body Discovery from these other ways of being intimate so you can experience being in the moment without trying to get somewhere in your lovemaking.

You can discover the joy of touching each and every part of your lover's body, and learn that every touch is potentially as satisfying and wonderful as any other. This is also an excellent exercise in which to move beyond the anxiety of responsibility to "perform" sexually, to make it happen for your partner.

Conscious Breathing

> "There is one way of breathing that is shameful and constricted. Then there is another way: a breath of love that takes you all the way to infinity."
>
> —Rumi

One of the essential tools of Tantric loving, conscious breathing not only brings you into the moment so you can participate fully in an intimate sexual exchange, it also fortifies your reproductive system and heightens your sexual pleasure. In addition, your overall health benefits when you breath properly—aches and pains, tension and anxiety disappear; your body cells charge up with more oxygen, and your brain energizes for clear thinking.

Breath control during lovemaking opens you up for extended pleasure and multiple orgasms. When you want more arousal and excitement, breathe rapidly (panting); when you want to sustain riding the edge of sexual pleasure, breathe slowly and deeply. Conscious breathing helps you learn to surrender and to ask for what you want. Focusing on a long, slow exhalation (twice as long as your inhalation) assists you to let go. Extending your inhalation for twice as long as your exhalation aids in developing your assertiveness and self-confidence so you can express your desires. As well, breathing in harmony with your partner is a powerful way to cultivate your sexual relationship and strengthen your energetic connection.

Deep Belly Breathing

This exercise helps you learn to breathe deeply and consciously:

- Sit, or lie down in a quiet, comfortable place.
- Loosen up by contracting and then releasing all the parts of your body.
- Start at your feet—tighten, hold, let go.
- Move to your calves—tighten, hold, let go.
- And so on, all the way up to your head.

- Remember the muscles in your face, neck, and scalp—you may be surprised at how much tension they hold.

- When your body is relaxed, begin to focus on your breathing.

- Place your right hand on your abdomen and your left hand along the bottom of your ribs on your left side.

- Inhale through your nose, slowly, deeply, naturally. Feel the air coming in through your nostrils. Follow it all the way

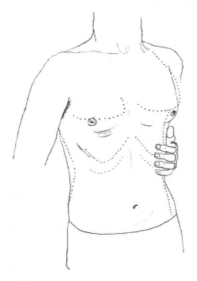

Deep Belly Breathing

down to your belly.

- Your belly should rise as you begin your inhale; you may even push it out a little to help you relearn to breathe very deeply.

- Continue to fill your lungs by expanding your rib cage.

- Feel your ribs moving outward as you inhale. You may even push them out a little to help you.

- Continue inhaling, filling the upper portion of your lungs.

- Inhale until your lungs and even your throat, mouth, and nose are completely full of air.

- Use a slow count of five to time your inhalation.

- As soon as you are full of air, begin to exhale.

- Do not hold your breath or stop between inhaling and exhaling.

- Allow a smooth transition from "in" to "out."

- Exhale slowly through your nose, counting to nine.

- Pay attention to the sensation of air as it passes.

- Inhale again and follow the breath down into your belly bringing with it vital energy.

- Exhale and imagine all negativity, illness, or tension leaving your body.

- Continue to inhale and exhale slowly.

- If thoughts intrude, gently call your attention back to your breath.

- Follow each breath, slow and deep.

- Do this exercise for a minimum of 10 minutes.

If you fall asleep while you are practicing, have a nice nap!

Harmonizing Your Breathing

During Tantric lovemaking, partners often harmonize their breathing. You can do this for different effects.

- At the outset of your loving time, sitting quietly together, looking into each other's eyes and breathing in synchronicity will help you tune in to each other and tune out the rest of the world. Breathing slowly and deeply in this fashion will also relax you and help you focus on the present moment.

- When you are both highly aroused and want to move the energy you have built up with your love play, stop active lovemaking. For instance, if you are engaged in intercourse stay joined but stop thrusting. Become still, look into each other's eyes, and breathe slowly and deeply together focusing on moving your high sexual energy up from your genitals throughout your body. This will also deepen your emotional and energetic connection and help you prolong your pleasure.

Experiment with these variations of breathing rhythm:

- Both partners inhale and exhale at the same time.

- One partner inhales while the other exhales.

Counting Breaths

Counting breaths is a familiar exercise for students of Zen. This is an excellent practice to help you learn to stay focused on the now moment. Begin to count your breaths up to 10. Then start over at one and count to 10 again. Repeat this for the period of time you have chosen for your practice. Keep your mind only on your counting of breaths. When other thoughts intrude, do not try to get rid of them, just bring your attention back to your counting. Try to work up to where you can do 300 counts (10 counted 30 times). This must be done without distracting thoughts of any kind before you can claim to have done it. Depending upon how slowly you breathe, counting to 300 will take close to three hours![3] A good start is to get as far as 30 counts (10 counted three times) without distracting thoughts.

Immersing Yourself in Experience

"The greater part of our happiness or misery depends on our dispositions and not our circumstances."

—Martha Washington

"I reckon people are about as happy as they make up their minds to be."

—Abraham Lincoln

Immersion is something you do, not something that happens to you. Realizing this is a key to opening yourself to experience immersion, which in turn is essential for experiencing ecstasy. Until you understand this, you may be tempted to give credit for the peak experiences you have to the circumstances of the experience or to the other person(s) involved, if there were any. Once you know that immersion is something you do, you can learn exactly how you do it and you can do it more often. With mastery, you can immerse yourself any time, in any experience you want to.[4]

Immersion Exercise

1. **Recall a peak experience from any time in your life**, one in which you were aware of some, but not necessarily all, of the following emotions and states of being:

☐ Joy

☐ Bliss

☐ Ecstasy

☐ Euphoria

☐ Happiness

☐ Excitement

☐ Freedom

☐ Sexually turned on

☐ Intellectually excited

☐ Extreme sensory richness

☐ Pleasure

☐ Trust

☐ Safe

☐ Secure

☐ Comfortable

☐ Appreciated

☐ Accepted

☐ Loved

☐ Cared for

☐ Beauty

☐ Tenderness

☐ Accomplishment

☐ Creativity

☐ Confidence

☐ Fun

☐ Playfulness

☐ Satisfaction

☐ Relaxation

☐ Contentment

☐ Peace of mind

☐ Spiritual awakening

☐ Unity

☐ Oneness with all things

☐ Direct connection with the Divine

☐ Positive hallucinations

☐ Out-of-body experience

☐ Psychic phenomena such as telepathy, remote viewing, moving objects at a distance, and so on.

2. **Describe the details of the experience.** Here are some of the things you can look for when describing the experience:

⚘ **What were you actually doing:** making love, dancing, singing, meditating, creating your art, competing, working?

⚘ Were you **alone or with someone** (a man or woman or many people)? Was it a **stranger or someone you knew**?

⚘ Was the situation **planned or spontaneous,** involving **surprise and/or mystery**?

⚘ Describe the **location:** Were you **inside or outside**? Was it **hot or cold**? Were you in or near **water**, in the **countryside**, in a **city**?

⚘ What did you **see:** colors, textures, motion, places, people, objects, animals, scenery, movies, theater?

⚘ What did you **hear:** sounds of nature, sounds of bodies, words, music (live or recorded), machinery?

⚘ What did you **taste:** food, drinks, bodies, semen?

⚘ What did you **smell:** bodies, scents, perfumes, flowers, air?

⚘ What did you **touch:** textures, bodies, materials, wet, dry, hot, cold, rough, smooth, soft, hard?

⚘ Were you **talking and sharing interesting ideas**?

⚘ Were you **being watched**?

⚘ Was **fantasy** involved in the experience?

⚘ Was what you were doing **forbidden, taboo, "bad," exotic**?

⚘ Was there **danger** or **violence**?

⚘ Were you in **control** or did you **surrender**, or both?

⚘ Were you **rescuing** someone, or being rescued?

⚘ Were you using alcohol, marijuana, or any **mind altering substance**?

☙ What **emotions, feelings, and states of being** did you experience? Check the ones that apply.

☐ Joy	☐ Tenderness
☐ Bliss	☐ Accomplishment
☐ Ecstasy	☐ Creativity
☐ Euphoria	☐ Confidence
☐ Happiness	☐ Fun
☐ Excitement	☐ Playfulness
☐ Freedom	☐ Satisfaction
☐ Sexually turned on	☐ Relaxation
☐ Intellectually excited	☐ Contentment
☐ Extreme sensory richness	☐ Peace of mind
☐ Pleasure	☐ Spiritual awakening
☐ Trust	☐ Unity
☐ Safe	☐ Oneness with all things
☐ Secure	☐ Direct connection with the Divine
☐ Comfortable	☐ Positive hallucinations
☐ Appreciated	☐ Out-of-body experience
☐ Accepted	☐ Psychic phenomena such as telepathy, remote viewing, moving objects at a distance, and so on.
☐ Loved	
☐ Cared for	
☐ Beauty	

3. **As you recall the experience, notice the part you played in it.** Look for the ways that you were responsible for it, how you created the experience, or allowed it to happen. *No peak experience just happens to you.* You are always an active participant in any experience of joy, bliss, ecstasy, and happiness. For example, ask yourself:

   ✍ "How did I choose to open myself to this experience?"

   ✍ "What did I do to help create my own joy?"

   ✍ "How did I put myself into the experience?"

   ✍ "How did I allow myself to go deeper into the experience?"

4. **Recall a second peak experience and describe this experience as you did the first one.**

5. **Look for similarities and patterns in the two experiences.** These similarities and patterns are your keys for allowing yourself to be immersed in ecstatic experience. Later, on your own, you can recall other peak experiences and get a more complete and clear picture of your "immersion pattern" (how *you* do immersion). Remember, it is not the circumstances themselves, but how you responded to them. Use the list from step number 2 for identifying the similarities and patterns. *Mark only the items that show up in both experiences.* Naturally you can add other things to the list.

> "Those who know are always drunk on the
> wine of the Self."
>
> —Ghalib

Chapter 7

Energy Delights

"Ecstasy is our very nature."

—OSHO

From the moment of our first Tantric lovemaking experience, we knew we were dealing with something beyond our regular understanding of our physical bodies. We experienced what we could only describe as an energetic phenomenon. This was foreign to us not only in its manifestation but also in its very idea. As children of a Western culture, "energy" was the electricity that powered our TVs and telephones and food processors, the stuff that was in increasingly short supply to fuel our cars and planes, and an element of some vaguely remembered Einstein equation from high school physics. It had nothing to do with how we moved through life, understood ourselves, or connected to others.

In Eastern societies it has everything to do with these and more. The idea that all of life is expressed in energetic flow is an underpinning of much of Eastern philosophy. Not only do human beings interact with this flow, it is part of their spiritual duty to conscientiously do so. There are numerous interpretations and classifications of "life force energy." The Taoists of China call it "chi," "ki," or "qi," and for them specifically, sexual energy is "ching." From India we have "prana" (from Sanskrit terms: "pra" meaning forward or before, and "ana" meaning breath), "kundalini," and "shakti"—the elemental life force in Tantric practice.

There are countless methods of working with energy, and Westerners are becoming increasingly familiar with them in areas as diverse as exercise, interior design, medical care, and sexuality:

- ⚥ Qi Gong (Chi Kung), Tai Chi, and Hatha Yoga, all methods of exercising and balancing your energetic as well as your physical body, are becoming the workouts of choice for everyone from executives to retirees to film stars.

- ⚥ Even conservative matrons are decorating their homes based on the harmonious principles of feng shui, which considers the combination of interior and exterior space, light, sounds, aromas, materials, placement of buildings and furnishings, and the energetic effect these combinations create.

- ⚥ Nurses at hospitals throughout North America regularly perform Therapeutic Touch, a healing process based on the assumption of a human energy field that extends beyond the skin.

- ⚥ Acupuncture, acupressure, Reiki, and a host of innovative therapeutic procedures, such as Awareness Release Therapy and Emotional Release Therapy, are gaining popularity, even with some medical doctors.

As modern science moves farther away from a Newtonian model of the universe as a giant machine and closer to an Einstein-influenced perception of it as energy in constant motion, the Western rational mind is more likely to accept the concept of "vital force" and the practices that accompany it. However, you do not have to understand it or even believe in it to begin to work with energy. Just jump in and see for yourself. Try some of these energy exercises that we employ in our life together and teach to others in our workshops. They are drawn from diverse traditions, ancient and modern. Some are general while others are specific to sexuality. As with all of the practices we present, we encourage you to thoroughly experiment, then retain those that work for you, and leave the rest behind.

Starting Out

You have already experienced your energy body, you just may never have thought of it that way. Whenever you know someone is coming up behind you, but you haven't seen them, heard them, or smelled them and they haven't touched you, you're feeling them with your energy body.

A simple way to begin to get in touch with your energy body is to briskly rub your hands together for about a minute. Then with your hands in front of you, palms facing each other, an inch or two apart, concentrate on the center of your palms. You may feel a tingling, or a pressure, or some other sensation. If you do, see if you can shape and play with this force. Move your hands farther apart, then closer together. What do you notice about this force as you mold it in your hands?

Grounding

Grounding, a simple, yet highly effective, practice that centers and stabilizes you, will change your life for the better. Through grounding, you direct energy down into the Earth. You can do this through your root chakra (an energy center that runs from the base of your spine to your pubic bone), through your feet, through your whole body if you are lying flat on the ground. There are many ways to ground, but this one is our favorite. We learned it from an extraordinary man named Denis Chagnon, whose loving touch has restored many to health.

Grounding Exercise

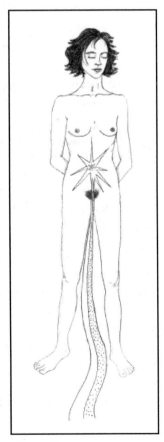

- Sit or stand comfortably—back straight but not rigid.

- Take a slow deep breath in through your nose.

- Let your breath flow slowly without pause—in and out.

- Focus your attention on your root chakra (your genitals to the base of your spine—more about chakras follows).

- Imagine a connection opening between your root chakra and the earth.

- This can take many forms and can be different each time you practice. Some see a tree trunk or roots, a hollow bamboo, a silver tube, a beam of light, a flow of menstrual blood, and so on.

- Visualize this connection extending from you down into Mother Earth, passing through the crust, the bedrock, deep into the molten core.

Grounding

- When you have your connection formed, allow any overwhelming sensations, any negative energies—anger, lethargy, hyperactivity, grief, anxiety, fear—to flow through your connection down into the center of Mother Earth.

- There, in a fiery blast, the energy is purified and returns back to you as safe, strong, peaceful life force.

- Maintain your flowing connection—overwhelming energy down and calming energy up.

We encourage you to practice grounding regularly. Try to do it consciously as you move through your day. Keep reminding yourself to ground, and then do it. Notice what a difference it makes in your stability and calmness.

But I Don't Feel Anything!

"And now here is my secret, a very simple secret: It is only with the heart that one can see rightly; what is essential is invisible to the eye."

—Antoine de Saint-ExupÈry, *The Little Prince*

"Love is what's in the room with you at Christmas if you stop opening presents and listen."

—Bobby, age 5

Some people are more sensitive to energetic phenomenon than others. As you begin your energy practices do not look for particular "special effects," rather be an observer of what is happening within you. If you do not notice anything at all while you are doing the exercises, be patient with yourself and keep going, even though your rational mind may want to conclude that this energy is not real and that nothing is happening.

Al's Experience: When we first began Tantric practice, I did not feel anything when I did energy exercises and my rational mind wanted me to reject the whole notion of subtle energy. What I did was I continued to practice the exercises, for example grounding, for several weeks, as if something real was happening. Then I stopped the practice for a week, added it back in for another three to four weeks, stopped for a week, and so on. I became aware that something very important was happening. When I did the grounding, my days went smoothly. I was able to handle stress without distress, making quick and effective decisions. I felt reasonably happy—life seemed generally good. When I stopped grounding, I found that within two to three days I became moody, and worried even about small things. I was picky toward Pala about nothing at all. I now do grounding each day as often as I remember to do it.

Pala's Experience: Like Al, I notice the difference that focusing on energetic connection makes to my life, but I am also aware of very specific sensations as I am in the energy practices. For instance, when grounding, my feet become very warm and rooted to the Earth, and my genitals tingle. I feel a release as negative energies leave my body and a lightness of being as Mother Earth energy comes in. If my eyes are closed, I often see colors.

You might notice colors, sounds, kinesthetic sensations, smells, electrical current, changes in temperature, goose bumps, hair rising up, and so on. Remember, the key is to observe, not expect. If you are looking for a specific outcome, you may miss what is actually going on.

Energy Centers—7 Chakras or Tan Tiens

"In Babylonia the spheres of the planets were called
'voices' and they were supposed to produce music.
According to Midrashic literature, the trumpet sounding
at Mount Sinai had seven different pitches (or notes), and
the rabbinical literature speaks of 'the heavenly music'
heard at the revelation."[1]

—I. Velikovsky

Chakra is a Sanskrit word meaning "Wheel of spinning Energy." The Taoist term for these energy centers is Tan Tien (pronounced Don Tyen). When we refer to chakras, we are referring to the subtle energy body, not the physical body. There are seven major chakra energy centers (some systems suggest as many as nine[2]) in the subtle energy body, aligned vertically up and down the spine, from the tip of the tailbone (coccyx) to the crown at the top of the head.

Each chakra vibrates to a distinct musical note, is connected with particular organs in the body, and relates to specific emotional, psychological, and spiritual issues. Particular colors, stones and crystals, essential oils, flower essences, shapes, symbols, and numbers influence these centers. Because each chakra represents aspects of your personality, character, and spiritual development, by working with them you can influence and direct your personal growth, healing, and spiritual progress.

Energy flows in to the chakras from the world around you and out to the world from within, as well as up and down between them. The chakras

Crown

Third
Eye

Throat

Heart

Solar
Plexus

Belly

Root

Chakra Centers

can become blocked, making you feel physically or mentally sick and out of balance. Fully open, clockwise-spinning chakras help energy to flow freely through your body and assist you in becoming a whole, healthy human being. In Tantric lovemaking, you direct the sexual energy that is passionately building in your genitals up through your chakra centers, share it with your lover, and pass it on to the universe. The more balanced and open these centers are, the easier it will be for you to move your energy.

First Chakra: Root or Base Chakra

The first chakra, the root chakra, is located at the coccyx at the base of the spine, and perineum, which is the spot of skin located between the anus and the vagina in women, and between the anus and scrotum in men. This chakra is the Muladhara Chakra. The sound of this chakra is LAM, in note C. The color of this chakra is red. Body parts associated with this chakra include the adrenals, perineum, anus, blood, the lymphatic system, and the skeletal system (teeth and bones).

When the first chakra is open, you will feel secure, calm, and motivated. You will welcome change, and adapt well to new circumstances. The adrenal glands regulate the flight or fight reaction in response to threats and danger with release of two hormones, epinephrine (adrenaline) and norepinephrine (noradrenaline). The adrenals determine how well you manage stress of any kind in your life. When your body manages stress well, you will have courage and calmness in the face of threats or danger and be able to act fearlessly.

When the first chakra is blocked or closed, you will feel insecure and may experience paranoia. Change will be threatening to you. Life seems beyond your control so you may try to compensate by overcontrolling little things, for example always eating at exactly the same time each day, always sitting in the same chair—"your chair." You may become fanatical about orderliness or cleanliness. You will tend to be incapacitated in the face of danger. You may bully those who are weaker and more vulnerable than you are.

Opening the First Chakra Exercise

You can stimulate any chakra, help it to open, and encourage it to spin, rotate, or vibrate by touching it. You can touch yourself or your partner.

- Lie on your right side. This will tend to open your left nostril and stimulate your right brain hemisphere.

- Reach around from behind and place your left palm on your sacrum (tailbone) with your middle finger (the longest finger) touching your coccyx.

- Reach around from the front and place your right palm on your perineum and your middle finger touching the middle finger of your left hand at your coccyx. In this position your are reaching down between your crotch, one hand from the front and one hand from the rear until your two longest fingers just touch, and with the rest of your hands against your skin.

- You can do this while clothed or naked; while naked is best.

- Hold this position while you visualize the color red, and make the sound *lam* (long vowel aaaaa).

- You may also place any red, black, brown, or silver stone or crystal between your hands and your body while you do this meditation.

131

- ঝ Visualize the energy in this chakra spinning, for example, smoke or fog swirling in a clockwise direction, or a propeller rotating in a clockwise direction.

The grounding exercise described earlier is also excellent for freeing up the root chakra.

Second Chakra: Navel/Belly/Hara/Sexuality Chakra

The second chakra is located at the belly, or hara, in the center of the space between your hipbones, about two finger widths below the navel. This chakra is the Svadhisthana Chakra. The sound of this chakra is VAM, in note D. The color of this chakra is orange. The body organs most closely associated with this chakra are the kidneys, bladder, small intestine, and large intestine (including the colon, rectum, and anal canal). Specifically for men, this includes: prostate, penis, scrotum, and testicles; for women: vagina, uterus, and ovaries.

When the second chakra is open and vibrating, you will feel confident and balanced, trusting that the universe will provide all that you need because you actually experience abundance. You will attract money and success easily and so will act with generosity toward others. You will feel comfortable with your sexuality, experiencing great passion. Men will be able to get and maintain erections. Women will be easily orgasmic.

When the second chakra is blocked or closed, you may be stingy and protective of what you have out of fear that you will lose it and not be able to get more. You may be overly materialistic, and not having enough money will be a constant worry. You may experience a lot of fear and this may be associated with health problems in the body organs associated with this chakra, for example, kidney infections, or a lot of grief associated with problems in the large intestine. Men may have trouble getting an erection, or may suffer from premature ejaculation. Women may have difficulty allowing themselves to surrender enough to become orgasmic.

Opening the Second Chakra Exercise

- ঝ Open your hands, keeping your fingers together and extend your thumb at a right angle to your fingers. If you look at your right hand when it is open this way, your index finger and your thumb form an "L" shape, and your left hand forms a reverse "L" shape.

- ❧ Place your thumbs on your hips, right thumb on right hip and left thumb on left hip. Bring your open hands around your front covering your abdomen until the longest finger on each hand just touches each other.

- ❧ Alternatively, bring your hands around your back until your longest finger on each hand just touches each other.

- ❧ Holding your hands in either of these positions brings healing energy to these organs and stimulates the second chakra. You can also lightly massage the area for additional stimulation. This is excellent for rejuvenating the kidneys and relieving lower back pain.

- ❧ Hold this position while you visualize the color orange, and make the sound *vam* (long vowel aaaaa).

- ❧ You may place any orange objects, for example crystals, flowers, or cloth, between your hands and your body while you do this meditation. Visualize the energy in this chakra spinning, for example, smoke or fog swirling in a clockwise direction, or a propeller rotating in a clockwise direction.

Third Chakra: Will/Solar Plexus Chakra

The third chakra is at the solar plexus located in the space from about one inch above your belly button up to the indentation of your breastplate, but not as high as between your breasts. This is the Manipura Chakra. The sound of this chakra is RAM, in note E. The color of this chakra is yellow. The body parts most closely associated with this chakra are the stomach, pancreas, spleen, liver, and gall bladder, the muscular system, and the skin as a system.

The third chakra is the center of your will. When the third chakra is open, you will be at ease in your body. Emotionally balanced, you will feel everything fully, both positive and negative emotions, but you will not be consumed by them. Self-motivated, you will be able to express your will in a way that is free of ego, getting what you want without placing anyone else at a disadvantage. You will be a good decision-maker and problem-solver, radiating a charisma that leads others to select you as a leader. You will be tolerant of those who have different viewpoints, lifestyles, values, and appearances from your own.

When the third chakra is closed, you will be unhappy with your body, perceiving it as too short, tall, skinny, fat, ugly, and so on, even though this may have nothing to do with any objective reality. Wildly enthusiastic one minute and depressed the next, you may experience life as an emotional roller coaster. Emotions may overwhelm you, or you may have closed them off and feel nothing at all. Struggle for power and influence may consume you. Certain that no one listens to you, you may feel that you have to prove yourself all the time. Worrying a lot, you may make selfish decisions without considering how those decisions affect others. Lack of motivation, depression, frustration, and tiredness may be your norm. Judgmental of others who have different viewpoints, lifestyles, values, and appearances from your own, you may openly ridicule them. You may experience liver problems and constipation because of repressed anger, or problems with your spleen, stomach, or pancreas due to excessive worry.

Opening the Third Chakra Exercise

- Gently thump your solar plexus with your open palm. Do not thump so hard that you bruise yourself or that it is uncomfortable. Thump in this manner 10 to 15 times.

- Then rub your hand, palm open, in a clockwise direction over the solar plexus for one minute. You can also do this for your lover.

- While you are rubbing your hand on the solar plexus chakra, visualize the color yellow, and make the sound *ram* (long vowel aaaaa).

- You may place any yellow objects, for example crystals, flowers, or cloth, between your hands and your body while you do this meditation.

- Visualize the energy in this chakra spinning, for example, smoke or fog swirling in a clockwise direction, or a propeller rotating in a clockwise direction.

Fourth Chakra: Heart/Love Chakra

The fourth chakra is located at the spot between your nipples at armpit level. This is the Anahata Chakra. The sound of this chakra is YAM, in note F. The color of this chakra is green. The body parts most closely associated with this chakra are the heart, breasts, lungs, thymus gland, and the cardiovascular blood circulation system.

When the fourth chakra is open, you will freely give and receive both romantic and unconditional love, easily forgiving hurts and extending compassion to all. Trustworthy and reliable, you will have a deep capacity for commitment. In the now moment, richly aware of your senses, you will also be in touch with your feelings, both positive and negative. Relationships will be high priorities for you and you will have strong connections to family and community. You will be happy in spite of the circumstances of your life rather than because of them, laughing frequently and sharing your joy. You will experience sublime moments of sexual ecstasy with your lover. For you, the glass is half full rather than half empty. Because the thymus gland is critical to immune system function, you will tend to be healthy most of the time, rarely getting sick, or healing quickly when you do.

When the fourth chakra is blocked or closed, you will have great difficulty in relationships, both friendships and romances. To protect yourself from being hurt or wounded as you were in previous relationships, you will remain emotionally closed. As you shut down your feelings, life may become dull and predictable. You may experience profound alienation from your lover, your children, your friends, your neighbors, and your peers at work, because you feel they do not understand you and disapprove of you. You may be alone, or move from one relationship to another as they disappoint you and fail. Rather than seeing that the root of your sadness is inside yourself, you blame your unhappiness on circumstances and other people. Thinking, reason, and intellect are your refuge. You can lose yourself completely in your work. For you, the glass is half empty rather than half full. Your grief may bring on lung disorders. To the extent that the blockage in this chakra affects your thymus gland, you immune system will not function optimally and you may find that you get sick easily and often and heal slowly.

Opening the Fourth Chakra Exercise

- With a set of colored pencils, draw a picture that illustrates how your heart is closed, protected, and shielded from negative feelings and emotions. For example you might draw your heart encased in a block of ice, or barricaded behind a wall of bricks and mortar, or enclosed in a suit of armor, or whatever image comes to mind for you.

- Lie down on your back with your chest bare.

- Dilute one drop of rose essential oil in one teaspoon of vegetable oil. Touch the fingertips of your left hand into the mixture and anoint your heart chakra by massaging the oil gently into your skin, circling your fingers in a clockwise direction.

- Put a piece of green silk on your heart chakra. Place several green stones (for example, jade or emerald) on top of the silk. If you have any rose petals, preferably fresh, place those on the green silk also.

- Place your left palm covering the objects on your heart chakra, and place the right palm covering the left palm.

- Softly chant the sound *yam* (long vowel aaaaa) as a mantra for four minutes.

- Repeat this exercise four days in a row. Gently wash the silk by hand after each repetition of the exercise to remove any residual oil it may have absorbed.

- The drawing of your heart is only done on day one and again on day four. There will likely be a noticeable difference in how you draw your heart on the fourth day, for example, the wall may be crumbling or the armor may have holes appear in it, or the ice may be melting or completely gone as you begin to open your heart to experience all emotions.

Emotional Release Exercises (see Chapter 5, page 100) are also very helpful for opening your heart chakra.

Fifth Chakra: Throat/Neck/Communication Chakra

The fifth chakra is located at the center of the throat at the level of a man's Adam's apple. This is the Vishudda Chakra. The sound of this chakra is HAM, in note G. The color of this chakra is sky-blue. The body parts most closely associated with the fifth chakra are the throat, thyroid gland, and parathyroid glands.

When the fifth chakra is open, you will find your voice, expressing yourself easily and clearly both verbally and nonverbally. You may take pleasure in singing and whistling. Sound may seem to have magical qualities to it and certain sounds will easily transport you into a delightfully altered, expanded consciousness. You will be a lover of music, perhaps making your own, either writing music or playing instruments. With no difficulty in expressing your point of view, you will easily take a stand on issues of importance to you and be known as a person who speaks their truth. A quick thinker and articulate speaker, you will be excited by ideas and take pleasure in the matching of wits with others in debate.

The thyroid gland acts as the body's "accelerator pedal." It speeds up the metabolic rate and the rate of chemical reactions inside cells, and this powerfully influences your energy level. When this chakra is open and the thyroid is healthy, you will easily maintain your ideal body weight without the need to carefully monitor what you eat, and you will generally feel full of energy and motivation.

If the fifth chakra is blocked or closed, you will find difficulty expressing your ideas and opinions. Speaking in front of people will make you nervous and writing will be difficult and frustrating. You will avoid taking a firm stand or position on controversial subjects, usually waiting for someone else to lead the way. Once someone else has articulated a firm position, you will tend to agree with that person and adopt the point of view as your own. You may change your mind a lot about many things, so that it is hard for others to know what you believe in. Because you are much more comfortable when everyone agrees with each other, disagreements, discussions, and even friendly arguments may frighten you. You may speak either very softly or very loudly, or you may mumble a lot. You may be apologetic for what you say or you may end many of your sentences with a rise in inflection, thus turning each one into a question, even when you are stating a fact. You may have a distinct preference for feeling and be distrustful of what you consider to be an overemphasis upon thinking.

When this chakra is blocked, you may find that it is very difficult to control your weight even though you pay careful attention to what and how much you eat. The parathyroid glands control calcium in the blood. If you are having problems with osteoporosis, loss of bone density with aging (most common with the onset of menopause in women), you may wish to concentrate on opening this chakra.

Opening the Fifth Chakra Exercise

- Alone or with a partner, make chanting sounds.
- Work your voice up and down the octave scale.
- The sound *ham* (long vowel aaaaa) is a good one to use.
- You may experiment with closing your eyes and visualizing blue as you chant.
- If you are with a partner, bring your chanting into harmony with each other.
- Do this daily.

Sixth Chakra: Forehead/Third Eye/Intuition Chakra

The sixth chakra is located at the forehead and is often referred to as the third eye. This is the Ajna Chakra. The sound of this chakra is AUM, in note A. The color of this chakra is indigo (deep blue), or violet-purple. The body parts most closely associated with this chakra are the pituitary gland (the master gland) and the pineal gland.

When the sixth chakra is open and vibrating, you will have an ability to "see" or understand what is actually going on in any set of circumstances very quickly. Blessed with insight, you will know what to do or not to do in almost any situation.

You will exhibit wisdom, a quality beyond intellect, knowledge, or experience. You will have vision, the ability to imagine how the future could be, and thereby gain considerable influence over how the future actually turns out. You will consistently be able to create the results that you vividly imagine. In spite of this, you may not be particularly goal-oriented, in the usual way that people set goals and then rely upon their willpower to achieve success. Rather, you will operate with *faith* in your higher self and in God that the universe is a place of abundance, and if you are doing your life's work, you will be supported along the way. Your life tends to be filled with amazement, astonishment, surprise, and delight, as what the universe presents to you is beyond anything your ego could have worked to create with willpower. You may have regular mystical/religious experiences, for example, satori or samadhi, that go beyond rational description, and you may be blessed with various forms of ESP (extra sensory perception) or other special powers.

You are the beneficiary of what we call the positive time paradox. Living in the now moment, you move slowly, yet time seems to fly by because you so thoroughly enjoy almost everything you do. In spite of this, you seem to have plenty of time to get everything done.

The pituitary gland regulates a number of key hormones including growth hormone, estrogen, progesterone, prolactin, oxytocin, and testosterone. If this chakra is open, you may find that you age gracefully and perhaps more slowly than others your same age, and that you maintain a high level of libido and sexual stamina. The pineal gland primarily regulates the sleep cycle. If this chakra is open, you will be able to sleep well and awaken fully rested.

When the sixth chakra is blocked or closed, you will place great importance upon education, acquired knowledge, and experience. You will rely upon your willpower to get what you want. You will feel reluctant to rely upon others, preferring to do everything for yourself. You may have a strong sense that only you can do it well enough or right.

You may have trouble even saying the word "God," let alone to rely in faith that what you need will come to you in some mysterious way. You may be strongly goal-oriented, creating a clear image in your mind of what you want to achieve, and then systematically plotting a course to achieve the success you want. You may indeed be highly successful at getting results, which confirms that what you are doing works. Your life has few surprises and little mystery. You are extremely skeptical of those claiming to have mystical experiences, and probably strongly deny the existence of any form of ESP.

You are the victim of what we call the negative time paradox. Most of the time, you are busy doing, and the very idea of just being seems like a boring waste of time. You may have a tendency to be a hyperactive workaholic. You move rapidly, but time seems to go too slowly, in the sense that you are always eager for some future result you are pursuing, and easily become impatient with the steps needed to get you there. Paradoxically, at the same time you never seem to have enough time to get everything done.

You may find that you age prematurely compared with others your same age. People might say that age was not kind to you. You may experience little interest in sexuality, instead channeling your energies elsewhere, for example into your work, as a diversion. You may regularly have trouble sleeping or find that your sleep is easily interfered with, and that jet lag is severe when you travel.

Opening the Sixth Chakra Exercise

- Lightly massage the third eye spot, the center of your forehead, with the first two fingers of either hand.

- Rotate your fingers first in a counter-clockwise direction and then in a clockwise direction nine times.

- Visualize the color purple and make the sound *aum* (long vowel aaaaa).

- Do three, six, or nine repetitions of this exercise daily.

Seventh Chakra: Enlightenment/Crown Chakra

The seventh chakra is the crown chakra located at the top of your head. The sound of this chakra is AH, in note B. The color of this chakra is white or mauve. The body parts most closely associated with the crown chakra are the central nervous system (CNS—brain and spinal cord) and the peripheral nervous system. The peripheral nervous system consists of sensory neurons that carry sensory input from receptors to the CNS, and motor neurons that transmit motor output from the CNS to muscles and glands.

When the seventh chakra is truly fully open and vibrating, you will be whole again. You will know what it means to live in a state of grace. The Kundalini serpent—a metaphor for pure consciousness and life force energy—will be uncoiled and released flowing freely up from the earth, through all seven of your chakras, out from your Crown, up to the heavens, and back down again at a high mystical rate of vibration. Your meditations will sometimes transport you into contemplative states in which the boundary between yourself and others will disappear. You will come face to face with the Creator, God, or the Divine in high states of satori, samadhi, and enlightenment. You may experience and possibly even perform miracles such as healing yourself and others. Your faith will be inviolable. You will operate in the world from a context of unconditional love and compassion for all sentient beings. You will be beyond desire, wanting, and karma. You will be free.

When the seventh chakra is blocked or closed, you will be very much caught in the endless cycle of birth and death, subject to the laws of karma. You may long to return home to God, but direct mystical experiences mostly elude you. You are still trying to make them happen and have not learned to surrender to allow them to happen. Intellectually, you may understand that the lower cannot command the higher, but you repeatedly fall back upon what you know how to do. Your ego regularly gets the front seat in your consciousness and your higher self recedes into the background. You have to work hard at reconfirming your faith, and it sometimes fails you completely. Regardless of your level of achievement and success in the world (power, position, wealth, sex), you are still prone to periods of spiritual darkness and fear of death. This compels you to try and get more of what you already have, even though you already have enough. You are still quite capable of operating selfishly and perhaps even violently toward your fellow man, even (or perhaps especially) those closest to you, including friends and family. You may be the envy of your peers because of your worldly success, but inside you still often feel like a fraud or a fake. You ask yourself repeatedly, "Is this all there is?"

Seven Chakras Meditation Exercise: Colors and Affirmations

Imagine you are lying in the sun. Feel the heat on your body and allow the light to permeate your cells. As your cells absorb heat and light, they begin to awaken and come alive. Allow your body to become transparent, like clear glass, as you allow the light to penetrate to the core of your being. Maintain your focused attention for five minutes or longer depending upon whether this exercise is working for you.

Chakra Meditation

Try to actually see your aura, or imagine your aura if you cannot actually see it, surrounding your body in a rainbow of vibrating, undulating colors. You will now shift your attention from one chakra to the next, pausing at each for at least two minutes, or longer if that feels right for you. With your attention focused on each chakra, put your left hand on the chakra, and at the same time hold your right hand over your body at that point but not touching. Rotate your right hand in a clockwise direction. At each chakra, imagine the color of light that is associated with that chakra, and imagine that light is cleansing, clearing, healing, and balancing the energy of that chakra. As you breathe in, life energy follows your breath to the chakra you are touching. As you exhale, any negative or excess energy flows out with the breath. Imagine that the chakra begins to spin in a clockwise direction.

First Chakra/Root Chakra: The light here is a sensual subdued red. Feel yourself solidly grounded to Mother Earth. Repeat the affirmation, "I am calm, safe, and secure. My body is a divine temple for experiencing this world."

Second Chakra/Belly Chakra: The light here is a deep saturated orange. Repeat the affirmation, "I am strong and confident. I am comfortable in my body. My body is beautiful. I enjoy a healthy, passionate sexuality. I am easily orgasmic."

Third Chakra/Solar Plexus Chakra: The color here is a bright yellow. Repeat the affirmation, "I am fully alive. I can feel everything. I love life and can create results that are important to me. I regularly experience success in the things I try."

Fourth Chakra/Heart Chakra: The color here is a deep, saturated green, the rich green of new life in springtime. Feel the warmth of love flowing in and out of your open heart, nourishing you as it flows in and nourishing the world as it flows out. Repeat this affirmation, "I am love. I give and receive love easily and unconditionally. Love is the reason I am in this body."

Fifth Chakra/Throat Chakra: The color here is blue, a pale blue as the sky or a dark, saturated blue as the sky reflected off water. Repeat this affirmation, "I am confident in speaking my truth. The truth sets me free."

Sixth Chakra/Third Eye Chakra: The color here is a deep, saturated royal purple. Imagine a third eye at the center of your forehead opening. As it opens, you are able to see and understand the meaning of all things. Repeat this affirmation, "I have access to wisdom and always know the right thing to do in every situation because I understand what things mean and what they are for. I act so that everyone will benefit."

Seventh Chakra: Concentrate on the color white, the purest, finest white imaginable, or alternatively the absolute clarity of a perfect diamond. Repeat this affirmation, "I am one with God. I am an enlightened being. Cosmic light, energy, intelligence, and wisdom flow through my body, mind, and heart. I am one with my beloved."

During our Tantric loving rituals, we will often do this meditation for each other by placing our hands lovingly on the chakra points and speaking words of encouragement, adoration, and reverence.

Energy Exercises With a Partner

"I feel my temperature rising
Help me, I'm flaming
I must be a hundred and nine
Burning, burning, burning...
...And you light my morning sky
With burning love"

—"Burning Love," music and lyrics by Dennis Linde

You may have experienced a sexual encounter that was physically satisfying, even satiating, but that nonetheless left you feeling very separate from your lover and internally empty. Although your bodies joined, your essential selves did not—there was no energetic bond, no joining of hearts and souls. Tantric lovemaking takes you beyond connecting your physical bodies to connecting your energetic bodies and ultimately to connection with the cosmic life force or God.

Psychotherapist Julie Henderson[3] has created an extensive program for getting to know your energy body. Her exercises, for working on your own or with a partner, are simple, practical, and thought-provoking. These are a couple of our favorites for connecting energetically with another in a non-sexual way. Knowing how to do this when you are unaroused makes it easier to do so during the heat of lovemaking.

Hands to Heart

Stand facing your partner, feet solidly on the floor, shoulder-width apart. Knees are slightly bent. Back is straight but not rigid. There are four sections to this exercise:

1. Vigorously rub your hands together, building energy in them. Feel this charge, your life force, in and around your hands. With palms facing toward you, slowly bring your hands, with their powerful energy, toward your heart. Notice when you start to feel the energy approaching.

2. Now begin to rock your pelvis back and forth and breathe rhythmically as you rock. Again, rub your hands together and bring them towards your heart. Notice when you start to feel the energy approaching. Is there a difference from the first time?

3. Continuing pelvic rocking, match your breathing rhythm to your partner's. Rub your hands together again. Move your hands, palms forward, toward your partner's hands. When do you feel contact?

143

4. Continue breathing in unison and rocking your pelvis. Charge your hands again. This time direct your hands toward each other's hearts. Notice when you make contact with your partner. Notice when you feel his approaching energy touch you. Be aware of and considerate toward sensory perceptions and emotions that may come up for each of you as you do this exercise. Let them flow freely. You might be drawn physically toward each other, for a hug, or you may feel the need to be very separate. Listen and do what feels right, without analyzing or judging.

Merging

Part One

& Stand facing your partner with enough space between you that you both feel distinct from each other.

& Your feet are solidly on the floor, shoulder-width apart. Knees are slightly bent. Back is straight but not rigid. Your eyes are closed.

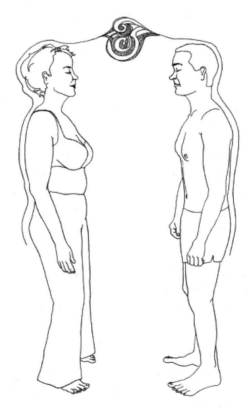

Merging

- Put your attention in your backbone. Feel the individual discs and bones. Feel your spine as a complete unit. Are there parts you cannot sense? Accept that without judging yourself.

- Gather your energy along your backbone. Picture it forming into a pillar that extends from your head down into the Earth. What sensations are you aware of?

- When your pillar of energy feels relatively steady, open your eyes. What happens when you look at your partner? Does your energy flow out toward her? If it does not on its own, consciously send it. Picture it moving from your back forward to join with her energy.

- Shut your eyes. Pull your energy back again into your supporting pillar along your backbone. Hold it there for a count of five.

- This time as you open your eyes, concentrate on holding your energy in its pillar for five more seconds.

- Now, let it go to unite with your partner's energy.

- Once again, shut your eyes and pull your energy back to form a stable pillar.

- Repeat this process five more times, endeavoring to hold your separate pillar and your merged energies a few seconds longer each time.

- If you want to, make sounds as you are merging and separating.

- On the last reforming of your energy pillar, keep looking into your partner's eyes.

- Finish with a hug if you like.

Part Two

- Do this merging exercise again, this time while doing pelvic rocking and breathing in harmony together.

- Perform six repetitions of gathering energy along your spine then sending it forward to join with your partner's energy.

- End with a hug if you like.

What differences were you aware of when doing this exercise standing still and doing it rocking? Was one easier than the other? Was one more powerful?

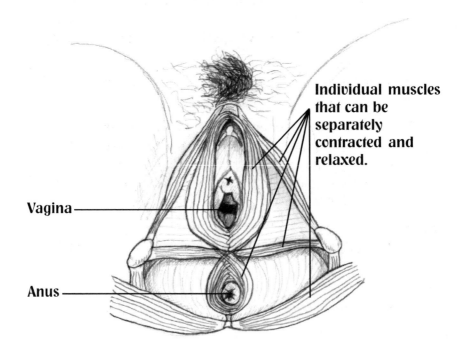

Individual muscles that can be separately contracted and relaxed.

Vagina

Anus

PC Muscles Female

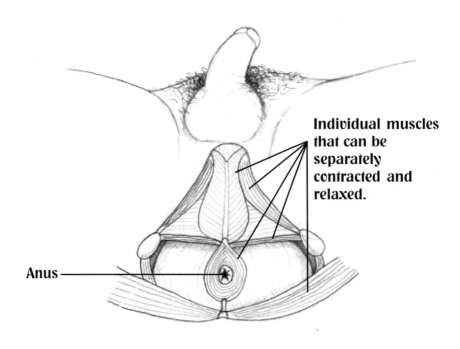

Individual muscles that can be separately contracted and relaxed.

Anus

PC Muscles Male

Sexual Energy Practices

PC Pumping

Without a doubt, the most important sexual energy exercise you can do is the PC Pump. It is standard in both the ancient Tantric and Taoist teachings of sacred sex. PC stands for pubococcygeous and refers to a group of muscles surrounding your genitals and anus. You may already know these exercises as Kegels, named for the American doctor who, during the 1950s, began prescribing PC squeezing to help prevent surgery in women with Urinary Stress Incontinence.

PC Pumping, or tightening and relaxing the muscles of your pelvic floor, does the following wonderful things. It:

1. Acts as a lock to keep your sexual energy in and a pump to push it up through your body.

2. Strengthens and tones the muscles in your urogenital area.

3. Prevents prolapsed uterus and incontinence in women.

4. Increases erection capacity for men.

5. Sensitizes and focuses women genitally, so their orgasms become stronger and more frequent.

6. Massages a man's prostate gland, helping it to stay healthy.

7. Adds extraordinary sensation when performed while making love.

PC Pumps are very easy to do. Simply pretend you have to urinate, but you are somewhere you cannot. You tighten up and hold it. You can actually begin your practice of PC Pumps by interrupting the flow while you are urinating. In addition to pulling your pelvic floor muscles up, PC Pumping includes lightly pushing them out. When you first start these exercises, you may find that your shoulders, your stomach, your buttocks, even your jaw, clench as well. However, within a short while you will be able to isolate and contract the many different muscles in your genitals while keeping the rest of your body relaxed. Try these variations:

Squeeze and Hold

- As you slowly inhale, contract your PC muscles.

- Keep the rest of your body relaxed, especially your shoulders.

- Hold your contraction as you hold your breath for a count of 10.

147

- Slowly exhale and relax your muscles.

- Repeat 10 times.

Squeeze and Push

- As you slowly inhale, contract your PC muscles.

- Keep the rest of your body relaxed, especially your shoulders.

- Hold your contraction as you hold your breath for a count of five.

- As you exhale for a count of five, gently push out with your muscles.

- Repeat 10 times.

Fluttering

- As you slowly inhale, contract your PC muscles.

- Keep the rest of your body relaxed, especially your shoulders.

- While holding your breath, quickly relax and contract your PC muscles five times.

- Slowly exhale and relax.

- Repeat 10 times.

Back to Front

This version helps you gain more control over individual muscles.

Women's Version

- As you slowly inhale:
  - Tighten your anus.
  - Pull up on your perineum.
  - Tighten the muscles inside your vaginal canal, one by one from the opening, all the way back to your cervix.

- As you slowly exhale:
  - Release your vaginal muscles, one by one, from your cervix to your opening.
  - Relax your perineum.
  - Relax your anus.

- Repeat 10 times.

Men's Version

- As you slowly inhale:
  - Tighten your anus.
  - Pull up on your perineum.
  - Pull your scrotum up close to your body.
  - Elevate your penis.

- As you slowly exhale:
  - Let your penis drop.
  - Release your scrotum.
  - Relax your perineum.
  - Relax your anus.

- Repeat 10 times.

Remember to PC pump everyday. You do not have to make extra time. PC squeezes can be done anywhere, as you are showering, driving, walking, waiting in line, working on your computer, or watching TV. The possibilities are endless, and no one can tell what you are doing, unless you have a smile on your face because it feels so good. Begin with 10 sets of the previous five exercises, then over a few weeks, work up to several hundred repetitions per day. You will soon notice a difference in sensitivity, capacity, and energy movement.

Sexual Fire Breath[4]

This is a very active breath technique to help you learn to move your sexual energy. Do this on your own to open yourself to your sexual potential. Do it as a charger-upper before making love. Do it during lovemaking as you are being manually or orally stimulated. Do it during intercourse, but be very observant and ready to stop in a flash in the early learning stages or the man may go beyond his point of no return—this exercise builds energy fast!

- Lie on your back. Feet flat on the floor/bed. Knees bent. Legs comfortably apart. Hands at your sides, palms up. Eyes closed.

- Breathe slowly and deeply into your belly.

- Focus your attention on your genitals and visualize drawing breath in and out through them.

149

- When you have a comfortable breathing rhythm established, begin to rock your pelvis, tilting it up toward the sky. Use your feet to slightly push off the floor so that you are not using your abdominal muscles to rock and they can remain loose and open.

- Inhale as you rock back. Exhale as you rock forward. (Note: Some bodies want to do it the opposite way—listen to yours and go with what feels right).

- Make sound as you exhale—AAAAAHHHH. (This is the most difficult part for many people but it helps enormously; sound carries the energy).

- When you are in a comfortable rhythm, add PC Pumping. Tighten your PC muscles as you rock back. Relax them as you rock forward. (Note: Your body might want to do it the opposite way; let it.).

- Begin to visualize your sexual energy as a great ball of golden fire in your genitals. As you rock, breathe, and pump, draw the golden fireball up through your chakra centers, one chakra at a time.

- Send the energy out through your crown chakra into the universe. Do not leave it to build up in your head. If you are making love with a partner, you can also pass the energy to him through your eyes, your kiss, your breath.

Fire Breath

- Pass your hands in flowing motions up your body to help with the energy movement.

- Breathe more rapidly to move the energy higher within your body, allowing yourself to open into its flow.

- When you reach a high edge of energetic arousal, you can maintain this level by deepening and slowing your breathing and keeping your body relaxed.

- Rest in stillness for a few moments when you are finished practicing so that the energy can continue to flow through you. Bring it back down and store it in your belly chakra for later use.

- If you have left a store of energy in your head and feel some congestion there, do grounding and apply firm pressure with your fingertips to your crown chakra.

The Passion Pump

The Passion Pump is an extraordinary tool for helping you to move your sexual energy. It combines deep, controlled breathing, PC pumping, slight muscle contractions in your head, and visualization of energy movement through an internal energy circuit—from your genitals, up your

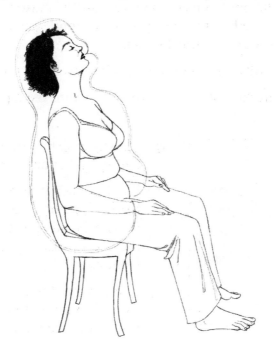

Passion Pump

back and down your front. It is based on the Taoist practices of master Mantak Chia. See Appendix A for some of the excellent books he has written.

❧ Sit comfortably, feet flat on the floor, back straight, shoulders relaxed, eyes closed, arms and hands loose in your lap or at your sides.

Breathing

❧ Inhale very slowly—to a count of five—through your nose, filling the bottom, middle, and upper portions of your lungs.

❧ Gently hold your breathe for a count of five.

❧ Exhale slowly through your nose, also for a count of five.

❧ Repeat three more times.

PC Pump

❧ As you are inhaling for the fifth time, tighten your PC muscles.

❧ Hold them as you hold your breath.

❧ Relax them as you exhale.

❧ Repeat three more times.

Head Action

❧ On the ninth inhale, squeeze your PC muscles. Then as you hold your breath, touch your teeth lightly together, and gently push your jaw straight back.

❧ You will feel a very slight pull in the back of your neck.

❧ Gently roll your eyes up to look toward the top of your head.

❧ These subtle movements help carry energy up to your crown chakra.

❧ Finally, touch the tip of your tongue to the roof of your mouth—your tongue in this position completes the energy circuit, joining back and front channels.

❧ Leave your tongue touching the roof of your mouth throughout the rest of the meditation.

Head Movements

- As you exhale, relax your jaw and teeth, roll your eyes down, and release your PC muscles.

- Repeat three more times.

Endeavor to keep the rest of your body relaxed as you work these specific muscles.

Moving Energy

- On the 13th inhale, as you squeeze your PC muscles, visualize pushing a bright beam of energy up your spine from your genitals.

- As you push your jaw back and roll your eyes up, the energy beam is pulled up to your crown chakra.

- As you slowly exhale, rolling your eyes down and relaxing your muscles, the energy spills over and flows down your front channel—through your third eye, your tongue, your throat chakra, heart, solar plexus and belly, back to your genitals.

- Repeat this sequence for 10 to 15 minutes:
  - Inhale.
  - Squeeze PC muscles.
  - Push energy up spine.
  - Hold breath.
  - Jaw back.
  - Eyes up.
  - Pull energy to top of your head.
  - Exhale.
  - Eyes down.
  - Tongue remains touching the roof of your mouth.
  - Relax PC muscles.
  - Energy flows down to genitals.

- On your last round, as your energy is flowing down your front pathway, bring it to rest in your belly chakra—your hara, your sexual center—instead of having the energy continue on to your genitals.

- Rest in stillness for several minutes and observe what is happening within.

Energy Storehouse

It is safe to store energy in your belly chakra. Later, when you want additional energy for other activities, put your attention in your belly chakra and bring some energy out. The energy will follow your attention. For instance, when Pala is driving and wants to be especially alert, she puts her attention into her hara, sends some energy down to her genitals, gives a little squeeze and zaps it up to her brain—voilà, instant alertness. Al sends energy into his hands for artistic activities. You can make use of the energy you store in your belly chakra for all sorts of wonderful purposes, such as healing, creativity, and decision-making.

At first, practice the Passion Pump meditation on your own in an unaroused state. When you have become fairly comfortable with it, add it to your self-pleasuring. Build to a high peak of excitement, then before cresting over into orgasm, circulate that hot sex energy through your body. Finally, bring it to your lovemaking with a partner. Do not try to add it too soon, unless you have a great sense of humor. This exercise is like learning to drive a standard transmission automobile. At first there are lots of bumps and jerks as you try to put all the bits together. But then when you have finally got it, the flow is so smooth and sweet, you are one with your car, and in this case, with your energy flow and your partner. It is easiest to circulate the energy through your pathways and into your partner with the Passion Pump when you are making love in upright positions—sitting or standing.

Balancing Male and Female Energies—Yin and Yang

"Consciousness and energy create the nature of all reality."

—Judi Pope Zion

In both Taoist and Tantric traditions, there are two opposite yet complementary forces at play in the universe, what the Taoists call Yin and Yang. Yin represents the feminine: cool, receptive, moist, and nourishing, and Yang represents the masculine: active, dry, and fiery. Women are mostly yin, men are mostly yang—what popular author John Grey calls Venus and Mars—but within each woman there is some masculine energy, and within each man, some feminine. Carl Jung called these forces animus and anima. In Tantric lovemaking, you share and thus strengthen and balance your masculine and feminine energies. The YabYum posture, outlined in Chapter 12 on page 249, is an extraordinarily effective, and pleasurable, position for exchanging sexual energy with your lover, as is the Lovers' Scissors.

Lovers' Scissors

This practice takes five to 30 minutes, depending on how much time you have. Do the Lovers' Scissors meditation before you get up in the morning or before you go to sleep at night. If you have been making love, you can also use this as your loving completion, to relax and merge your energies. Although there is genital connection, this meditation is not intercourse for sexual arousal—there is no active thrusting or drive to complete an orgasm. It is for balancing your energies and connecting to your lover. Experiment with doing this every day for several weeks and then not doing it for a few days. You will notice that its effects are cumulative. When you do the exercise daily, you will relate to each other more respectfully, appreciatively, and lovingly. You will also have greater personal resilience and resources for dealing with all the stresses and challenges of living. When we do this regularly, we are calm and loving toward each other. When we skip it for a while (more than four days in a row), we can start to get antsy and even a little snarly with each other.

Lovers' Scissors

- The man lies on his side and the woman on her back. The woman's leg closest to her lover goes over the top of his hip. Her other leg goes between his legs. This is the "scissors." You are at a 90-degree angle to each other. Your heads are apart and your genitals are connected.

- Slide penis into vagina. Soft entry works fine—use saliva or lubricant as needed.

- The key is to be able to stay relaxed, connected, comfortable, and still.

- Breathe slowly and deeply—harmonize your breathing; if you wish, look into each other's eyes.

- Place your hands on each other's heart.

- Simply allow yourself to BE in the experience.

- Be silent.

- If you drift off into sleep that is fine, but do not allow your mind to intrude with thoughts unrelated to your loving connection.

When you have some experience working with your sexual energy, add these more advanced elements to your connection:

- Focus on the energy connection between you, extending out from your genitals.

- You may occasionally tighten your PC muscles to help focus your attention on your genitals and to move energy up from them.

- Bring energy from your genitals up to your heart.

- Allow your heart to open to your lover.

- Allow energy to flow from your heart to the top of your head, then down to your eyes and through your eyes into your lover.

- Direct energy that comes from your lover in through your eyes down to your genitals. Or put it in your belly chakra for later use. Or send it to whatever part of your body may need healing.

- If you become "spaced out," anxious, or hyperactive, because you have accumulated a high energy charge, do grounding.

"My heart was split, and a flower
appeared; and grace sprang up;
and it bore fruit for my God.
You split me, tore my heart
open, filled me with love.
You poured your spirit into me;
I knew you as I know myself.
Speaking waters touched me
from your fountain, the source of life.
I swallowed them and was drunk
with the water that never dies.
And my drunkenness was insight,
intimacy with your spirit.
And you have made all things new;
you have showed me all things shining.
You have granted me perfect ease;
I have become like Paradise,
a garden whose fruit is joy;
and you are the sun upon me…"

—*The Odes of Solomon*, Ode 11[5]

Chapter 8

Ejaculation Mastery and Male Multiple Orgasm

"The chicken and the egg were lying in bed one
night, when one turned to the other and said,
'Well, now we know.'"

—Unknown

One of the best-kept secrets of our time is that men (not just women) can be multi-orgasmic. Not only can a man have several orgasms during one session of lovemaking, but he also can do it and still have lots of energy and desire. "Oh sure," you may be thinking, "maybe Superman or super stud, but not me." Actually most "ordinary" men can, you can—the key is learning to separate orgasm from ejaculation. Because ejaculation follows orgasm so closely—within a split second—most people think they are one and the same, but they are two distinct phenomena. In Tantric loving, you learn to experience the pleasure of orgasm without the accompanying letdown of ejaculation. There are only two things you need to learn in order to be able to separate your orgasm from your ejaculation:

⚜ Stay relaxed no matter how aroused you are.

⚜ Move your hot sexual energy up and away from your genitals.

Any man who does this and makes love long enough to build a very high sexual charge will eventually spontaneously experience non-ejaculatory orgasm.

3 Types of Orgasm

The Ejaculatory Orgasm

Most men are happily familiar with a regular ejaculatory orgasm during which the whole body tenses, and the prostate gland vibrates strongly, propelling semen forcefully out of the penis. For a few seconds there is intense pleasure, and then a refractory (or recovery) period sets in. The body relaxes; the erection subsides and with it goes interest in further sexual activity. Sleepiness sets in. How long it takes before energy and interest return depends on a man's age, health, libido, and frequency of ejaculation. Some men, usually young and strong men, may be able to retain an erection in spite of ejaculation by continued thrusting, or they may gain another erection almost immediately.

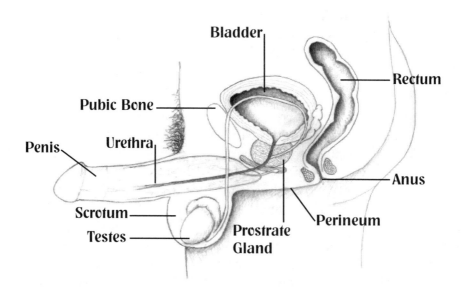

Male Anatomy Side View

No matter how good it feels, repeated ejaculation with its accompanying loss of sexual energy can deplete your body's strength and vitality. If the energy drain is extensive, it can lead to unconscious resentment of your partner for "exhausting your manhood."

The Prostate Orgasm

Although the prostate orgasm is also accompanied by ejaculation, less fluid is expelled. Because the contractions of the prostate are much less powerful, the ejaculate dribbles out and pleasurable sensations are felt more internally. The usual tiredness following orgasm is noticeably reduced.

Some men experience prostate orgasm occasionally and unexpectedly. For those practicing the art of Tantric loving, it is a sign that you are learning to keep the muscles around your genitals relaxed even during high arousal and vigorous activity. It is a marker along your road to mastery.

The Non-Ejaculatory Orgasm

By building a high sexual charge and moving it up through your body rather than releasing it through ejaculation you can discover non-ejaculatory orgasm. Your whole body can become an orgasmic erogenous zone, with orgasmic sensation in your toes, for example, or intense orgasmic rippling through your entire body rather than just your genitals. There are no limits to how many of these orgasms you can have, with the intensity of each one varying from mild to overwhelming. A non-ejaculatory orgasm does not result in any loss of energy. On the contrary, your energy can build indefinitely to higher and higher intensities. You may experience the opening of your higher spiritual centers, specifically your throat, third eye, and crown chakra energy centers. Furthermore, you can build up reserves of sexual energy and use it for other purposes, such as physical healing, spiritual awakening, enhanced creativity, or excellence in science, business, and sports. Any man who learns to do this will gain a serious competitive advantage.

A non-ejaculatory orgasm usually feels different from a regular ejaculatory orgasm, although sometimes the sensations that accompany a normal ejaculation are also experienced in the non-ejaculatory variety. That familiar intense pleasure that starts in the vibrating prostate and typically travels out the end of the penis with the ejaculate instead travels upward along the energy meridians of the chakra centers to the top of your head. As this energy moves, you may experience intense sensations of pleasure throughout your body. These sensations are not the same as the sensation located in the genitals during ordinary orgasm, but they are superb. My body often contracts and jerks involuntarily with the force of this flow of energy. This rush of sensations lasts much longer than a genital orgasm, for example from several minutes up to a timeless, continuous bliss state.

I do love to have an ejaculation, but I do not enjoy the accompanying energetic letdown and loss of desire. After an ejaculation I do not even feel like cuddling—I want to roll over and go to sleep. I experience this depletion whether my ejaculation is involuntary or voluntary, and it gets worse with each passing year. By comparison, a non-ejaculatory orgasm leaves me relaxed, but not tired. I do not lose my capacity to keep or regain an erection. I still have intense desire, which I do not experience as discomfort but rather as vitality and vigor. I bask in an afterglow of high energy, an intensification of sensation, and creative potential. This does not interfere with sleep, because there is a sublime combination of aroused excitement with complete relaxation.

Ejaculation Mastery

"The archer strikes the target—partly by pulling;
partly by letting go."

—Unknown

With regular lovemaking, there is a steady buildup of sexual excitement to ejaculatory orgasmic release, which usually ends the sexual activity. Tantra sacred sex is high-energy sex. You make love for a period of hours, building higher and higher concentrations of energy, stopping before you let go into ejaculation, relaxing a little, then building excitement again and again. By delaying ejaculation, you accumulate enough sexual energy to open your spiritual centers, plus you last long enough so your lover may experience multiple orgasms.

But don't make the mistake of putting all your effort and attention into simply preventing ejaculation, as I did at first. When your focus is on *not* ejaculating, your mind is still locked on *ejaculation.* Remember the Doer consciousness from Chapter 2? The Doer consciousness only notices the object of your attention. If you focus on "I do not want to ejaculate," the object of your attention is ejaculation, and you are going to get more of that. Instead, your effort should be positive, on learning to accumulate and then circulate more and more sexual energy. Using your imagination to think about and visualize working with your sexual energy is one of the positive methods you can use to replace the negative idea of not ejaculating.

Mapping Your Sexual Arousal Process

There are a number of techniques you can use to successfully prolong lovemaking and build a high sexual charge. The first is to create a scale from 1 to 10 for your sexual arousal cycle—one being the lowest level of arousal, and 10, the highest level. Ten does not mean ejaculation, but is the level where you may experience whole body orgasms, profound connection with your lover, and altered states of consciousness. At 10, you may have direct experiences with the Divine.

Ejaculation may take place at any level on the scale and it is important that you know where on your scale ejaculation becomes unpredictable. Unpredictable does not mean imminent. For instance, you might find that any time you get to a seven on your scale you cannot control when ejaculation will take place. One second you are fine and the next second you have lost it. You could last two more minutes or another hour, but you cannot tell which it will be. By the way, do not worry about how your scale compares with anyone else's; the important point is to know your own number.

How can you identify this "point of no return" on your scale? Learning about your arousal cycle is a little like potty training. As a young child, at first you did not pay any attention to the signals your body gave that you had to go to the bathroom. In fact, you did not even know that your body was giving you these signals until someone taught you what to look for. Once you knew what you were supposed to do, you became so sensitive to the signals that you could always get to a bathroom on time and avoid embarrassing mistakes.

In a similar way, you may not know what signals your body is giving you that ejaculation is very close. You will not know what to do to delay ejaculation unless you become aware of these signals. What are some of the signs your body uses to tell you how excited, turned on, and close to ejaculation you are?

Body Signals for Ejaculation Mastery

4 Stages of Erection

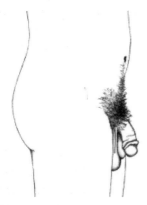

Stage One Erection

One of the most easily identifiable signs, for both you and your partner, is the stage of your erection. There are four.

Stage one is a flaccid, limp penis, revealing no evidence of any sexual excitement. Nevertheless we refer to this as stage one because you are aware of sensation in your penis, you are thinking about sex, and may want to touch yourself, or be touched by your lover. Intercourse is not possible in stage one.

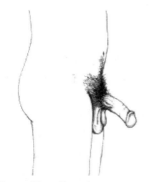

Stage Two Erection

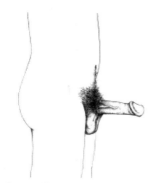

Stage Three Erection

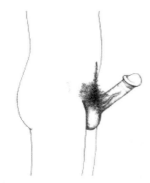

Stage Four Erection

Stage two is a partially erect penis. Although starting to stand up, it is not straight-up saluting. This degree of erection is enough for intercourse if you help insert the penis into the vagina with your hands in a "soft entry." To begin intercourse with a soft entry, you can stimulate a stage one limp penis to a stage two erection by using your hand to rub the limp penis against your lover's vagina, being sure to apply suitable lubrication, such as saliva, vaginal fluids, or water-based or silicone-based lubricant. While stage two is sufficient for penetration, it will not usually provide maximum sexual satisfaction for your partner.

Stage three is an erect penis that is standing straight up and saluting. Stage three can be orgasmic-level arousal for you, and is quite adequate to give your partner pleasurable intercourse. Stage three allows you to be fully engaged in active intercourse, and able to delay ejaculation for prolonged lovemaking.

Stage four is a "boner." Because the penis is fully engorged with blood, a stage four erection is rock hard. It feels very hot to the touch and changes color, becoming a brighter or darker pink, red, purple, or deep black depending on your skin color. For most men, stage four means ejaculation is unpredictable, perhaps imminent. You must change or stop what you are doing and allow the penis to subside to a stage three erection, which will allow you to continue lovemaking almost indefinitely.

Erections Come and Erections Go

With regular lovemaking, a man usually gets one erection, which proceeds from stage one through to stage four, then ejaculation occurs, and the lovemaking is over. During Tantric extended lovemaking, a man does not get and keep one erection for four hours or more. This is not desirable or healthy. An erection is a cardiovascular event. The penis becomes erect when blood is trapped inside, and stays erect for as long as that blood remains. Blood entering the penis carries with it oxygen and hormones. During active lovemaking, the oxygen is depleted, the hormones are chemically transformed, and waste products build up. Many men involuntarily ejaculate out of sheer penile exhaustion when they try to maintain their erection too long. It is a good idea to allow the erection to subside to stage two or even disappear entirely every 30 to 45 minutes. This allows the old blood to be removed along with waste byproducts, and when active lovemaking is resumed and fresh blood flows into the penis, the supply of oxygen and hormones is renewed. You are then fresh and virile and able to delay ejaculation quite naturally.

There is a psychological issue of great importance involved with this. If you and your lover make losing an erection into a problem, fear and performance anxiety can severely interfere with the normal spontaneity of healthy lovemaking. This can be easily avoided if you both understand that in prolonged lovemaking, there will be a number of erections that naturally come and go over a period of hours. This is not only desirable, it is a necessity.

Pre-Cum

When you are fully aroused in either a stage three or stage four erection, pre-cum may drip from the end of your penis. This fluid is very slippery. The popular silicone-based lubricants are copies of how pre-cum feels. Do not mistake this fluid with urine or semen. Completely clear and relatively tasteless, it is a unique fluid that helps lubricate the vagina during intercourse. You may emit this fluid continuously for hours if your arousal is maintained sufficiently for stage three erections, but if the fluid becomes cloudy, some ejaculate is mixed in with it, and your point of no return may be fast approaching.

Other Ejaculation Alert Signals

As a man approaches the point on his scale where ejaculation becomes unpredictable, he may also exhibit one or more of these signs:

☂ *Breathing* becomes much more rapid, uneven, jagged, or raspy.

☂ *Sound*—unless he is intentionally being quiet, his natural response is to become noisier. He will start to make all sorts of sounds including animal growls, grunts, and screams.

☂ *Tension* will be apparent in either his entire body or parts of it. He may clench his fists, squeeze his lover very tight, flex his stomach muscles, and contract his buttocks.

⚜ *Flushing* may occur in the upper torso of a light skinned man. Due to increased blood circulation, his upper chest, neck, face, ears, nose, or all of them may turn bright red.

⚜ *Testicles* pull in close to the body and *eyes* glaze over just before ejaculation. Unfortunately, these two signals happen so close to ejaculation that there is not much reaction time.

Internal Body Signals

As you go through many repetitions of observing your sexual arousal, you will become attuned to the subtle internal signals that your body offers alerting you to approaching ejaculation. These internal signals are the most reliable and the ones you will pay most attention to as you gain mastery in making ejaculation voluntary.

As the sexual energy builds with arousal, your prostate will get to a point where it feels as if the orgasm is just starting to happen. This sensation is unmistakable—it feels exactly like the onset of ejaculation. If you have slowed down and are being very observant, you will definitely feel it. This sensation does give you enough warning to be able to change what you are doing and allow the energy to subside to a more manageable level. You can then resume lovemaking and build to another energy peak.

Going the Distance—It's Your Decision

You will soon find that mapping your arousal scale and identifying your signals at the point of no return is the easy part. What is much more challenging is making the choice to do something about it! The urge to go on to ejaculation may be overwhelming—like trying to stop a team of wild horses. However, if you do want to make that next step toward ecstasy, for yourself and your partner, here are some simple hints.

Stop

Stop whatever you were doing to build your sexual excitement and become still. This is almost guaranteed to work unless you have waited too long and ejaculation has already started. If necessary, you can interrupt intercourse—as you gain mastery it may be sufficient only to slow down without actually coming to a complete stop. Wait for the excitement to subside and your sexual energy to become more manageable before resuming active intercourse, oral sex, or manual stimulation.

Breathing

Just as rapid breathing helps to build your excitement and effectively indicates how aroused you are, slow, deep breathing calms and relaxes you. By paying very close attention to your breath, you are also taking your attention away from your genitals, so your urge to ejaculate lessens. There are a number of effective breathing exercises in Chapter 6, beginning on page 117.

Sound

You may have noticed that when martial artists are making a hit, they often give a loud yell. The sound carries their energy with it. You can use sound to circulate your sexual energy up out of your genitals and through the rest of your body. It really does not make much difference what sounds you make. Experiment—yell, scream, make animal sounds, talk into each other's ears, say or sing words of love and adoration. Talk wildly and lewdly when the level of excitement and passion builds to the right fever pitch. If you are used to being quiet when you make love and you want to add in some sound effects, you may wish to alert your partner beforehand.

We highly recommend that you both make noise while you make love. The more noise you make, the better. Besides moving energy, it gives your partner feedback about what you like and do not like, and your rising level of excitement.

Testes Tug

Because a man's scrotum pulls up tight to his body just before ejaculation, an effective delaying action is to gently tug the testes down periodically during lovemaking. You can do this yourself or your partner can do the honors with hands or mouth, pulling gently or more firmly according to your preference.

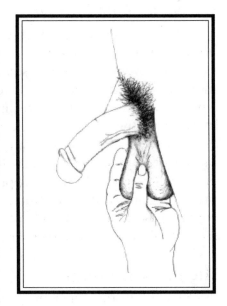

Testes Tug

Penis Tip Squeeze

This technique works best with masturbation or manual or oral stimulation by a partner and is especially effective during your early days of learning. It can be used in conjunction

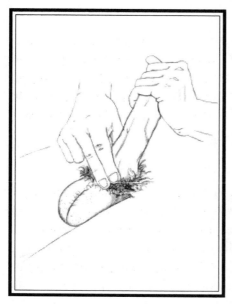

Penis Tip Squeeze

with intercourse, but requires complete withdrawal. At the beginning of a stage-four erection, firmly grasp the tip of the penis in one hand so that the palm of your hand closes over the tip of the penis. Do not try this if ejaculation has already started—it will be ineffective and painful. Combine this technique with applying pressure at the base of the penis where the shaft rises out of the pubic bone. One hand presses against the pubic bone, with the thumb on one side and the first two fingers on the other side of the shaft, while the other hand squeezes the tip of the penis.

Wear a Condom

Experiment with wearing a condom[1], not for the purpose of safe sex, but to decrease the sensitivity of your penis. This may make quite a bit of difference in how long you can maintain your erection.

Focus On Your Partner

Train your mind to think of something other than ejaculation. We do not recommend reciting sports stats or in any way diverting your attention from lovemaking. It is essential that you be fully present from moment to moment. However, instead of thinking about ejaculation, or worrying about ejaculating too quickly, we suggest you think about pleasing your partner. Learn to take pleasure for yourself by pleasing her. Notice how she reacts when your tongue is exploring around her clitoris, but also notice how her clitoris feels on your tongue. Notice how she enjoys when you suck on her nipples, but also notice how her breasts feel pressed against your face. Notice how she moans when you gently run your fingers up the inside of her thighs, but also notice how her skin feels so soft and warm against your fingers.

The Passion Pump

Switch into the YabYum position, Chapter 12, page 249, with the woman on top, straddling the sitting man, and facing him, then become still. Open your eyes and make eye contact. Run your hands up each other's backs from the coccyx to the crown of the head to help move the sexual energy up. Do some PC squeezes or the complete Passion Pump exercise (see Chapter 7, page 151).

Affirmations

Using affirmations before, during, or after lovemaking may help your staying power. Affirmations are a form of communication between your conscious and subconscious layers of mind, but not all affirmations are equal—many are a disguised form of lying to yourself. For example, if you ejaculate prematurely and you say to yourself as an affirmation, "I can last for hours without ejaculation," you are lying to yourself, which will cause inner resistance and stress.

Generally, you do not want to say to yourself that you can do what you have not been able to do. Rather, select words that state the possibility of doing what you want to be able to do. For example, you might rephrase the ejaculation affirmation in any of the following ways: "I am learning to master delaying ejaculation." "With practice I will become a master at being able to delay ejaculation." "Learning to delay ejaculation is fun and easy." Make sure any statement is true. Do not add words such as "fun" and "easy" if they are not true.

I have three affirmations that are my regulars: "I am a healer." "I am a winner." "I am a finder." I woke up one morning with one of those "ah-ha" flashes of insight, the kind of knowing where you just see and understand what is. This is the kind of knowing that is beyond believing. The very concept of belief implies doubt, as does faith. The insight was for the affirmation "I am a finder." I suddenly knew, in an epiphany of higher consciousness, that it was not really accurate to say I found what I was looking for, but rather that what I was looking for bumped into me. In a paradoxical sense, what I was looking for found me as much as I found it. It is as if what I am looking for is drawn to me or comes to me, as if it and I were magnetized to pull each toward the other. It quickly followed that what I would win, would also come to me, and any healing I did would come through me. All of these things were gifts, not accomplishments. Any effort I made was not really the point. What I was looking for would come to me after the effort, not because of it.

There is a great scene in the popular movie *The Matrix*[2], where the hero is being taken to meet the oracle to try to determine if he is "the one" chosen to defeat The Matrix. He is ushered into a waiting room with many other candidates. One is a young boy who is holding a large metal spoon, bending and twisting it with his mind. Our hero stoops down in astonishment at this phenomenon. He takes the spoon from the boy and tries to bend it with his mind.

The boy speaks: "Do not try and bend the spoon; that's impossible. Instead, only try to realize the truth."

"What is that?" asks our hero.

"There is no spoon."

"There is no spoon?" echoes the hero.

"Then you'll see that it is not the spoon that bends, it is only yourself."

This is an illustration of union of all that was formerly separate. This is the same state that is the culmination of Tantra, the joining of the lovers and God—the healing of separation. In this state, there is no controlling of ejaculation, no ejaculation mastery; rather, there is a state of high satori or samadhi. This culmination is not the result of any effort you have made to learn about delaying ejaculation, but it does follow that effort. Experiencing this is not an accomplishment, but rather a gift.

Masturbation

"Masturbation: the primary sexual activity of mankind.
In the nineteenth century it was a disease; in the
twentieth, it is a cure."

—Thomas Szasz

Learning how to circulate your sexual energy requires many arousal repetitions while paying exquisite attention to your arousal scale. It is difficult to do this during intercourse, particularly in the early days of your practice and especially if you always take the active role. Both masturbation and a loving partner who actively assists you are the best ways to learn.

For the most part, our culture still views masturbation as a rather furtive, solitary release for a buildup of sexual tension. It is a second-best substitute for "real" sex and we are embarrassed by it. There are few who, like noted sex-expert Betty Dodson, view masturbation as "the ongoing love affair that each of us has with ourselves throughout our lifetime."[3]

In the practice of sacred sex, masturbation is not only a beautiful and loving act, it is also a key for learning. Eastern philosophies view the body as a microcosm of the universe—all that is in the heavens and the earth is contained in the human body. So to make love to oneself is to make love to the All. We are blessed with highly sensitive, erogenous bodies. To give yourself pleasure through caressing and stimulating your body in a loving way brings sensual satisfaction and emotional richness.

On a practical level learning to lovingly arouse yourself, discovering what turns you on and heats you up, pacing yourself to ride the wave of high excitement, prepares you to be a fulfilling partner. You become truly and freely responsible for your sexual satisfaction. When you know your body thoroughly, you can share it totally with your partner, helping her to learn the delightful intricacies of loving you. Even more to the point, the line between riding the wave of orgasm and falling over into ejaculation is a fine one. Attentive, joyous self-pleasuring gives you the essential "hands-on" capacity to see your line coming, to change what you are doing, and to allow your excitement to subside at the critical moment.

Man Self-pleasuring

Masturbation Ceremony for Men

Arrange a loving space for yourself—soft lighting, comfortable pillows, sensuous music, aromatic scents, and beautiful objects. Set the scene as if you were going to seduce the most desirable lover you have ever met. Make sure you will not be disturbed for at least an hour.

Approach your loving from the outside in—start with delicate strokes of your arms, face, neck, and thighs. Use your fingertips, a feather, or a piece of silk to lightly tantalize your hungry flesh, and gradually increase the pressure. This may be uncomfortable for some men because men are more accustomed to diving straight to the genitals and to approaching their bodies with firm handling. But what you are doing is helping to arouse and excite your entire body, to make your whole body an erogenous zone, not just your genitals.

If it helps to arouse you, begin your self-loving with an erotic fantasy. But once you are turned on, let the fantasy go and focus on what is happening in your body. Remember, to fly free in sexual bliss, you must leave your "daily mind" behind.

Caress, fondle, and tweak your nipples. Nipples are big turn-on zones for men, too! Run your hands down over your belly. Stroke the inside of your thighs. Tease yourself a little before you latch onto your penis—or lingam as it's called in Tantric practice. Pull the crinkly hair of your pubis. Using plenty of good quality lubricant, massage the muscles around the root of your penis and down into your strong inner thighs and the crease of your groin. Push on your perineum, feeling the spongy nut of your prostate under the skin, circle it with loving pressure first counterclockwise then clockwise. Trail your fingers to your anus, run them round the sensitive rim and allow a finger to move inside for exciting exploration. This can be very pleasurable and can help you learn the joy of surrender to penetration as well as being the active "penetrator."

Caress your scrotum. Tickle your balls, pull them gently away from your body, and then increase the pull. Finally, move to your penis. Stroke its full length and lightly squeeze its head. Vary the speed, length, and pressure of your strokes. Try the "corkscrew," gently twisting your lingam as you pull it up and away from your body. At the same time twist and pull your scrotum down and away.

Remember to pay attention to the rest of your body. Run one hand up and down your belly, massage your ears (they are full of highly sensitive spots), and suck on your fingers. To increase the connection between sex and loving, place one hand on your heart chakra and cradle your genitals with the other.

As you love yourself, notice how your penis moves through distinct changes before orgasm and ejaculation—he is not just soft and then hard and spewing. Through attentive self-arousal, you can learn how to stay for longer periods of time in the exciting, but less explosive, third stage of firm erection. When you feel yourself moving into the hard, hot level, stop stimulation, relax, and pay attention to your breathing. Breathe slowly and deeply. The first number of times you practice this you may need to apply the Penis Tip Squeeze (page 167). Later, add the Passion Pump (Chapter 5, page 151) to move the energy up through your body. Do not focus on stopping ejaculation; instead, focus on moving that wild sexual energy up through your body. Run your hand(s) in stroking movements up over your belly and chest to your head and crown. Sound helps, too—make lots of it. With practice you will be able to surf the intense wave of high sex energy for longer and longer periods of time without cresting over into ejaculation. If you do ejaculate, enjoy it!

To complete your self-loving ceremony, rest for a while, breathing deeply, and enjoy the sensations coursing through your body. Massage your perineum to help disburse any energy still congested there. Thank yourself, *aloud*, for giving yourself this wondrous gift.

Help From Your Partner

A common misconception many women have is that the way to satisfy your man is to make him ejaculate. This is not the case. While men certainly do enjoy ejaculating, what many men would really like is to be able to be fully sexually aroused and maintain that peak state of arousal for as long as possible. Any woman who can help her man learn to ride the wave of sexual bliss will have a very happy and satisfied man. She will also benefit because the longer the lovemaking goes on, the more sexual energy is available, and the greater the likelihood that she will experience multiple orgasm. Taking an active role in lovemaking—exploring your lover's body fully, paying careful attention to his rate of arousal, assuming woman-on-top position as part of your intercourse—can give him great pleasure and help him to delay his ejaculation.

Some Tips for Loving a Man

Stimulate your man with your hands or mouth: for instance with firm rapid strokes of his penis—use lots of lubricant—or long licks with your tongue along his shaft followed by dainty flicks of your tongue on the tip. Try different speed and pressure of strokes with your hands—change from gentle holding to very firm, short strokes to very long ones. Use the "corkscrew"—grasping and twisting the end of his penis very gently. Touch other parts of his body as you are stimulating his genitals—his nipples, belly, and back. This helps to sensitize and arouse all of him. Caress his perineum spot and massage it to help him disperse the pressure building there. Let him know that you love what you are doing to him through sounds, words, and looks of love.

Paying very careful attention to the stage of arousal of his penis, bring him close to the edge. When his penis begins to get very hard and hot, slow down or stop your movements. Encourage him to breathe deeply into his belly. Match your breathing to his. Keep one hand at his genitals (perhaps pushing on the perineum, squeezing near the glans of his penis, or pulling his scrotum gently away from his body) and move the other up his body in streaming motions as he relaxes himself into the energy flow. It is easier for him to learn to move the energy through when he is passive, not moving, and you are the one that is taking the initiative.

During intercourse, it is equally important to be aware of your partner's arousal state. You may be rocking wildly against him, close to orgasm yourself, but if your partner moves into the hard and hot fourth stage of erection you *must* stop your movement or he will crest over into ejaculation. It may be difficult to stop, but it will be well worth the effort in the long run. Understanding and compassion are also called for. If your partner does slip over into ejaculation do not berate him or sulk. Performance anxiety is a passion killer. If you are still very eager for an orgasm give yourself pleasure, with love, and unselfconsciously. With practice and attention from both of you, your lover will soon learn how to maintain his erection for significant periods of time.

You will progress more quickly and more smoothly on your Tantric path if you work together. Consideration, timing, and playfulness are essential elements of Tantric loving, but when you are aching on the verge of an orgasm it is not always easy to remember any of this! We went through our periods of mismatches and disappointment in the beginnings of our Tantric practice, particularly during intercourse when Pala was cresting into climax and I was at the point of no return. Here is how Pala describes our adventure:

"It was difficult for me at first if, when during intercourse, both Al and I were close to coming. My body insisted on wildly thrusting and moving towards completion. If we did not stop and he went over into ejaculation but I did not quite make it, I would be disappointed and let it show, sometimes rather ungraciously. This was when I still thought my satisfaction was my lover's job. Then I began to be more aware of his arousal state and how my response was critical to how long he could last. I learned to stop movement when he got too close to the edge. Although he did not ejaculate, I did not get my orgasm at that moment either. I was not satisfied but I looked at it as a sacrifice for more pleasure to come. This 'martyr' syndrome was not particularly helpful either. Eventually I understood that when Al was getting very close to his line, it was an excellent opportunity for *both of us* to stop and circulate our energy—not just for Al to move his, but for me to move mine as well. I chose to go farther rather than grab that instant gratification. By building and circulating my energy, I went on to higher and higher peaks of pleasure and connection."

174

Setting Up a Feedback System With Your Smooth Muscles

As your Tantric practice progresses—with regular PC pumping (Chapter 7, page 147), delaying ejaculation, and moving your sexual energy—you may gradually begin to gain some mastery over the smooth muscles in and around the penis, scrotum, and anus. The walls of hollow organs such as blood vessels, the gastrointestinal tract, and the bladder are composed of smooth muscles. Contraction and relaxation of these muscles is controlled automatically by the body's autonomic nervous system and is normally involuntary—hence their alternative name, involuntary muscles. Slow and steady smooth muscle contractions, for example, process food through the intestines and force urine from the bladder. Stronger and more rapid smooth muscle contractions expel semen from the penis in involuntary ejaculation. The prostate contracts one to two seconds before ejaculation and expels the seminal fluid into the urethra.

You can learn to voluntarily relax your smooth muscles, which enables more blood to flow into the penis than flows out, thus maintaining erection and delaying the ejaculation response, while at the same time allowing the orgasmic response to continue. Becoming intimately familiar with that part of your body is the first step to becoming aware, on a very subtle level, of what is happening with your internal smooth muscles. In addition to the techniques we have described for building strength, stamina, and focus—particularly PC Pumping—you can also set up an internal feedback through temporary use of the amino acid arginine.

Arginine

Your body releases nitric oxide (NO) in your genitals in response to sexual stimulation. This encourages your smooth muscles to relax and blood flows into the penis resulting in erection. If there is not enough NO, erection won't occur. Arginine has been shown to enhance NO levels in your body.[4]

From six to 18 grams of arginine are needed to produce the effect of smooth muscle relaxation. This is six to 18, 1000 mg. capsules, or about three heaping teaspoons of arginine powder dissolved in a liquid, such as orange juice. If arginine works for you, within 30 minutes you will notice a major difference in your staying power. If you pay very careful attention to exactly what is happening in your body, with several repetitions you may begin to be able to do yourself what the arginine helped you to do.

Caution: Large doses of arginine before lovemaking do not replace PC exercises and concentration. This is a *temporary* practice only, to enable you to actually feel smooth muscle relaxation and differentiate it from involuntary contraction. Diabetics, borderline diabetics, pregnant or lactating women, cancer patients, persons with phenylketonuria (PKU), or persons who have had ocular or brain herpes should not use arginine. High dietary levels of arginine may cause reactivation of latent herpes viruses in a few susceptible individuals. If this occurs, discontinue use. **Consult your physician before using any supplements.**

Prostate Health

We are suggesting that you delay ejaculation not just for a particular session of lovemaking, but over days, weeks, and even months of frequent lovemaking. Many men ask how often they should ejaculate. The answer is, as infrequently as possible. One way to determine when to ejaculate is by paying attention to how your prostate feels.

Probably every man who begins to practice delayed ejaculation with extended and frequent lovemaking will experience prostate discomfort. Perhaps as a young man, you had the experience of "blue balls" after several hours of petting (kissing and touching genitals) without the release of ejaculation. If you extend lovemaking to several hours, the prostate may become swollen or enlarged because you have stimulated such a buildup of sexual energy. When this happens, allow yourself to have an ejaculation. This instantly relieves the pressure and you will feel comfortable again. Renew your practice, once again retaining your sexual energy by delaying ejaculation. The length of time between ejaculations will get longer and longer, as you become more successful at circulating your sexual energy away from your genitals.

Delaying ejaculation is completely safe, but when you have not moved all your sexual energy away from your prostate, the resulting pressure causes discomfort. If you have any concerns about this, be sure to consult your physician, especially if your prostate is still sore after you ejaculate. Let him know that you are beginning to explore retaining your sexual energy by delaying ejaculation. Ask him to check your prostate and confirm that you are indeed healthy. Your doctor can then monitor your prostate, genital, and urinary tract health over time to eliminate any concerns you may have.

As well, health food stores carry safe, natural herbal supplements to help maintain optimal prostate health. Saw Palmetto, Stinging Nettle, Pygeum, and Lycopene are some of the best herbs for this purpose. Zinc is also an important nutrient for maintaining healthy prostate function. Many nutritional companies offer an excellent formula combining several or all of these ingredients in one capsule.

For some reason still unknown to scientists, the prostate tends to swell as we age. This condition, called benign prostate hypertrophy

(BPH), is common, is uncomfortable, is not usually dangerous, and can be easily treated. Some medical researchers claim that more than 75 percent of men over 50 years of age have a somewhat enlarged prostate. Because the prostate is wrapped around the urethra, any swelling can cause difficulties with urination, such as the need to urinate more frequently, having to get up in the middle of the night to urinate, urgent voiding, or the feeling that you have not emptied out your bladder completely when you are done urinating. An enlarged prostate can greatly diminish your libido and your capacity to engage in or enjoy sex—so take care of it. Prescription medications, such as Hytrin and Proscar, also exist to relax the prostate and shrink the gland. Ask your doctor.

Regularly stimulating your prostate through PC pumps and external perineum or internal anal massages (see Chapter 11, pages 220 and 221) will help to keep it healthy. Before we became involved with Tantra, I had some prostate problems, but with PC squeezing, massages, and nutritional supplements, my difficulties completely disappeared.

Am I Sure I Want to Do this?

Remember, you do not have to give up ejaculations in your Tantric loving practice; you can ejaculate anytime you want to. In fact, you will have to ejaculate in order to protect the health of your prostate while you learn how to successfully move your sexual energy. At some degree of mastery, ejaculation may become totally irrelevant in your lovemaking—but orgasm will not. You will discover many levels of orgasm.

You can also have quickies. We love quickies, but if your lovemaking regularly ends in five or 15 minutes, especially with an ejaculation, you will not be able to experience the higher spiritual sexuality that comes with building elevated sexual charge. Our quickies do not end with ejaculation; they are brief interludes of teasing and enticement. These delightful, often raunchy encounters provide excellent stimulation and preparation for our extended lovemaking sessions—not a substitute for them.

Multiple non-ejaculatory orgasms differ greatly from ejaculatory orgasms. Are they better? You will have to decide for yourself, but for me, an orgasm with ejaculation, even though extremely enjoyable, is now experienced as a letdown. It ends my pleasure and depletes my energy. In fact, ejaculation is one way that men commonly deny themselves pleasure. There is nothing wrong with ejaculation, but there is something better—multiple, non-ejaculatory orgasms. Until you experience it for yourself, you may be skeptical, but if you persevere you will find great pleasure, renewed vitality, and the possibility of sexual/spiritual ecstasy.

Chapter 9

Freeing the Female Orgasm

"When mom found my diaphragm, I told her it
was a bathing cap for my cat."

—Liz Winston

Women are blessed with an extraordinary capacity for physical pleasure. When we are fully awakened sexually, we can experience a veri-
table cornucopia of orgasms—genitally and beyond. We even have a
special body part, the clitoris, whose only function is to make us writhe
and moan with delight. Why is it then, when nature has kindly endowed us
with such intense possibility, that so many of us ever realize only a fraction of our pleasure potential?

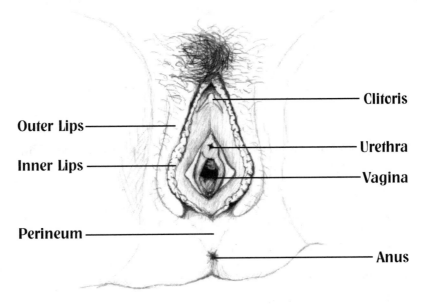

Female Anatomy Front View

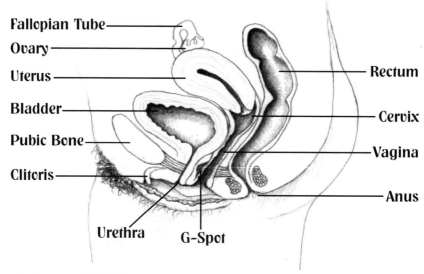

Female Anatomy Side View

Quite simply, our heads get in the way. "The mind," which one workshop participant reproachfully described as "not the friend you think it is," interferes. Its attitudes, assumptions, and conditioned beliefs are your biggest blockages to sexual fulfillment. But take heart, you can pass through these mental barriers to emerge fully orgasmic. There are only two things you really need: permission and time—permission *from yourself* to allow your sexuality to blossom, and enough time during lovemaking for your body to become thoroughly aroused.

Permission

"I wrote the story myself.
It's about a girl who lost her reputation
and never missed it."

—Mae West

There are a variety of strategies you can employ, on your own and with your partner, to open your mind to "yes":

1. Accept that *you* create your orgasms.

2. Drop shame and guilt.

3. Cultivate your erotic self.

4. Communicate what you want.

5. Befriend your body.

6. Build your yoni power.

7. Play with self-pleasuring.

8. Welcome your lover's support.

9. Stay focused.

It's Up to You

"The older one grows, the more one likes indecency."
—Virginia Woolf

First, we women must take responsibility for our own sexual satisfaction. We have to give up the idea that a Prince Charming will come along and do it for us—despite how enticing or preferable romance novels make that seem. Yes, you do want an attentive lover, but no matter how skilled or caring he may be, unless you are willing to allow yourself to surrender to orgasmic pleasure, it will not happen. Although bliss is your birthright, it cannot flow through you if you are tightly trying to stay in control.

To welcome ecstasy, it is also necessary to relearn that your sexuality is a *good* thing, in the face of a culture that constantly tells us the opposite. Despite the progress that's been made since the sexual revolution of the 1960s, a double standard still exists. It's not quite so flagrant, but it's there. Even today, a young man who actively explores sex is an adventurous stud, but a young woman who does the same is a promiscuous slut. A woman who engages lustily in the delights of the body is somehow morally questionable. On an intellectual level, we know that is nonsense. We can tell ourselves quite rationally that we have left behind such outdated thinking, but underneath, in our heart's core, that nasty message still holds too many women hostage. The virgin or the whore split is alive, well, and feasting on each of us.

How do you step out from under this ancient yoke? Retrain your mind; make it your tool, not your master. Learn to identify and alter any sex-negative messages you give yourself. For example, notice what you say to yourself about:

⚜ Initiating sex.

⚜ Asking for what you want in bed.

⚜ Your children hearing you make love.

⚜ The sex appeal of your body.

Drop Shame and Guilt

How loud are your voices of shame and guilt? Negative messages can be subtle as well as overt, so be vigilant, and catch those thoughts as they start to damn you, gently release them, and replace them with sex-affirming concepts. Remind yourself that your sexual fulfillment brings benefits to other aspects of your life and to the people around you. Remember that your partner wants you to be satisfied, through and through. So, for example, if you are like many women who fret about how your lover could possibly want to have his face at your genitals for as long as you need to reach orgasm, replace that thought with the knowledge that female pheromones, male attractants called copulins, are only produced in the vaginal canal. Of course he'd want to have his face there as much as possible—he's chemically programmed for it!

Cultivating the Erotic You

> "Good girls go to heaven,
> bad girls go everywhere."
>
> —Helen Gurley Brown

Besides simply substituting sexually expansive messages in place of restrictive ones, you can go a step further and deliberately cultivate your erotic imagination. Everyone has moments of daydreaming—make some of yours a conscious focus on kindling your sexual nature. Indulge in fantasy, imagining all the wonderful things you would like to do with, and to, your lover.

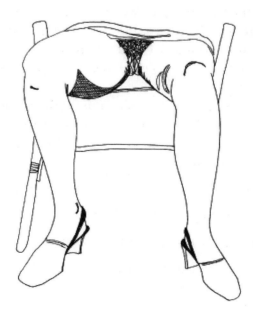

Yoni Power

182

Be audacious. Give voice to your sexual enthusiasm. Identify your sexual stumbling block, and as is the Tantric way, jump on it. One of my big sexual issues was "good girls don't." My bad girl could, but I wanted all of me—good, bad, and in-between to be freely sexual, so to rid my-self of this weighty carapace I forced myself to push my envelope of propriety. For about a year and a half during our lovemaking, as I was wildly riding Al, bouncing about in sexual abandon, I would make my-self roar, "I'm a *goooood girl.*" I felt simultaneously afraid and elated, shy and bold—and very, very free. That roaring helped me absorb throughout my entire being the knowledge that *this* good girl does.

Asking for What You Want

"When the sun comes up, I have morals again."

—Elayne Boosler

Part of giving yourself permission to fully enjoy your sexuality is daring to tell your partner what you want. It is essential that you let him know exactly what turns you on. If you are not comfortable telling him during lovemaking, talk about it at another time. Be explicit—explain to him how, where, and when you like to be touched. A frank and play-ful conversation about your sexual desires can be a tremendous turn-on for both of you. Remember to phrase your requests in terms of what you like that he's already doing and what you would like him to try, not what you think he's doing wrong.

During lovemaking, when your partner caresses you in ways or on erogenous spots that excite you, let him know with words, sounds, or body movement. As Al says, "It is easy to train your man to do what you like. Give him a big reaction." For example, I love it when Al nuzzles my neck—it zaps me all the way down to my groin—so I communicate my pleasure with wiggles and giggles and moans. My response inflames him—he nuzzles more, I wiggle more, and our circle of reciprocal turn-on builds.

Love Your Body

Get to know your body. Become its lover and friend, not its critic. If you are not comfortable with your body, it is hard to let it have its way in sex. As you follow the path of sacred sex, you begin to love and appre-ciate your body for what it really is—an extraordinarily complex organ-ism, capable of amazing feats and home to your true self, your Spirit. Facilitate this shift in attitude by taking a loving tour of your body.

Looking at Yourself Through the Eyes of a Lover

- ❧ Allow at least an hour of undisturbed time for this marvelous tour.

- ❧ Begin with a bath or shower.

- ❧ Create a loving ambience—warm room; lighting bright enough to see by but soft and caressing to your skin; music that relaxes you and makes you feel sensual.

- ❧ You will need a mirror, preferably two—a full-length mirror and a hand mirror.

- ❧ Before you begin, say aloud to yourself, "I come to this exploration with love and acceptance." Start with your head and work your way slowly down your body, looking, touching, sniffing, tasting. Feel the texture of your skin. Follow the curves and angles of your outline. Appreciate the differences in color from top to bottom. As you are exploring, picture all the marvelous things you can do with your body.

Love Your Body

ଛ If negative thoughts and images come up during your discovery (my breasts are too small, my butt has too much cellulite, my legs are too short) do not get caught in them and do not admonish yourself. Acknowledge the thought ("Oh, that is a judgment") and then purse your lips and blow it out and away from you, down to the Earth for cleansing. If you find you cannot let the negative images go, stop the exercise, do some emotional release, and come back to it again later. You want to make this a positive loving experience. With practice, you will.

ଛ Continue your exploration with a long loving look at your genitals. You may be most comfortable doing this lying down, your head propped on pillows, using a hand mirror to see all your glory.

ଛ It is strange that in a society so obsessed with sex, we seem particularly embarrassed about our genitals. Many women have never looked closely at their genitals, or yoni, as this marvelous feminine body part is called in Tantric practice. We all have a yoni, but each is as different and individual as our faces. Some are small and delicate, folding in on themselves like pale ferns; others are bold and glistening with dark lips protruding from tangled jungles. All of them are glorious flowers mirroring the beauty of Mother Nature. There are heart shapes, diamonds, and bells, plump and juicy or slender and angular. As you look, appreciate your uniqueness, the elements of your body that make you exclusively you.

ଛ Put your fingers gently inside. Smell and taste your delicious self. (Do this "taste and smell" exercise several times throughout the course of your monthly cycle. Notice the differences.)

ଛ To complete your loving tour, kiss your hands, hold them for a moment on your love grotto, then place them over your heart and give yourself thanks. Say thank you aloud and say your name.

ଛ As an additional affirmation, write down 10 things you like about your yoni—become a genuine admirer of your feminine glory.

Yoni Power

Ancient Eastern lovemaking traditions revered the yoni—the source of life. Its juices were considered ambrosia, rejuvenating nectar. You can cultivate the power of your yoni by consciously building its strength and sensual capacity. Basic PC pumping (Chapter 7), works very well, but I suggest going a step further and using a vaginal exerciser. These come in a variety of styles and shapes, but my favorites are vaginal eggs, which are about the size of a chicken egg and are manufactured of various kinds of crystal and stone. They come complete with instructions, but the basic exercise is to gently insert the egg comfortably into your vagina, then push it down, but not out and pull it back up again.

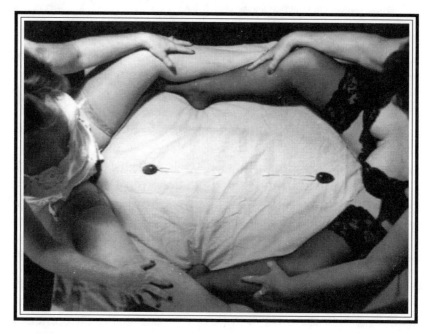

Yoni Eggs

If you are nervous about inserting a vaginal egg—afraid that it will get stuck inside—relax. Usually the difficulty is having enough muscle tone to keep it in. Because you do these egg exercises standing up, it is a good idea to stand over a soft rug or to wear panties to catch the egg in case it pops out.

Not only do these exercises tone your muscles and give you added pleasure, but also the deliberate act of strengthening this part of your body with a beautiful object is empowering. You are acknowledging your feminine capacity for sexual freedom.

Masturbation

> "Lead me not into temptation; I can find the way
> myself."
>
> —Rita Mae Brown

Learning about masturbation is an essential element of your self-love process, of taking responsibility for your sexual fulfillment. In order to get what you want, you have to let your partner know. In order to be able to tell or show him, you have to know yourself. Find out what you like through self-pleasuring.

Learn to thoroughly love yourself in masturbation; do not just rush through to a tension release. Take your time, seduce and pleasure yourself so that you can begin to peel back your layers of unawakened passion. Tease and tantalize yourself, allowing yourself to thoroughly catch fire. Gradually increase the length of your masturbation sessions, building up to almost climax, then relaxing and slowing down, building again and so on. Not only will you have more pleasure when you do let go, but this is also an excellent way to learn how to relax while carrying a high-energy charge.

When you are ready, masturbate for your partner. It is a wonderful way to ask for and show him what you want. Self-loving while he watches makes you at once vulnerable and powerful. If you are fearful that you will not look sexy enough because your body is not the currently ideal type, understand that it is your excitement, your wantonness that inflames your man, not the perfection of your shape.

Masturbation Ceremony for Women

If you have not already done so, take yourself on the Looking At Yourself Through the Eyes of a Lover tour. Arrange a loving space for yourself—soft lighting, comfortable pillows, sensuous music, aromatic scents, and beautiful objects. Make sure you will not be disturbed for at least an hour. This is very important because getting out of your mind and into your body is key to opening up to full sexual pleasure. If you are worried about being interrupted, you will not be able to let go into your play.

Approach your loving from the outside in—start with delicate strokes of your arms, face, neck, and thighs. Use your fingertips, a feather, and a piece of silk to lightly tantalize your tender skin. If it helps to arouse you, begin your self-loving with an erotic fantasy, but once you are turned on, let the fantasy go and focus on what is happening in your body. Remember, to fly free in sexual bliss you need to leave your "daily mind" behind.

Begin to massage your breasts, try a light touch with large circles—counterclockwise then clockwise and gradually increase the pressure. Move slowly in toward your nipples. Experiment with tweaking them, pulling them, gentling circling them until they are stiff and tingling. You may feel a direct line of heat from your breasts down to your genitals.

Trail one hand down across the flesh of your belly, reveling in the softness of your skin, its warmth and sensitivity. Feel your pulse racing beneath its surface. Flutter your hand across the fluffy bush of your pubic hair. Delight at its texture—is it thick and crinkly, long and fine? Is there a light dusting of hair or a full coarse bush?

Move gently to explore your vulva—the fleshy outer lips and the welcoming inner lips. Explore with delicate, tentative, and awe-filled fingers. Find the clitoris—its hood, shaft, and glans. Slip your fingers gently past your perineum and on to your anus. Allow yourself to consider this "forbidden gate" as a source of potential pleasure.

Begin the dance of your fingers. Use plenty of good quality lubricant. Stimulate your clitoris, start slowly and build up speed and pressure. Try different spots—the sides and the head. Build your pleasure up and then slow it down. Tease yourself with loving playfulness. With your other hand, continue to stroke your body or brush your nipples. Touch your heart chakra to deepen the connection between sex and loving.

Woman Self-pleasuring

Dip your fingers into your honey pot. Squeeze your fingers with your ever-strengthening PC muscles. Moisten your fingers with your juices—smell them and taste them. There are many female aromas and tastes—tart, pungent, salty, and sweet. Yours are uniquely you.

Increase the speed and pressure of your stimulation. When you find a stroke or combination that gives you particular pleasure, continue it. If you have not had much experience with orgasm, if your clitoris does not seem particularly sensitive to stimulation, you may want to experiment with a vibrator or a vaginal sensitizing cream such as Vitara or Viacreme. Perhaps you may want to use one hand to stimulate your clitoris and the other inside your pulsing vagina, or you may want to use a dildo for vaginal pleasure. Lightly tap your perineum as if you were pulsing out a rhythm on a fine hand drum. Circle your anus; teasingly insert a brave finger inside. Dare to feel everything you have dreamed of. Doing the Sexual Fire Breath (Chapter 7, page 149) as you love yourself will help to increase your pleasure.

As you practice self-loving, do not hurry to reach orgasmic release. You are your own lover—you have all the time in the world to come to bliss. Increasingly bring yourself to the edge of orgasm, then slow down and practice the Passion Pump (Chapter 7, page 151) to move your energy through you. When you do go into orgasmic contraction, use slow, controlled breathing to ride the wave longer and longer. Your orgasms will increase in intensity and will move throughout your body rather than be centered in your genitals.

To complete your self-pleasuring ceremony rest for a while, breathe deeply, and enjoy the sensations coursing through your body. Thank yourself, aloud, for giving yourself this wondrous gift. Tell yourself, aloud, "I love you, _____(speak your name)."

Your Partner's Help

"Women's virtue is man's greatest invention."
—Cornelia Otis Skinner

One of the reasons for the suppression of women's sexuality is the sheer awesomeness of its power. Because of our physiological differences, a sexually ripe woman can literally suck dry an unskilled male lover. It's been far easier to brand Woman as evil strumpet than to learn how to match her capacity. Some version of the dark goddess Kali—standing on the body of her lover Shiva, his severed head in one of her hands and a cup of his blood in another—threatens many a man's sexual security, albeit on a deeply subconscious level. Just as it is essential for a woman to examine her approach to sex, so it is for her lover to consider his response to her sexuality. He must search his psyche and weed out any remnants of the misogynist belief that women cannot be wholesome and still be fantastic lovers.

A man who wants a truly satisfying sexual life with his mate can help her break through conditioned, pleasure-stifling attitudes by letting her know how much he respects, admires, and cherishes her fully female, sensual self. He will tell her often, especially when making love, that it thoroughly turns him on to see her let loose the passionate side of her nature. His words will be encouragements to her hot-blooded self, not a demand for it. Through love and acceptance of her unique sexual needs and wants, he can create a safe place for her to open to the joy of sex. Making it safe is one of the greatest gifts a man can give.

Al helped me unite my good girl with my lusty animal by verbally combining those two seemingly contradictory elements. During sacred loving he'd whisper in my ear, "You are so sexy and you are an amazingly kind, caring woman. You are a wild thing and a marvelous mother. You are so hot and such a creative business partner." His understanding and support made it easier for me to allow myself to be and do what I really wanted.

Staying Focused

"Only good girls keep diaries.
Bad girls do not have time."

—Tallulah Bankhead

Besides worrying about whether they are "bad" if they really enjoy and want sex, women can worry about enjoying sex the "right way." You may worry about how you look, smell, and taste. You may worry that the cellulite in your upper thighs or your slight bulge of tummy fat may quiver unattractively. You may worry about being clean "down there." You may worry about how long it takes to reach climax, how much time your man has to spend stroking, licking, and caressing to help you fly over the mountain. All of these thoughts take you out of lovemaking.

When thoughts drive you into your head, you can bring yourself back into your body through:

- Breathing consciously—slow, deep breathing to relax and connect with your lover and rapid, shallow breathing to increase your excitement.

- Concentrating on your senses—touch, smell, and sound.

- Opening your heart—feel how much you love your partner.

190

- Making sound—everything from little "mmm" to medium size "oooo" to gigantic "yes, yes, yes."

- Moving your body—especially rocking your hips.

The Sexual Fire Breath (Chapter 7, page 149) is particularly effective—the rocking, breathing, squeezing, making sound, and focus on energy movement make it pretty hard to have your attention elsewhere!

Time

After you have given yourself permission to open fully to your body's pleasure potential, you need time to allow it to happen. One of the occasionally frustrating differences between men and women is rate of arousal. Men are naturally most akin to fire—heating up quickly and burning out just as fast. Women are water—slow to reach boiling point but then able to bubble happily along for quite a while. In much "regular" lovemaking, a woman may be just becoming totally fired up as her partner is ready to roll over and go to sleep. Because Tantric lovemaking takes place over a period of hours, women are able to reach numerous peaks of arousal and experience multiple orgasms. Tantra includes lots of what we normally call foreplay. Your partner helps you reach orgasm with his fingers, tongue, and lips before you even start to have intercourse.

As you become more adept at sacred sex loving, connecting energetically, not simply physically, you will come to understand that all moments of sexual intimacy are of equal value and potential for bliss. The genital orgasm, the goal of so much of our regular lovemaking, is no longer the focus, but rather building and moving your sexual energy so that your entire body, indeed your whole being, becomes orgasmic.

Some Tips for Loving a Woman

"It's not the men in my life that count,
it's the life in my men."

—Mae West

Most men enjoy having their genitals touched at any time, whether they are sexually aroused or not. This is not usually the case with women. One of the most common complaints we hear from them is about the Bull's Eye Syndrome—immediate honing in on breasts and genitals. Think of the vagina as a "potential" opening, a magical door that will happily open wide to receive you, but only after you have called ahead to ensure your welcome. Be certain she's eager for your genital explorations by focusing loving attention on other parts of her body first—lots of kissing, neck nuzzling, tender strokes on back, shoulders, and arms, then adoring caresses of her breasts. Build her arousal from the outside in. That is, start with her head, neck, hands, feet, then move in toward breasts, belly, and vagina. Only after you sense she's ready, through signs like rapid breathing, flushed skin, hardened nipples, or enticing moans should you move to her vagina. Once your hand or mouth is at her sweet honey pot, begin to explore it also from the outside inward—outer lips, clitoris, inner lips, vaginal canal.

Pay particular attention to her love button, the clitoris. The skin of your fingers is not nearly as sensitive as her clitoral tissue. But the tissue of your mouth and tongue is an almost perfect match. Begin with oral stimulation then move on to manual pleasuring. For some women the head of the clitoris, the pointed tip, is too sensitive for much direct pressure, so focus your attention on the sides. Touch around it and along the shaft until her excitement increases. Start slow and soft, then experiment with different pressures, strokes, and speeds. Ask her which ones she likes best. A good way to do this is to try two different touches, then ask her which one she likes better. If she's willing, invite her to masturbate for you so you can learn exactly how she likes to be touched. Many women are shy to do this at first but with some gentle encouragement she may really show her wanton self. It can be a great turn-on for both of you.

Once you do begin to explore her grotto of love, continue the movement of outside to inside—gently stimulating the outer lips, and especially the clitoris before you dip into the well of life. It is a good idea to wait until she is very aroused before entering her yoni either with your fingers or your penis. It should be wet and juicy before you go exploring. Generally, if she's not wet, she's not ready. It is as simple as that. If your lover does not have a lot of natural vaginal juices, even when she is fully aroused, be sure to use a good silicone or water-based lubricant. Nothing can be a quicker turn-off than rough, dry skin rubbing on soft vaginal tissues. Water-based or silicone lubricant is better because oil can clog the sensitive vaginal tissue. A delightful turn-on is to ask your woman, reverently and hotly, if you may enter. If she says she would like you to play a little more on the outside, do so with grace and love.

A wonderful way to make the transition from the outside of the yoni to the inside is to keep pleasuring her clitoris with your tongue as you slip a finger inside. Begin to stimulate her G-spot. Move your index finger or your first two fingers in a "come hither" motion (as if you were asking someone from across the room to come over to where you are) and gently stroke her.

Women respond strongly to multiple points of stimulation—for instance, your tongue on her clitoris, your index finger in her yoni, your baby finger lightly circling her anus, and your other hand caressing her breasts. Another key to pleasing a woman is this: When you find a stroke or movement that feels good to her, (for instance a long, slow rhythmic sliding on the shaft of her clitoris, or a short, rapid, medium-pressure stroke on her G-spot) *keep on doing it!* A common tendency is to want to add more—more speed, more pressure—or to move to some other spot. Instead, stay where you are and keep doing *exactly* what you are doing until she indicates that she would like something else, either by words or body movement.

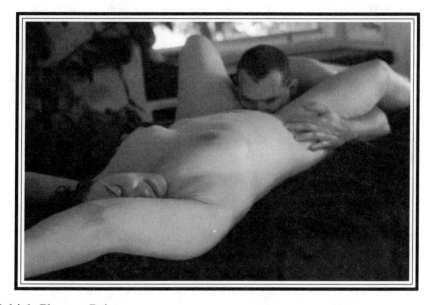

Multiple Pleasure Points

Sometimes after a woman has had a clitoral orgasm, her clitoris feels too sensitive for continued caresses, particularly of the same intensity. Rather than moving on to some other delightful activity, you can help her to build to multiple clitoral orgasms with this simple technique:

- ❀ Maintain very light contact between tongue and clitoris, keeping absolutely still.

- ❀ After a short period of time, 10 to 30 seconds, move your tongue ever so slightly.

- ❀ If her response lets you know it is too much too soon, stop but keep the connection.

⚕ After another brief pause move your tongue again.

⚕ Keep doing this until her body has calmed enough for you to resume active caressing, taking her up to yet another climax.

It is also important that you let your lover know that you are enjoying pleasing her. Remember, many women begin to worry that they are "taking too long" for their partner, that he is losing interest. This takes focus away from the pleasurable sensations in her body and jumps your lover into her head, just the opposite effect from what you would like—a letting go into the delights of your touch. So let her know by sounds, by words, that you love giving her this pleasure.

An intercourse technique that is highly pleasurable for women is the "shallow-deep thrust." This powerful thrusting method mixes a series of shallow thrusts—usually nine, an auspicious masculine number in Eastern philosophy—with one deep. Air is pushed out of the yoni by one deep plunge. The following shallow thrusts, which penetrate only the first inch and a half to two inches of the vaginal canal, create a vacuum that aches to be filled by the next deep one. These short strokes also stimulate the nerve-filled, most sensitive part of the yoni, increasing the woman's desire. Besides giving her great pleasure, this technique helps you last longer because shallow thrusts do not build your excitement as quickly.

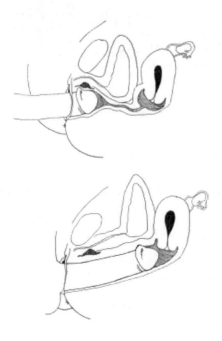

Shallow/Deep Thrust

An Orgasmic Cornucopia

Each woman has her own "orgasmic fingerprint" as sexologist Lonnie Barbach describes it. Many women reach orgasm through stimulation of the clitoris, others through internal vaginal stimulation, and others through a simultaneous combination of internal and external pleasuring. Some tip over into climax with breast play, others by squeezing or applying pressure genitally, others through the power of erotic thought. The important thing is to relax into the delight of finding what your unique pleasure pattern is, not to make it essential to have a particular type of orgasm.

Generally, women reach climax most easily through clitoral stimulation, even during intercourse. Because the clitoris is extremely sensitive to touch of all kinds, experiment with caressing all the parts of it in different ways with a variety of things—tongue, fingers, vibrators, feathers, and so on, and remember, it is quite acceptable for you to be playing with your love button while your lover is exciting you in other ways.

The most sensitive part of a woman's vaginal canal is the first inch to two inches. It is here that most of the nerve endings are located. The G-spot is the "female prostate gland." It surrounds the urethra (the same way a man's prostate surrounds his urethra) and is felt through the upper or top vaginal wall about half way between the back of the pubic bone and the cervix. With proper stimulation and high states of sexual arousal, the G-spot can become very sensitive and may be a source of great pleasure, but many lovers report difficulty locating it. Imagine a glass lying on the floor. If you reach your first two fingers into the glass at the top, that is, toward the ceiling rather than the bottom towards the floor, you should find it.

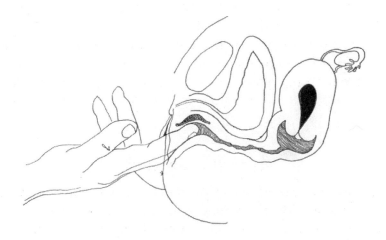

G-Spot Stimulation

Most important to finding the G-spot is *when* to look—it is often only identifiable after a woman is very excited and has had considerable external pleasuring. Typically, the G-spot swells as you become more and more sexually aroused. It can reach the size of a walnut and may feel like a bumpy or raised area of skin. The best way to know you have found this highly intense love spot is by the pleasurable sensations you experience. It is difficult to reach the G-spot with the penis through intercourse, especially in the missionary position, although you can have some success with woman-on-top and rear-entry positions. It is much easier with fingers, or specially formed dildos and vibrators.

Stimulation of the goddess-spot can produce extraordinarily intense orgasms. As you are approaching a G-spot orgasm, you may feel like you have to urinate (probably because of the pressure against the urethra as the female prostate surrounding it swells). This may provoke you to tighten up, stop, and pull back from the edge of bliss. If, instead, you can stay relaxed or even push out a little with your vaginal muscles, that "have-to-pee" sensation will pass and you will likely move on into deep waves of sexual delight. You may also have an ejaculatory orgasm. A fluid that resembles watered down fat-free milk—often lots of it—may spurt out from the urethra. It may have a slightly sweet taste. According to research by Dr. Beverly Whipple and others, the female ejaculatory fluid contains simple sugars—glucose and fructose—as well as other ingredients.[1] When it dries, it leaves no mark. This fluid is assumed to originate in the paraurethral glands, in the spongy tissue around the urethra. It is not urine, but if you are worried that it is, go to the bathroom before stimulating the G-spot.

As you become more and more open and charged up through extended lovemaking your entire yoni may come alive with sensation so that you experience orgasm deep within the vaginal canal. Continued PC squeezing magnifies the intensity.

Women do not usually notice a loss of sexual energy after orgasm. In fact, one orgasm can be the building block for the next and the next. However if you do find your desire diminishing after a particular type of orgasm, delay it, building up to several peaks and backing off before you let go.

On to the Mystery

As you become more easily orgasmic during your sacred loving sessions, experiment with postponing orgasm, building up a higher and higher sexual charge. Do the Passion Pump (Chapter 7, page 151) and/or Sexual Fire Breath (Chapter 7, page 149) as you are reaching a high state of arousal but before you spill over into orgasm. Stop stimulation, breathe slowly and deeply, relax your body, tighten your PC muscles, run hands (yours or your partner's) up from genitals to crown, and visualize your molten heat spreading. Repeat this several times to expand the sexual energy throughout your body. It is in this way that you move on to whole-body orgasms and mystical states of consciousness.

Allow the awakening of your unique orgasmic self to be a gradual, loving, and delight-filled process. Do not rush or push yourself to achieve climax, to make it happen, or feel that you must have it a particular way. Instead, permit your pleasure pattern to unfold naturally. Think of your opening to orgasmic bliss as a journey of discovery without end. It is a lifelong education. My personal process began as a girl by discovering how to masturbate to clitoral climax, then as a young woman experiencing clitoral orgasm with a partner, at first occasionally, and then most of the time. As a mature woman in Tantric practice, I have extended my experience to G-spot and ejaculatory orgasms, deep vaginal orgasms, full-body orgasms and mystical, energetic beyond-body connection. Variations of these pleasures await you as well. All you need is permission and time.

Chapter 10

Planning and Ritual in Sacred Loving

"The very best impromptu speeches are the ones written well in advance."

—Ruth Gordon

Your intention is the key to transforming regular sex into sacred sex. Intention affects emotions, energy, and consciousness, which govern how you perceive your lovemaking. You can be engaged in exactly the same actions with your body—deep kissing, hungry licking, wild thrusting—but have vastly different experiences depending on your intention. If you are simply concerned with releasing pent up sexual tension, that is likely all you will get. If you are making love because it's your Friday night routine, then routine sex is probably in store. If you are filled with the desire to merge wholly with your lover, then you may elevate your lovemaking to holiness. That is the intention of Tantric sex—to unite with your beloved in all ways, and in so doing connect with the Divine.

Planning

"Failing to plan is planning to fail."

—Effie Jones

Planning assists intention. When you want to create a fantastic event, you prepare ahead. You make careful arrangements for cocktail parties, business meetings, touring holidays—your sacred loving time deserves the same attention.

We schedule a lengthy Tantra session once a week. Day and time are slotted into our planners and as soon as that date is set we start getting ready. Couples often say to us, "Doesn't planning for lovemaking take away its spontaneity?" It could if you orchestrated every detail and held rigidly to that prescribed scenario, but that is not what we are advocating. Approach your Tantra date as you would an intimate dinner party with close friends—select the menu, arrange the setting, consider a few topics for conversation, then bring your guests together and let the evening magically unfold. Sacred loving sessions are similar, you can be spontaneous precisely because you have put thought in beforehand. When everything you may want for your romantic play is close by, you can relax and go into a loving flow. When you have prepared for different types of activities, you have plenty to choose from to suit exactly how you are feeling in that moment—passionate, tender, playful, quiet, lusty. Remember, sacred loving includes much more than explicit sex. It incorporates a wide variety of intimate, loving connections that are limited only by your imagination. Suggestions for activities follow in this chapter and appear in Chapters 7, 11, and 12.

Here is a short list of elements to include in your loving plan:

1. **Location:** at home or elsewhere and in which room(s)?

2. **Physical properties of the setting:** lights, music, scents, and furnishings.

3. **Food and drink:** for nourishment and sensual arousal.

4. **Clothing:** to put on and take off.

5. **Loving activities:** games, rituals, massage, bathing, dancing, and energy play.

6. **Shutting out the world:** no phones, no visitors.

Sometimes your planning may be elaborate, at others very simple and open-ended. Always it provides a framework within which your exquisite union can blossom. Consciously preparing for your Tantra date helps build anticipation and excitement, readying you emotionally and energetically for your day of love, plus, if you have become unaccustomed to spending several hours together only as lovers, a basic outline can help relieve anxiety about what on earth to do.

Ritual

The rituals of Tantric loving help you keep focused on your intention of absolute union with your partner, and because ritual acts reach beyond your conscious mind deep into your unconscious, they increase the *power* of your intention.

At first, you may be uncomfortable about deliberately bringing ritual into your sex life. Most likely your participation in rituals has been in the context of an organization—probably a religious organization, but perhaps also in clubs, fraternities, military or sports associations. You may feel that those organizations are the only authorized and valid places for ritual expression. You do not have the right to do it yourself. Because ritual is so powerful, any practice outside formal institutions may also be subconsciously associated with danger and evil—black magic. As well, if your experience with ritual has been solely within a formal framework you probably have not learned how to create any on your own.

In Tantric loving, you learn to associate ritual with pleasure, playfulness, and spiritual awakening. Give yourself permission—it is okay, it is fun as well as profound, and it has great benefits. Ritual helps your consciousness create results. The more you believe, the more likely you are to create the results you want. At first, you may have to suspend your disbelief (just like you do when you watch a movie) in order to practice ceremonial lovemaking, but when you do, because ritual is so powerful, the positive feedback you will get will encourage you to go on.

At the outset of our Tantric practice, we were nervous and shy about ritualizing our sexuality. Pala, who has a natural ceremonial orientation, most often prepared and led our rituals, but she had to overcome her fear that Al would judge her or refuse to participate. She was afraid he'd think, "What is this crazy woman doing waving incense and chanting? No way am I making a fool of myself." However, fortunately he respected her enough, had a good sense of humor, and a powerful intention of his own for sacred loving to act despite his self-consciousness. Now rituals are second nature to us—a joyous and essential aspect of our loving.

For your practice, begin with the rituals we have included here or borrow some from other cultures: native North American, Asian, and African. Alter them, if you wish, to suit your circumstances, your traditions and your sensitivities. Then when you are feeling more confident, when your imagination has awakened to the possibilities, dare to create your own.

Creating a Temple for Love

When celebrating sacred sex it helps if you create the proper atmosphere. Set up part of your home, bedroom, living room, or den, as a "Temple for Love."

     ⚬ Begin by giving each other a warm embrace then proceed in
        silence to arrange the space you have chosen.

- Make sure it is tidy—vacuumed, dusted, and general clutter removed. Do not spend more than five minutes cleaning up. If it is messy, straighten up beforehand. This is your time for loving not housework.

- Soften hard surfaces with beautiful fabric. If there is a TV in the room, hide it under sensual cloth. Better yet, if the TV is in your bedroom take it out, permanently. TV is one of the biggest distractions from each other.

- Bring in plants or flowers and other beautiful objects that have special meaning for you: pictures, sculptures, and craft pieces. Arrange them artfully around your space.

- Include plenty of pillows for supporting your bodies in delightful sexual positions.

- Ensure that the room is warm enough for comfortable nakedness.

- Pay special attention to the lighting. Drape colored cloth over lamps or use candles, red lightbulbs, dimmer switches and if you have it, firelight. Watching flames of a fire can bring on alpha and theta brain states. Alpha brain waves are associated with relaxation, visualization, and creativity. Theta brain waves evoke deep trance states, sexual ecstasy, shamanic visions, out of body experiences, and other profoundly altered states of consciousness.

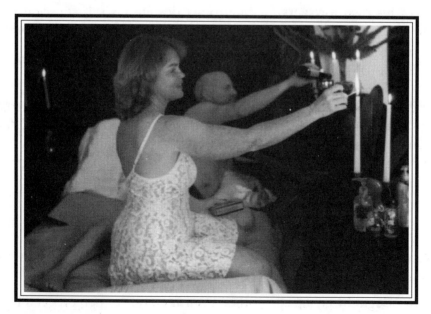

Sacred Space

- ❧ Aromatize your temple with incense, essential oils, scented candles or fresh flowers. Use scents that you both like.

- ❧ Set out an assortment of music to accompany your moods of love.

- ❧ Arrange close to hand any oils, lubricants, and sex toys you may want to use.

- ❧ Bring in drinks and light snacks.

- ❧ When you have finished, take a few moments to admire the transformation you have wrought.

Arranging your temple should take 20 minutes or less—you have thought about and gathered most items earlier. Move deliberately, and gracefully, with your intention always in mind—to create a beautiful space for sacred loving. Each time you set up a loving temple, make it somewhat different. You want it to be freshly appealing, not a familiar habitat that you no longer really see.

Each time we create a sacred space, Al revels in a sensual experience of pleasure through sight, smell, touch, and sound. As the room is beautifully transformed, it is as if he were in a completely different place. He senses a newness that is erotic, arousing, and mysterious.

For Pala, creating a temple of love helps her move out of any habitual lovemaking mode. She becomes consciously aware of acting differently. It stimulates and humbles her to set up a temple for honoring her higher self, her beloved, and the Creator.

Psychic Protection

When you have finished arranging your temple to your satisfaction, you can further sanctify it through an assortment of rituals. In Tantric lovemaking, you desire to go beyond your limits, to break down any walls that may separate you emotionally or energetically from your lover and from the Divine. Trust and vulnerability are essential. Psychic protection rituals reach past your rational mind to your inner core evoking safety so that you can truly let go into love.

Pala finds that purifying rituals instill a deep sense of relaxation and security throughout her entire being. Because she feels confident and protected, she is able to unreservedly open to Al in all ways.

Al's use of psychic protection rituals is based on the premise that negative energies or entities cannot come into you or your space without your permission and that they have to leave when you tell them to if they are already there. Positive energies and beings will respond to your invitation to enter.

✢ You may burn sweet grass, cedar, or incense, passing it over and around the space, and say words like, "I purify and sanctify this space. I make it holy and safe through my love and my intention."

✢ You may walk three times counterclockwise round the perimeter of your temple, saying as you walk slowly and reverently, "I send out from this space all negative energies—fear, doubt, anger, complacency…" Include anything you do not want in your space or yourself. Then reverse your path and walk three times clockwise around the perimeter, saying as you walk, "I welcome into our special place all positive energies—joy, wisdom, passion, love, wonder…" Include everything you want to be present. Counterclockwise direction disperses energy and clockwise builds it. Speaking aloud—naming—gives more weight to your words than shyly, silently thinking them.

✢ You may ring a bell, bang a drum, or strike a gong as you walk. One of our favorite instruments is an exquisite Tibetan singing bowl of hammered brass.

✢ You may envision a golden ball of light surrounding your space, a permeable force field that allows in all that is good and repels any evil.

✢ You may put on a special robe or other costume for your ritual. Let your imagination guide you.

✢ You may light candles in each of the four corners of the room, calling upon the power of the four Directions: East, South, West, and North. Different sources equate different qualities to the four Directions, these are the meanings we use[1]:

  ✢ "East is Air—the majesty of mind, the purity of thought. As I light this candle in the East, I unlock my mind to conscious knowing."

  ✢ "South is Fire—the power of spirit and energy. As I light this candle in the South, I open myself to creative energy flow."

  ✢ "West is Water—the power of emotion and feeling. As I light this candle in the West, I allow myself to feel all, to reveal all."

  ✢ "North is Earth—the wonder of the body. As I light this candle in the North, I invite the mystery of the world."

Endeavor to relax and enjoy yourself. These are joyous, celebratory, and holy rites. A magical transformation will take place, brought about by your intention, your sacred focus on creating a space of beauty, safety, and honor in which to celebrate your love of yourself, each other, and God.

The Lovers' Purifying Bath

Enjoy a luxurious bath or shower together as an introductory segment of your loving time. Symbolically, bathing together cleanses and purifies you, washing away the accumulated emotional and psychic grime of the world. You are reborn in the healing waters. Physically, a good soak relaxes your body and makes it fresh and clean so you look and feel your best for your lover. Bathe together, playfully and tenderly washing each other's bodies. Lovingly rub each other dry with fluffy towels. Reverently anoint each other with oils and perfumes and creams.

Lovers' Bath

Honoring Your God and Goddess

Sacred sexuality seeks to bring out the best in lovers. You perceive yourself and your lover as manifestations of the Divine and seek ways to make this so. In traditional Tantric practice, lovers see themselves as the god Shiva and the goddess Shakti. Therefore, throughout your Tantra loving session you treat each other with respect and adoration. These love sessions are not times to be critical of each other or to discuss worldly affairs such as finance, children, or employment. Only words of endearment and elevation are spoken—how much you love each other, how happy you are to be together, how blessed your union is, what delights you about your lover, how your passionate sex awakens your spirit.

Harmonizing Ritual

Before you begin your lovemaking, gaze into each other's eyes for two minutes, without speaking. Harmonize your breathing as you do so. Ask your partner's permission to embark on an erotic, spiritual journey with you. Speak from your heart as you tell each other what you want to do during your time together. Be sexy and spiritual. As you address your lover, look for and encourage the Divine to come out to play.

Examples:

    ❧ "My magnificent Goddess, I am aching to make love to you. My heart is so full when I look at your beauty. I want to make you moan with pleasure as I caress all your sweet and juicy spots. I want to join with you in every way. May I show you my love?"

ᘓ "My dashing Hero, I want to show you how much I love you. I want to tease you and please you and let you know just how wonderful a man you are to me. I want to nibble you, suck you, and rub myself all over you. I want my heart and my soul to open to you. May I please love you up?"

Mantras

Mantras, resonant sound syllables that focus your mind and protect it from unwanted thought, are used throughout Tantric lovemaking rituals. They may be chanted or whispered, alone or in unison, or repeated internally in silence. Besides assisting with mental focus, the resonant sounds of mantras vibrate your body's energy centers helping to open them and free up energy flow.

OM, AH, HUM is one of the most frequently used mantras. According to Tantric scholar Nik Douglas, the meaning of this mantra is: OM—purity of spirit, AH—Divine Love, HUM—Eternal Union.[2]

Experiment with incorporating these sounds at various times during your lovemaking:

ᘓ Chanting together at the outset of your loving time to aid in letting go of the world and connecting with each other.

ᘓ At the height of sexual excitement to reinforce your intention of uniting sex and spirit.

ᘓ Whenever you find your mind begins to wander.

In addition to traditional mantras, Pala also mentally repeats inspirational phrases during lovemaking. "Our love is the gateway," her favorite, always opens her heart and reminds her of her intention. Create your own intention phrase and repeat it as you would a mantra.

A Lovers' Ritual

There are likely as many versions of Tantric rituals as there are Tantric lovers. This particular ritual, one we find very powerful, is an adaptation of an ancient Tantric "Secret Rite" described in Nik Douglas and Penny Slinger's extraordinary book *Sexual Secrets*. It recognizes and balances the different arousal rates of women and men, first focusing on the woman, bringing her to sexual life, then moving on to honor the man. The distinct stages in the ritual include: purifying; relaxing and energizing; harmonizing; focusing; honoring the feminine; honoring the masculine. Throughout the ritual, endeavor to remain aware of your intention to elevate your sexuality to extraordinary heights of spiritual bliss.

Purifying

    ᘯ Bathe or shower together.

Relaxing and Energizing

    ᘯ Give each other a brief (five minutes) massage.

    ᘯ Dance together or do stretches.

Partner Yoga

Harmonizing

- Sit side by side with the woman on the man's right.

- Breathe slowly and deeply in unison for several minutes.

- Chant a mantra or sing an uplifting song.

Focusing

- Concentrate on the intention of your ritual: to connect in love and passion and open to the Divine—become Divine.

- To assist your energy to flow, picture a golden ball of heat and light beginning to pulse at your genitals.

- As you progress through the ritual, the ball elongates and undulates in golden waves up your spine—this is the kundalini power awakening.

Honoring the Feminine

- The man sits in front of the woman, looking lovingly at her and thinking of all the things he adores about her.

- He massages her feet with scented oil paying particular attention to and spending most time on her big toes. There are acupressure points on either side of the big toe, which will calm her spirit and clear her mind. As he massages, he may hum a mantra and visualize his lover as a goddess arousing under his loving touch.

- The woman, too, pictures herself as a goddess and begins to awaken and move her sexual energy by squeezing her PC muscles and gently swaying back and forth.

- To further stimulate her passion, as his lover is rocking, the man slowly and gently moves his hands up her body in this order, which corresponds to her natural rhythm of desire: right toe, right foot, right knee, right thigh, yoni, right buttock, belly button, center of chest, right breast, right side, right side of neck, right cheek, bottom lip, right eye, top of her head, left eye, top lip, left cheek, left side of throat, left side, left breast, center of chest, belly button, left buttock, yoni, left thigh, left knee, left foot, left toe. At each point he pauses and sends loving energy through his hands.

- Moving his gaze from his lover, the man meditates for a moment on the flame of a candle. Then returning to his beloved, he applies scented oil to her chakra points, visualizing his touch fanning the flames of her sexual fire.

- He continues to honor his goddess by decorating her with flowers or body make-up or jewelry or sensual cloth. He may anoint other parts of her beautiful body with perfumes or oils—her hands, breasts, inner elbows, and hair. He touches her with sensuality and reverence, not in a sexually demanding or aggressive way. Even though he may be becoming very aroused, he remains calm, relaxed, and focused.

- When the man has completed his devotional arousal of the goddess, the woman then moves to his left.

Honoring the Masculine

- The woman is now the active partner, honoring her beloved.

- Circling their bodies with incense, moving in a clockwise direction, she builds a protective shield of love. She may dance seductively for her lover as she passes the incense around them.

- She further arouses her lover with her hands and mouth, moving lovingly over his body.

- Picturing her lover as a Divine god, she pays homage to his lingam, his wand of light, massaging it erotically with scented oil.

Now the lovers begin their joyous and passionate lovemaking, merging god and goddess in ecstasy.

Renewing Your Vows

One of the most meaningful rituals we perform is our renewal of vows. Every year, usually in the autumn, we go to a very special place nearby and recommit to each other. "Our spot" is a sparsely treed and seldom frequented ridge overlooking a broad expanse of rolling hills and shining water. Hawks are our only companions, wheeling high above. It seems to us they come to bless our union.

In our backpacks we bring lunch—not standard picnic fare of sandwiches and sweets, but delectable foodstuffs, such as strips of tender

Renewing Vows

grilled chicken with a sweet, spicy mango sauce; cucumber rounds marinated in basil vinegar; pasta salad with sun-dried tomatoes, black olives and crab; crusty French stick with dilled cream cheese; fresh peaches, sliced and sprinkled with Cointreau; a slab of dark bittersweet chocolate. Wine and water and hot espresso quench our thirst.

After our picnic, we begin our ceremony of connection. Each time it is different, reflecting what is currently in our hearts and minds. Some things remain constant—we dress up in costumes of various sorts; we each prepare a significant part of the ritual in which we both participate; we make our vows of commitment; and then seal them with sacred loving under the majesty of the sky and the watchful eyes of the hawks.

For our ceremonies, we bring distinctive objects from home—a golden goblet, a decorative candle, a silver dagger, tinkling chimes, iridescent crystals—and combine them with particularly striking things we find at the site—an odd shaped rock, a dusky hued feather, a perfect leaf. We may wear masks, light robes, body paint, or unusual jewelry. Most things we bring are light and easily portable—it is a long hike up that cliffside.

211

Our vows are written at home with thought and care, revealing our love in this moment and our hope for the future. They take different forms: prose, poetry, or song. They may be short or long as our mood dictates. In closing, we make passionate love and ask God and Mother Earth and all the elements to sanctify our joining.

Reconnecting this way year after year strengthens our bond. It requires us to look at where we are *now* in our lives and consider where we want to be in the future. Most of all it reminds us how blessed we are to have found each other. We encourage you to do the same.

Chapter 11

Erotic, Relaxing, Healing Touch

"Touch-A, Touch-A, Touch-A, Touch Me."
—Music and lyrics by Richard O'Brien,
from *Rocky Horror Picture Show*

"And when I touch you
I feel happy inside
It's such a feeling that my love
I can't hide"

—*"I Want To Hold Your Hand,"*
music and lyrics by John Lennon
and Paul McCartney

Close your eyes and feel:

Sensitive, knowing hands firmly kneading the ache from your shoulders.

Soft, moist lips gently nuzzling the excitable nape of your neck.

Strong, loving arms enfolding your grief-shaken body.

Tantalizing fingertips tracing fire up your eager inner thighs.

Touch, glorious touch, one of the greatest bodily pleasures, is an extraordinary resource for conveying love, relieving stress, and nurturing health. The North American medical community is gradually recognizing what millions of people worldwide already know—touch can heal. Touch Research Institutes lists more than 70 scientific studies that show massage therapy has helped more than 30 types of ailments from asthma to diabetes, high blood pressure to multiple sclerosis, depression to migraine headaches.[1] Responding to the positive effects of the 60 million visits Americans make to body workers every year, major insurance companies are slowly adding massage to their coverage.[2]

When you are touching and being touched your body secretes endorphins and oxytocin. These powerful chemicals make you feel good and at the same time build the desire for more of that marvelous holding and stroking. You can literally take your lover's well being into your own hands simply by touching more. Through your touch you can offer comfort, relaxation, arousal, and healing—separately or in imaginative combinations.

One of the most stress-relieving gifts you can give your mate is the solace of touch for comfort's sake. When Al falls into his insecurities, bombarding himself with self-criticism and self-doubt, Pala's reassuring words cannot break through those barriers. His doubts are not rational thought that can be set right with ideas, no matter how heartfelt and real her ideas may be. But her "comfort touching," not sexual, but quiet holding, pressing him to her bosom, stroking his hair, rubbing his back and legs, massaging his shoulders, makes it through every time. It lets him know he is safe and okay—*he* is all right.

For a man who is really stressed and tired a loving massage is better than sex. Firm, deep pressure in the large muscle groups—neck, shoulders, back, and thighs—relaxes him, allowing him to slow down, slough off the weight of the world, and rest. Giving your man a relaxing deep massage can let him know that you are not always expecting him to perform sexually. Your loving ministrations might lead to arousal but you are not expecting or demanding it. On your Tantric journey it is essential to learn to touch each other without assuming it will lead to sex. Your touch is not a means to an end but a mutual pleasure freely given. When there is no pressure your partner can open and relax and arousal might or might not occur.

In the early days of our Tantric learning, as Pala's sexual appetite was burgeoning and Al was still learning how to delay ejaculation so he could maintain high sexual stamina, Pala would sometimes be eager for sex when Al was worn out. She learned that one way to satisfy her hunger was to thoroughly work Al's body lovingly and sensually but without expectation that her massaging would turn him on. Often, he revived under her unconditional stroking and then, because he was relaxed and energetically open, his interest and stamina intensified. Crucial to his awakening was the fact that her touch was not conveying a demand to do so. The quality of your touch reveals your intention, so, in this, as in all Tantric connection, you are remembering your intention is to unite with your lover and bring pleasure to you both. You are not caressing him to get something else.

214

This is true for women as well as men. Affectionate touching without obligation reaches a woman's heart. It makes her feel adored and, more importantly, respected. Sadly, many men have not been on the receiving end of much physical affection as they were growing up and really do not know how to touch a woman. Women can help themselves and their partners if they let go of the expectation that he does. Assume you must teach your man how to touch you and assume, *without judgment*, that because he's not had much previous instruction, the lesson may take awhile. Let him know playfully what you want him to do, with encouragement and love, not a chastisement that makes him feel what he is doing now is wrong. When he does touch you in ways and places you like, give lots of happy feedback, with sounds or body movement or words of appreciation.

Al's advice to women is, "If you are not getting what you want you are probably not asking for it. Most men would give their woman anything if they just know what she wants. They would love to be heroes and satisfy her through and through." As a basic starting point, the song "Slow Hand"—"I want a man with an easy touch"—is excellent guidance for any man. The slow tender approach works, whether it is during massage, explicit sex, or an everyday hug.

Most women have body image issues so combining appreciative sounds or words with your touch helps her get out of her thoughts and into her sensations. Tell her you love to touch her and be specific in what you admire about her body. Comment only on what you like—the softness of her skin, the curve of her hip, the shape of her nipples. Never, never be critical—especially about her weight.

Men usually enjoy it when women take the lead and initiate touching. An exception to this general rule is touching in public. Some young men may use public touching as a sign of their power, but because of long-term conditioned behavior, for many men public displays of affection, particularly around other men, can be acutely embarrassing. It can mark a man as soft or a sissy. Do not take it personally and do not challenge your man about it, but instead share with him your own desire for affection. Help him understand that his loving attention to you makes you feel wanted and respected. Begin to slowly acclimate him with small doses of affectionate touching in places and situations where he feels safe.

When a man rejects his woman's touch, especially if it is a sexual overture in private, it can seem to her that she herself is being rejected and judged. Men, over years of making passes through the teens and beyond, some of which were accepted but many of which were turned down, are accustomed to "no." They may not like it, but it is familiar. For a woman, being refused when she has taken the bold step of being overtly sexual can be devastating. Feelings of shame and guilt may arise, so it is important to let her know it is not her or her behavior that is unwelcome. It is about you right now, not her, and even though you may not be feeling particularly sexual, you would welcome her affection. Do not berate yourself either—let go of the idea that you should be a "sex machine" and allow yourself to simply enjoy the comfort of touch.

Right now start adding more touch into your life together with simple things like cuddling while you watch TV, holding hands when you go for a walk, embracing in a full body hug—toe to toe, groin to groin, heart to heart—when you depart in the morning or return at night. Also, explore some special touching with the techniques below, either as part of your weekly Tantra date or at another time, just because you love each other and want to feel fabulous.

With all of the marvelous practices discussed here, **the most important point for the "toucher" to remember is to focus on what you are doing.** The beneficial effects of your touch are magnified when you put yourself completely into sending love, or healing or arousal, as the case may be. Your lover deserves your full attention and you will get more out of it too.

Massage

Massages are easy to do as well as fun to give and receive. You do not have to have any training to give your mate a thoroughly satisfying massage, although if you would prefer more guidance, there are some excellent books, videos, and courses available. You will find some in our References and Resources section.

Giving each other a massage as a first course of sexual play adds to your entire experience. Both partners are able to relax, leave the world behind, and be in the moment together. With massage, a woman's body begins to awaken for arousal—her erotic side receives the time and attention she needs to "get in the mood." A man whose body is relaxed so that his energy can flow more freely is able to last much longer.

You can perform massages just about anywhere—bed, floor, couch— but most comfortable for the masseur is a table at about hip height. It is not likely you have a portable massage table at home, but you do have a kitchen or dining table. With firm cushions, a foam mat, or even an air mattress on top covered by a sheet, they make great massage surfaces. If the kitchen or dining rooms do not afford you as much privacy as you would like, move the table into your bedroom.

Give a dry massage without oil, or a wet one with oil. The market is flooded with wondrous potions, lotions, lubricants, and oils—scented, unscented, edible, warming, cooling—take your pick. You can also make your own with a light vegetable oil, such as safflower, sunflower, jojoba, or canola-grapeseed, and add your own essential oils to create a scent you prefer.

This is Al's refreshing, and lightly spicy recipe, for the massage oil we supply in our lover's kits at our Tantra weekends:

4 oz.   canola oil (or substitute as above)
4 drops   YlangYlang essential oil
1–2 drops Black Pepper essential oil
          (1 in summer, 2 in winter)
1–2 drops Clary Sage essential oil (1 in winter, 2 in summer)

Whichever products you choose for general body massage, it is best to use water-based lubricants for massaging a woman's genitals. Other lubricants may clog her pores and encourage vaginal infection.

Massage Strokes

If you are unsure how to begin to give a massage, there are a few simple strokes you can learn to master easily:

* Long, smooth, firm strokes following the line of muscle up and down his body.

* Circular motions, especially at joints.

* Kneading—slowly and firmly squeezing muscle between fingers and palms of your hands, then letting go and repeating—particularly in large muscle groups like shoulders, back, buttocks, and thighs.

* Feathering—very light fingertip strokes—primarily for erotic massage, the arousal of skin-to-skin contact.

* Rocking—with one hand on either side of your partner's body, or a particular part of it, her buttocks for example, gently rock back and forth.

You cannot go wrong by starting out with slow, gentle pressure in your strokes. Ask your partner to tell you if she would like more intensity as you go. The more massages you give each other, the easier it will be to know what is needed through the messages your hands give you. Nevertheless, whenever you are receiving a massage, communicate your desires and sensations with loving requests and appreciative sounds— give your masseur informative and thankful feedback.

Starting Your Massage

An excellent starting point for a relaxing and invigorating massage is the back.

❧ Begin at the base of his spine with your palms on his sacrum (just above his tailbone).

❧ Inhale.

❧ As you exhale slide your hands up his back on either side of his spine.

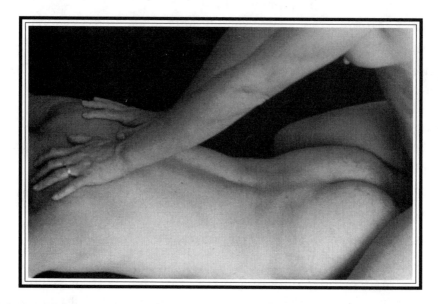

Relaxing Massage

❧ With a firm touch, follow the line of his shoulders out from his neck.

❧ Slide your hands down the outer sides of his back, coming to rest again at the base of his spine.

❧ Do it again and again and revel in his sighs of pleasure.

❧ Move on to his buttocks or shoulders or neck or arms— wherever your hands feel compelled to go.

❧ If you are giving your lover a full-body massage, make sure to cover every part of his body—ears, toes, eyes (very softly), fingers—not just the major sections like legs and back. His whole body has skin hunger.

Massage Variations

7-Minute Massage

It is a delicious treat to receive a full-body massage that lasts any-where from 30 minutes to a couple of hours, but you can also give your lover a boost with a massage "quickie." You can effectively energize and loosen him up from top to toe in five to seven minutes. Try this in various situations:

❧ Near the beginning of your Tantra loving time.

❧ As a refreshing pause from strenuous sexual activity.

❧ To start or end your day.

Up and Down

Working a massage from the top to the bottom—starting at her head and shoulders and finishing at her feet, with most of your strokes in a downward motion—is generally relaxing, draining tension away and down. Working in the opposite direction—starting at her feet and fin-ishing at her head with most of your strokes going up her body—can be extraordinarily enlivening as energy builds and moves upward.

Erotic Massage

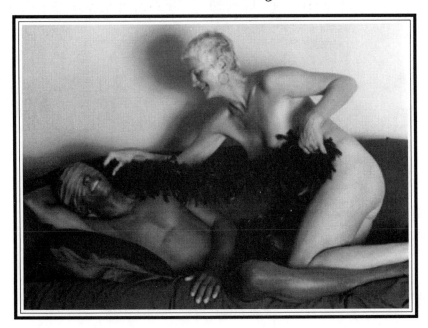

Erotic Massage

Primarily for arousal, erotic massage focuses, although not exclusively, on tantalizing skin-to-skin contact that becomes increasingly sexual as the massage continues. Using light, feathery touches, begin moving inwards from the extremities of your lover's body, for example from her toes, up her feet, to calves and thighs, stopping just short of her genitals, or her fingers to palms to inner elbows to armpits and almost to her nipples. Only slowly, as her body awakens under your teasing touch do you move on to actually caress her hot sexual spots.

With erotic massage you may use not only your hands but also your tongue, lips, hair, or other exotic aids such as feathers and even ice cubes. Add more spice with a blindfold or by loosely binding your lover's wrists and ankles to the bed corners so she is at your tender mercy.

Perineum Massage

The perineum, that small patch of skin between a man's anus and scrotum or between a woman's anus and vagina, is a powerful point of pleasure that is often overlooked. Lightly tapping, pressing, or massaging it during lovemaking can be highly arousing.

For a man who is learning ejaculation mastery, massaging the perineum regularly is essential to help him move accumulated sexual energy away from the genitals where it can cause discomfort. Begin by pressing on the perineum, back towards the anus where you will feel a small indentation—this is the "P-spot," for prostate gland. The prostate feels like a firm lump about the size of a large grape or a small walnut. Gently push

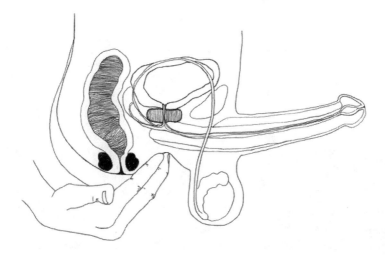

Perineum Massage

and probe the entire area with your fingertips. Especially delightful is massaging the perineum in circular motions, first clockwise and then counterclockwise, with a piece of folded silk (two layers). Either you or your lover should do a prostate massage after every lovemaking session. Or you can add it as part of your continual loving touch during sacred sex. You can also massage the prostate directly through the anus.

Anal Massage

The anus is a common holding spot for tension—just think of the term "tight ass" and the personality that comes to mind: rigid, irritable, tense, picky. The anus, although culturally taboo because it is considered "dirty" or associated with homosexuality, is a nerve-filled, highly erotic part of your body. Massaging first the buttocks and then the tender tissues around your "rosebud" gives amazing release.

Internal prostate massage—through the anus—not only keeps the prostate healthy, but is also one of the best ways for a man to learn surrender. At the very thought of penetration most men tighten right up, memories of uncomfortable visits to the doctor foremost in their minds. Yet if a man can relax enough, and if his partner is sensitive and gentle, he may find it exquisitely pleasurable.

- To begin, the man lies on his stomach. You might place a towel-covered pillow under his hips for a better angle of penetration.

- Help him to relax by first gently rocking his body back and forth and then massaging his shoulders, back, and buttocks.

- Wearing latex gloves and using copious quantities of lubricant, massage the tissues around the anus with circular motions and gentle stretching.

- Remind your lover to breathe slowly and deeply.

- Spend as much time here as needed until the anal muscles begin to relax.

- When you feel he is ready, very, very slowly insert your index finger. Your palm is facing down toward the pillow.

- Not far inside the rectum, about an inch or two, you will feel a lump below your finger about the size of a small walnut or a large grape. This is the prostate gland. Gently massage it—circling and pressing.

- With your other hand massage his buttocks, stroke his back or thighs, or press the heel of your hand on his sacrum.

- When you have completed the internal massage, remove your finger ever so slowly.

- Always wash your hands thoroughly after anal play.

Yoni Massage

The Yoni Massage, or female genital massage, brings healing and emotional opening. Your intention is not arousal, or orgasm, although these may well occur, but rather to help your lover become more sensitive, relaxed, and connected to her yoni—her sacred temple. Much frustration, pain, and trauma are held in the tissues of the vagina; loving massage can help discharge them. This process may bring up strong emotions—feelings of fear or anxiety and joyous outpourings of release. It may take several sessions before her yoni has healed so that she can fully enjoy the range of sexual pleasures it holds.

- Your lover lies on her back, a towel-covered pillow under her hips.

- Her legs are apart, knees slightly bent.

- Sit between her legs.

- Look into each other's eyes and breathe slowly and deeply together.

- Gently massage her legs, belly, and torso, advancing without haste to her inner thighs and pelvis.

- When she is relaxed, move to her yoni, and, asking permission to honor this most sacred spot, pour a good quality, water-based lubricant on her mound and begin to massage it slowly. "Slowly" is a key point for this entire massage.

- Gently squeezing each outer lip between thumb and forefinger, stroke up and down.

- Ask her to tell you if she wants more pressure or speed or softness.

- Repeat the stroking, squeezing motion on her inner lips.

- Move to her clitoris, circling, squeezing, and gently pulling.

- When you feel she is ready, ask permission to enter her enchanted garden and gently insert your finger—some women prefer two fingers.

- Crook your finger in a "come hither" motion and press it against the walls just inside the entrance of her vaginal canal.

- Explore all around this wonderful opening, fraction of an inch by fraction of an inch.

- If you encounter spots that are painful or tight, stop movement but continue to press your finger there.

- Breathe together. You may notice tingling or heat as the tension releases.

- Move in a little deeper and again press all around.

- This is the area of the G-spot, which can be extremely sensitive—its spongy tissue is a storehouse of sexual frustration and pain—so move respectfully.

- Some women feel a burning or a desire to urinate when the G-spot is awakening; continue to apply pressure and allow the sensation to pass.

- Move deeper still, straightening your finger and pressing along the sides as you go farther back toward the cervix.

- Wherever she feels trauma or pain, stop movement, press the spot firmly, breathe deeply, until there is a release.

- If your lover would like you to, as you continue your internal massage, begin to stimulate her clitoris with your other hand awakening her to a state of high arousal.

- She may experience orgasm—clitorally or vaginally or in combination.

- When she feels she has had enough, slowly take your hands away.

- Complete your massage by gently holding her in your loving arms.

Lingam Massage

Men, too, need gentle healing of their genitals—a purging of emotional and energetic blockages. When a man holds frustration and hurts in his genital region, the muscles can be tight, affecting his capacity for erection and his ability to master ejaculation. The lingam massage relaxes these tense muscles and helps a man open to his receptive side so he may experience deeper levels of pleasure. If the massage brings up strong emotions for your lover, encourage him to allow them out.

- Your lover lies on his back, a towel-covered pillow under his hips.

- His legs are apart, knees slightly bent.

- Sit between his legs.

- Look into each other's eyes and breathe slowly and deeply together.

- Gently massage his legs, belly and torso, advancing without haste to his inner thighs and pelvis.

- Ask permission to honor his "wand of light," and with a quality lubricant deeply massage the muscles at the top of his inner thighs, in the crease where his legs and pelvic floor meet. Work along the connecting bone and muscles, releasing tension as you go. "Slowly" is a key point for this entire massage.

- Ask him to tell you when he wants more or less pressure or a change of stroke or to touch a different spot.

- Massage above his lingam on the pubic bone.

- Move down to the scrotum, gently kneading and pulling his testicles.

- Pay special attention to the perineum, circling and pushing the tissues there.

- Bring your loving touch to his lingam, stroking the shaft with varying pressure and speed. With alternating hands slide up from the base of the shaft to the head and then off. Repeat this movement and then reverse direction—slide from the top down.

- Hold his lingam by its head and gently shake it back and forth.

- Thoroughly massage the head of his lingam.

- He may or may not get an erection. If he does, it may come and go throughout your massage.

- If he feels he is coming close to ejaculation, slow down or stop your massaging, or move to a different spot, for instance the perineum. Breathe deeply together.

- Move from perineum to testicles to lingam and back again, paying attention to different areas as he rises to a peak and then backs off. The lingam massage is a great aid to learning ejaculation mastery.

- Perhaps he would like to ejaculate at the end of the massage or he may want to retain his sexual energy. Whatever his preference, when he feels he has had enough, remove your hands slowly and reverently.

- He may want you to hold him in your arms to complete your session.

Acupressure

There are more than 350 points along your body's energy pathways where tension can gather, causing blockages and discomfort. Pressing firmly on those spots relaxes the tissues, increases blood circulation, and allows energy to flow more smoothly. Some spots are also highly erotic. On the following pages, we describe a few of our favorite points for relaxation and arousal. Some of them are among the spots that noted acupressurist Dr. Michael Reed Gach refers to as "the top six sets of acupressure points for lovers."[3] For more in-depth study, we highly recommend his excellent books and videos.

Acupressure spots are generally located in indentations of bones or along ropes of muscles. The more you practice, the easier it will be for your fingers to find the right points. Continual communication with your partner helps, for example, "Move a little to the left, please," or "Try a quarter-inch farther down." To touch the points, you use the pads of your fingers and press straight down, leaning in with the weight of your body. You might also try a slight circular motion or rhythmic pulsing.

Each person likes different strengths of pressure at different times on different parts of the body. Because you press very softly at first and only gradually increase the pressure, you do not have to worry about pressing too hard. Besides, your partner will let you know if she wants more or less pressure. If your partner wants a lot of pressure, you can use your thumbs, knuckles, or the heel of your hand instead of fingers. We have even had therapists at our workshops who use elbows and feet.

As you apply pressure to your lover, breathe slowly and deeply in unison. Hold each acupoint for a minimum of one minute—two or three is better—to allow the tissues to properly relax. You may feel a pulsing sensation that increases as the congestion leaves the area.

The acupoints are identified by a series of letters and numbers corresponding to their position on the energy meridians. In the Chinese system of acupressure, the points have been given poetic names, which we much prefer, and offer here.

Shoulders

Everyone seems to gather tension in their shoulders. Pressing on this acupoint, "Shoulder Well," melts that tension away. You can find Shoulder Well at the height of the shoulder muscle, on each side, approximately an inch out from your lover's neck.

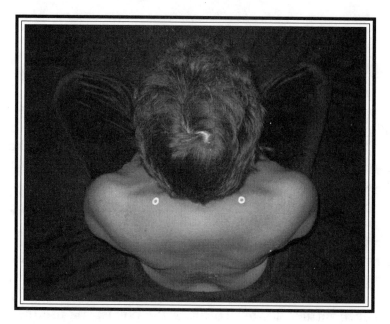

Acupressure: Shoulder Well

Base of the Skull

"Wind Mansion" is located at the base of the skull in the hollow where the head and neck meet. It is a great spot for calming your thoughts and awakening your spirit. When touching this point, angle your pressure slightly upward toward the top of the head.

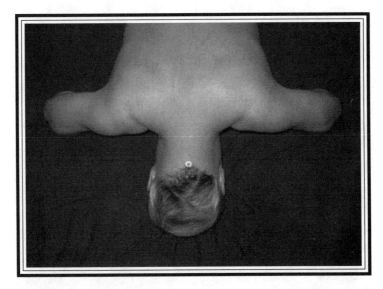

Acupressure: Wind Mansion

Lower Back

The "Sea of Vitality" is Al's absolutely favorite acupoint. He can be frazzled and tired out, but with a few minutes of pressure on these spots, he is raring to go. To find the Sea of Vitality, trace your finger on a line around from your lover's belly button to his back. There are two spots on either side of the backbone—the first about an inch and a half out, the second about three inches. Use your thumb and index finger to press there, or the heel of your hand.

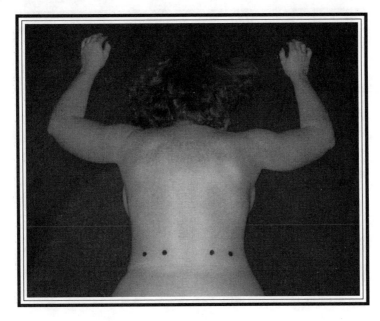

Acupressure: Sea of Vitality

Base of the Spine

Your "Sacrum" has a series of indentations in the bone. Your lover can press these with fingertips or, as many prefer, with the palm and heel of his hand cupping you as if you were sitting on his hand. Pushing here touches the sacral nerve sending pleasing sensations to your genitals.

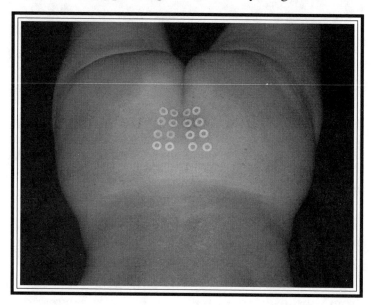

Acupressure: Sacrum

Belly

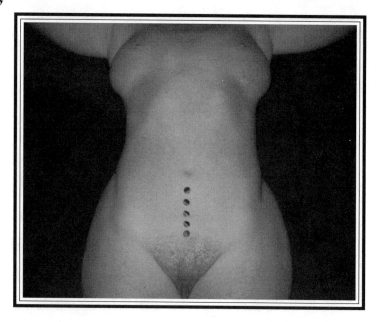

Acupressure: Sea of Intimacy

The "Sea of Intimacy" corresponds to your belly chakra. It is a series of spots relating to your reproductive system and your feelings about sexuality. The acupoints run from about an inch and a half below the navel to just above the pubic bone. One of Pala's most loved acupressure spots, it is highly erotic, and works wonders for menstrual cramps, too.

Groin Creases

In the center of the crease where your legs join your body and on either side of the artery that runs down into your legs are "Rushing Door" and "Mansion Cottage." These acupoints increase sensitivity and circulation in your genitals and your legs.

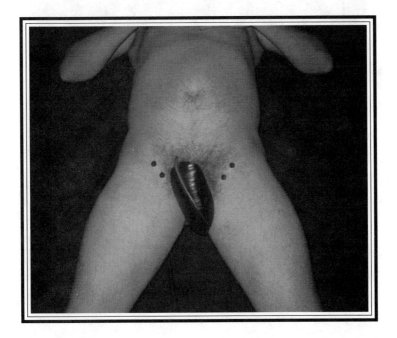

Acupressure: Rushing Door and Mansion Cottage

Heart Center

The aptly named "Sea of Tranquility" is in the center of your chest on a line between your nipples. Relating to the heart chakra, it brings calm and peace with gentle pressure. Try looking deep into each other's eyes as you lightly touch this sensitive spot with the palm of your hand.

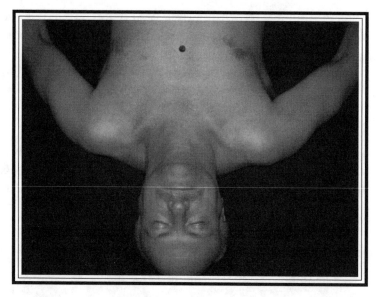

Acupressure: Sea of Tranquility

Reiki

Reiki is the ancient Japanese art of healing through touch. Its basic premise is that the person giving the Reiki treatment acts as a channel for cosmic energy, "rei," to pass through her body and out her hands into the person she is working with. This cosmic energy unites with the other's "ki" energy, or life force, and promotes healing. Trained Reiki masters are adept at deep healing of emotional and energetic, as well as physical, traumas. You can practice a simple version with your lover.

- ⚜ Place your hands on a part of your sweetheart's body that is tired, achy, or injured.

- ⚜ Breathe slowly and deeply in unison.

- ⚜ Ask for the loving energy of the cosmos to enter and pass through you to heal your lover.

- ⚜ Ask to be protected from any negative effects of the energies that may be released in your partner during the healing process. Be sure to be grounding the whole time (see Chapter 7, page 127).

- ⚜ Visualize healing energy entering the top of your head, passing through your body, and out through your hands into your lover's body.

❧ Focus on sending your love along with the energy.

❧ You may feel heat as the energy builds and releases.

❧ Hold your hands on the spot for three to five minutes.

❧ When you feel it is time to let go, remove your hands very slowly and reverently.

❧ Shake them to disperse any accumulated energy or, if they are very hot, rinse them in a pan of cool, heavily salted water.

Mix and Match

You can experiment with each of the techniques separately, as a unique exploration of loving touch. Press your lover's Sea of Vitality or Sacrum as you hug him goodbye in the morning. With your hands on her brow, send healing love into her tired brain after a hard day at the office. Awaken her to the delights of her sexual power with a slow, sensitive yoni massage.

You can also combine these practices, as we do, in a marvelous mélange of comfort, arousal, and healing. Begin lovemaking sessions with a mix of massage, acupressure, and Reiki—lingering over especially sensitive spots, tantalizing some, and soothing others. Revive each other with a brisk five-minute massage during erotic loving and follow it with special attention to favorite acupoints. Tenderly press your lover's heart center while you are joined together in ecstatic genital connection.

Whatever your personal preference of mix and match, you will improve your health and your relationship by touching and touching and touching even more.

"Dancin' in the dark, middle of the night
Takin' your heart and holdin' it tight
Emotional touch, touchin' my skin
And asking you to do what you've been doin'
all over again"

—"It's Your Love,"
music and lyrics by Stephony Smith

Chapter 12

Sexual Play

"A kiss is a lovely trick designed by nature to
stop speech when words become superfluous."
—Ingrid Bergman

Tantric loving is serious business. After all it brings you face to face
with profound issues such as: "How do I welcome God?" and, "Am I
living my life to my full potential?" Because it deals with weighty matters, you might assume that Tantra is solemn, even grave. You may also
suspect that even though Tantra includes sex, because it is "spiritual"
sex, it is likely sedate—a polite sexuality with much earnest eye-gazing
and not lots of juicy bits. Well, you would be partly right. There is much
about Tantric loving that is thoughtful and decorous, but the Tantric
scope encompasses *all*,
uniting seemingly dis-
parate polarities into an
integrated whole, so
reverence and raucous-
ness, piety and playful-
ness are equal partners
in your lover's bed. You
engage in all sorts of
wild and wonderful acts
to build your sexual
charge then focus your
thought to elevate that
charge, thus connecting

Sexual Play

your animal body with your ethereal spirit. In this expansive view, you
push your limits, allowing and encouraging each other to be imaginative, vulnerable, and bold.

Perhaps you feel you aren't innately daring or sexually adventurous—well, the best suggestion we have ever gotten for this self-sabotaging argument is: Make it up! You might not think you are particularly wild but, ask yourself, *if* you were, what would you do? Then do it. You may surprise yourself, and your lover, with your ingenuity. Use the suggestions in this chapter to kick-start your creative process. An effective approach is to each assume responsibility for investigating a different activity and then share what you have learned. Select something that appeals to you and plan how you will include it in your next Tantra date. Take turns from week to week or both pick one treat to contribute. Remember to be flexible as you create your scenario—you are simply setting the stage and providing the necessary props for an inspired improvisation.

Location

In Chapter 10, we outlined elements of creating a sacred space for your Tantric lovemaking. Most likely, your love temple will usually be at home and probably in your bedroom, but a change of scene can add excitement and mystery. If you have the privacy, move around from room to room, christening your tables and countertops, rugs and window seats, infusing every part of your home with the electrical charge of your blissful connection. When our house was being built, we would slip in at night and consecrate specific areas with our fiercely magical mating, until

Outdoor Romance

we had covered the entire building. We have continued the practice, regularly blessing every delightful nook and cranny through our ceremonial sexuality. You can feel the love as soon as you step in our door.

Occasionally, making the shift to a locale away from home injects the spice of newness into your sacred sex time. Slip off to a nearby motel for a lovers' afternoon rendezvous. Set up a love nest in a tent in your backyard or trade apartments with your friends for the weekend.

Food and Drink

Sex and food are inseparable, or they should be. Palate-pleasing food and drinks are essential elements of extended loving sessions. For one thing, you need them to keep up your stamina, but besides that, their aromas, flavors, textures, and appearance nourish your senses. They also remind you to be grateful for the many bounties of the Earth.

Cooking is an erotic experience for us, so sometimes preparing food together is part of our sexual play. Eating definitely is: tenderly feeding each other tasty finger foods; slurping succulent tidbits off each other's bodies; enjoying a formal candlelight dinner with amorous interludes between courses; sharing sacramental dishes during reverent ceremonies. If you are not into cooking, order in, buy some frozen gourmet specials, or go minimalist with raw fruits, nuts, and vegetables escorted by intriguing sauces. Whatever your method, be sure to give yourself the sensual delights that can accompany fueling your body.

Love Snacks

Ancient Tantric rituals incorporate food and drink—grain, fish, meat, and wine—and sexual union as sacramental symbols of the five elements. Grains represent Earth, fish–Water, wine–Fire, meat–Air, and coitus–space—the all-pervasive element that is part of all the others. In traditional Tantra, various intoxicants were also employed: alcohol and drugs, such as marijuana. They were included as enhancements to lovemaking—aids to alter consciousness, not escape from reality. Moderate consumption of wine or spirits over an evening of high-octane sex is pleasurable and manageable; too much dulls your senses. The same restraint applies to eating—not to your enjoyment of the food—but to the amount you consume.

Erotic Words and Images

"All really great lovers are articulate, and verbal
seduction is the surest road to actual seduction."
—Marya Mannes

Some say the brain is the most influential sex organ. Steer it in the right direction with erotic words and images.

Poetry: Poems speak the language of love, whether whispered in your sweetheart's ear, written to him on a mushy card, or read seductively to her as she soaks in a scented bath. Be courageous, write your own poem and read it to your mate on bended knee. Let go of the need for your ode to be publishable; as a private expression of your love and desire, your heartfelt sentiments will endow it with grace. Mix in selections of erotic or spiritual or amorous verses by some of the world's greats, such as Rumi, Octavio Paz, Elizabeth Barrett Browning, Walt Whitman, Emily Dickinson, Rainer Maria Rilke, and Maya Angelou.

Prose: There is nothing like a steamy story to set the mind reeling and the blood rushing. On a languorous Tantra afternoon, in between your own passionate entanglements, cuddle up and read sections aloud, each taking on different parts. Alternatively, for a provocative aural adventure, have your beloved close her eyes while you read sexy passages to her in a deep, throaty voice. Vary your selections from classic to modern: *The Story of O, Emmanuelle, Justine, Lady Chatterly's Lover, Pleasures: Women Write Erotica*.

Visuals: Feed each other eye candy:
  ⚶ Coffee-table books featuring erotic nude photography from the explicit to the ephemeral—Robert Mapplethorpe, Herb Ritts, Imogen Cunningham, Barbara Bordnick, Helmut Newton, Edward Weston, Jan Saudek.

☥   Fancifully illustrated versions of pillow book classics such as the *Kama Sutra*.

☥   Paintings, sketches, and drawings that feature the bawdy side of artists and illustrators from Ingres and Picasso to Aubrey Beardsley and Guido Crepax.

Videos: If your thighs tingle when you tune in to pornographic videos, stimulate your appetites with short snippets from your favorite films. On the other hand, if you want some explicit guidance watch 10 to 15 minutes of an instructional video about massage or sexual positions. Limit your viewing during your Tantra sessions—this is *your* time for action; watch the others doing it later.

Clothing

"Love is when you tell a guy you like his shirt, then he
wears it every day."

—Noelle, age 7

What you wear affects your mood and your energy level and influences what you will and will not do. For example, every sport and many workplaces have uniforms, which contribute to the perceptions and

Lovers' Costumes

performances of those wearing them and those watching them. This holds true for lovemaking as well. The clothing you select for your Tantra tete à tete can turn you on or off, inhibit you or unleash mad passion. Because a sacred loving session takes place over several hours, you have the opportunity to dress and undress more than once. Choose a variety of outfits—casual, conservative, elegant, provocative—clothes to unlock a particular persona and its accompanying behaviors.

Experiment with makeup for men as well as women. Add to your mystery and liberate your libido with masks, from basic black Zorro to bejeweled and befeathered African queen. Costumes give you permission to bring out qualities and aspects of yourself that do not necessarily fit elsewhere in your life. You can playfully and healthfully welcome *all* of you out into the safety of your lovers' world.

We love to dress up and down for each other—formal evening clothes for candlelight and wine; thongs and sarongs for indoor winter picnics; flashy, slinky half-undressed for private dance parties. As a birthday gift to Al, Pala once transformed into seven different women in one day, from sophisticated courtesan to devilish dominatrix to Virgin Island goddess.

Scent

"Love is when a girl puts on perfume
and a boy puts on shaving cologne and they
go out and smell each other."

—Karl, age 5

Enticing aromas are magical—you open immediately to someone who smells good. Make use of a variety of personal scents as preparation for, and part of, your erotic rituals. Buy the best you can afford and only wear those you both like. Apply small amounts of different scents to individual parts of your body, for instance: feet, knees, pubic bone, navel, chest, ear lobes, wrists, and hair. Tantric ceremonies often include anointing your lover with scented oils of musk, jasmine, rose, patchouli, and sandalwood.

Sex Toys

Sex toys are moving out of the shadowy world of "nudge, nudge—wink, wink" and into the light of respectable merchandise. Most major cities now boast sex shops that include sex education as part of the package. Knowledgeable staff will help you choose the best toy for your desires and tell you frankly and comfortably how to use it. Online storefronts offer discreet shipping of high quality goods to most countries around the globe.

Tantalizing weapons for the skilled warrior of love, sex toys open up a world of playful possibility. They offer variety in activity and sensation, and practical solutions to some intriguing sexual challenges. For instance, vibrators are fabulous devices for helping a woman learn to become orgasmic. Anal beads and butt plugs help men learn to relax, surrender, and go to another level of pleasure. A skillfully wielded dildo can keep a woman rolling in satisfaction while her male lover takes a much-needed break from thrusting his own tool. A moment or two to retreat from the precipice and he can plunge in to match her once again. Nipple clamps, vibrators, and anal toys provide multiple points of stimulation, building sensation throughout your body. Just watching you deploy your arsenal of love devices for the evening's encounter can set your partner's pulse racing.

Fantasy

"I married a German.
Every night I dress up as Poland and
he invades me."

—Bette Midler

If you can give each other and yourself permission to allow your imagination out to play, fantasy can be tremendously exciting and exhilarating. Fantasy adds newness and variety and stimulates creativity. It builds trust and encourages vulnerability, because you risk judgment and rejection when you reveal your fantasies to your lover. Sexual fantasy is one of the few places you can safely explore your Dark Shadow so that it does not come out in harmful, antisocial ways. One of Carl Jung's important teachings is that you cannot get rid of your Dark Shadow, but you can find ways to let it out safely so it loses its power.

For example, when Pala imagines being ravished in the woods by a handsome stranger, she tells Al, then goes for a walk in the woods, cape and basket and all, and waits to be set upon and lovingly devoured. She does not need to go out looking for excitement in situations that are truly dangerous; she can have all she wants in complete safety.

To help you break through self-consciousness about creating or revealing your own fantasies you might start with books and games containing inventive scenarios. Selections such as *101 Nights of Great Sex* and *101 Nights of Great Romance* lay out everything for you in sealed packets containing seductive instructions for him and her.

We have only three rules for fantasy. Decide what yours may be, then dive in.

1. We are both willing participants. There is no pressure to do anything we do not want to do.

2. Neither of us gets hurt—physically or emotionally. Stop means *stop instantly* so it is safe to go to the limits of our imagination, even to the dark, dangerous areas.

3. We only play with fantasies that bring us together and strengthen our relationship, rather than taking us away from each other or threatening our connection. Consequently, we explore situational fantasy ("me Tarzan, you Jane") and stay away from fantasies about specific other people (I'm really hot for our new neighbor Fred; let's pretend you're him).

Shake Your Booty

Body movement—dance, stretching, and partner yoga—livens up your loving by keeping your body loose and helping you stay in touch

Energy Dance

with it. Give your lover the wonderfully erotic gift of a dance especially and only for him—or her, women love to watch their man move. Try a spur of the moment striptease, a carefully choreographed bump-and-grind, or an impromptu undulation. Let your feet flow and your hips shake and your arms wave in glorious celebration. Dance together, alternating hot, fast numbers with slow, romantic grinders. If you arrive at a momentary lull during your hours of a Tantra date, dancing is the perfect answer to, "What will we do now?"

Sounds of Love

Tantric loving is completely unrestrained and uninhibited. A sure-fire way to blast the fetters off your boisterous hidden lover is to make sound, lots of it. Along with body movement and breath, sound is one of the three keys for moving energy. We are continually dumbfounded that people do not seem to have many qualms about their kids hearing them argue, yet heaven forbid a sound of love should reach the children's ears.

So, please, when you are in the throes of passion let passion guide your voice—soft moans of surrender, exuberant shrieks of conquest, throaty growls of lust. Intone mantras for concentration and connection. Howl and twitter and shriek in animal abandon. When you are caught in the frenzy of God's love, open your mouth and allow yourself to speak in tongues. Lilt sweet sighs of satiation. At the peak of fervor, chant together—"OM." You may feel uncomfortable at first, but the beauty of the sound that emerges, propelled forth by your pure energy, will drown out your fears.

Talking can be love sounds, too. Tell each other over and over what you love about each other and how happy you are to be together—you can never say it or hear it too often. Words weave magic spells—words of endearment and adoration, desire and lust, love and devotion, spoken or whispered or sung.

Singing to your beloved, especially if you do not usually sing, is a first-class heart-melter. Pala came completely undone the first time Al, who has little confidence in his singing voice, shyly offered her his rendition of Springsteen's "Tougher Than the Rest." Serenade your sweetheart with lullabyes, love songs, and rollicking ditties.

Scratch My Back, I'll Scratch Yours

An oh-so-simple yet heartily appreciated act of love is to do something personal for your lover that she would normally do for herself:

- Dress and undress her—slowly, seductively, attentively.

- Wash his hair—massaging his scalp, cradling his neck.

- Bathe her body—with soapy suds on loofah sponges.

- Shave his beard—carefully, conscientiously, and sensually.

- Shave her legs or other body parts—as above.

- Give her a pedicure—with skin sloughing ointments and refreshing foot creams.

- Give him a manicure—complete with polish, clear or colored.

- Treat her to a facial—the works: cleansing, massaging, toning, and moisturizing.

Playful Positions

"After all, if words cannot be found then it is
the body that must talk.
Especially tender words."
—*The Zebra*, by Alexandre Jardin

There are six basic lovemaking positions:

- Man on top.

- Woman on top.

- Sideways.

- Standing.

- Sitting.

- Rear entry.

With subtle, or if you prefer, dramatic shifts in placement of legs, feet, hips, and hands you can transform these six fundamentals into scores of titillating variations. Each basic posture contributes its own distinct pleasure, so during extended lovemaking, partners shift from position to position in a glorious lovers' dance. With practice, you can retain genital connection while gracefully making your moves. Try a little pre-love sexual choreography with your clothes on to playfully rehearse a series of potential bedroom ballets.

Man on Top

Man on top positions are good for starting and ending intercourse. As you are beginning intercourse, shallow strokes are often most pleasurable for the woman, allowing her yoni to gradually expand and welcome you.

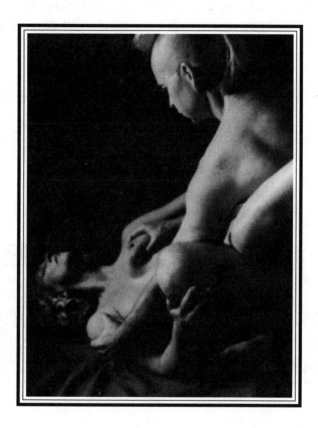

Man on top

Position Variation: Man on top, woman flat on her back her legs wrapped around your thighs.

After you have been making love in other poses for some time—both of you at fever pitch, your beloved panting for you to fill her completely— return to the man on top position with this pleasing ***Position Variation:*** man on top, woman's hips raised on a pillow, her legs over your shoulders or spread wide to enfold your upper body. She can take you deep, deep into her enchanted garden.

For a couple whose genital match is smaller man–larger woman, these positions are the best because they offer maximum penetration.

Woman on Top

Woman on top positions give women most control over the angle and depth of penetration, plus they leave the man's hands free to stimulate other parts of her body—clitoris, breasts, back, and buttocks. Because the man can relax his body, remaining relatively still and passive, it is easier for him to delay ejaculation in these positions while his partner continues to build her ardor with movements that particularly turn her on.

Woman on top

Position Variation: Man flat on his back, woman crouches above him. With your feet flat on the bed on either side of his hips, your knees bent, ride up and down his magnificent jade stalk. You might need to maintain your balance by holding on to a headboard. This position gives you the added bonus of a strenuous thigh workout.

These are particularly good positions if the genital match is larger man–smaller woman.

Sideways

Sideways positions—that is, lovers lying on their sides—are generally slower and more relaxed because your range of movement is more restricted. These are good transition poses, in between very active ones—you remain connected but your arousal level can level off. Sideways postures are especially lovely if you are tired or low on energy. You gain the benefits of loving union without a lot of physical exertion.

Sideways

Position Variation: Lie on your sides facing each other, sharing a slow soul kiss, hands on each other's shoulders. Your thighs gently close around the shaft of his lingam, its head nestles inside the mouth of your honey pot. Gently rock back and forth together.

These variations are particularly effective for a large man with a small woman. Although there is shallower penetration so she is comfortable, he receives sensation along his full length.

245

Standing

Standing positions are great for highly charged quickies. Because in most of these variations, the man must support much of the woman's weight, you usually cannot sustain them for very long. Also there is not a lot of range for thrusting, but because you are in an upright stance, there is lots of potential for energy circulation.

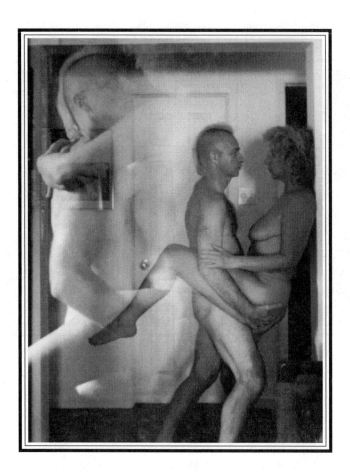

Standing

Position Variation: In a narrow doorway, the woman leans back against one of the door frames, lifts her legs up around your waist and supports some of her weight by pressing her feet against the opposite door frame. She wraps her arms around your shoulders. As you rotate your hips in a circular motion, screwing far inside her, you help to hold her up with your hands beneath her buttocks.

Sitting

Sitting positions are in essence vertical varieties of woman on top; only in this case, it is woman on lap. Again, there is not a lot of thrusting range, but if you both lean back on your arms you can get a lot of up and down rubbing action happening, which can make a woman's clitoris very happy.

Sitting

Position Variation: Experiment with sitting on a range of chairs, stools, sofas, of different heights, widths, and degrees of firmness.

Rear entry

Rear-entry positions are wildly exciting. Mimic your animal friends' mating habits in more than just their "attack from the rear" stance, by adding their love sounds—growls, howls, and roars. Because of the angle, a well-aimed thrust from the rear stands the best chance of finding a woman's G-spot. In this pose, a woman's vaginal canal tightens, so it is also a good one for men who have erection difficulties.

Rear Entry

Position Variation: As the woman bends over and grasps her ankles, you take her swiftly from behind. It's particularly erotic if she is wearing a long, loose skirt that falls forward to envelope her upper body.

This is excellent for a small man–large woman combination, because you can achieve very deep penetration.

Position Tips

The person who is on the top during active lovemaking generates the most energy, which is passed to the partner on the bottom. Take turns sending and receiving by switching top and bottom throughout your sacred loving. If one of you is tired, or recovering from an illness, then spend most of your time underneath.

Face to face positions with similar body parts touching (mouths kissing, hearts together, genitals joined, hands linked) encourage emotional union and energy circulation. Postures that combine opposites (rear entry, head to feet, mouth to groin) build excitement and generate a high sexual charge. Establish a rhythm of active postures for increasing arousal followed by very slow or still poses where your focus is on moving the energy you have fired up, then build again, circulate again, and so on in a series of peaks. Nine peaks of arousal and energy circulation are considered particularly fortuitous in the Eastern view.

Tantric Love Posture Supreme: The YabYum Position

The YabYum position is ideal for moving and exchanging sexual energy. In this position, almost all of you is pointing up, even the man's penis inside his partner is in an upward slanting position. Move into this posture when you are both highly aroused, after active lovemaking has built your sexual charge. The man sits cross-legged, in the lotus position, with his partner on top of his lap. You may support his thighs and back with pillows. If the lotus position is too difficult, he may sit on the edge of the bed or on a straight-backed chair with his legs out in front of him and feet on the floor. Another variation is for the woman to kneel on the man supporting some of her own weight with her thighs. It is important that you find a variation that is comfortable for you both so that you can maintain it for a while.

Once you are snugly connected, be still and harmonize your breathing. Look into each other's eyes, connect your mouths with a kiss, or touch third-eye points. Focus your attention on moving your sexual energy up from your genitals through your chakra centers and then into your partner and/or out into the cosmos. The Passion Pump (Chapter 7, page 151) is particularly effective in this position. Experiment with making a sound at each chakra point, chanting or "toning" together to focus the energy.

Hands help to concentrate and circulate the energy as well. Place your left hand at the base of his spine and your right hand on his back at the heart center. Alternatively, place your left hand at the base of his spine, and with your right hand, press the "Wind Mansion" acupoints at the junction of skull and neck. Another variation is to run your hands in flowing motions up his spine. Experiment!

YabYum

When your sexual excitement begins to subside, speed up your breathing and undulate your bodies to build the charge again and move it up. Even with rapid rocking and breathing, there is little actual thrusting happening, so the man is able to last longer. Some delightful yoni squeezing will help him to maintain an erection without going over into ejaculation.

You can easily roll from this position into man or woman on top or face to face on your sides while still maintaining your genital connection. Some lovers also enjoy the YabYum position as a way to tune into each other early on in their lovemaking. Then they return to it when the sexual charge is high.

Chapter 13

Soul Sex Simple Summary

Tantra, sacred sex, is a practical key to unlock your potential for an intimate, passionate relationship. The approaches and exercises you have just read about can bring great meaning to your life, as they have to ours and to hundreds of our students. All that's required now is some effort on your part. You can try as many or as few of the techniques as you want to. Even if you only add daily PC pumping (Chapter 7, page 147)—which doesn't take extra time, just a little discipline—you'll see a noticeable difference. But to receive the maximum benefits you deserve, we suggest you take the following steps as well. They will likely require some shifts in attitudes and behaviors, but you and your relationship are worth it!

- ⚜ On your own, and with your partner, examine your beliefs about sexuality, spirituality, and relationships. Replace unwanted negative messages with supportive, positive ones.

- ⚜ Make your relationship a top priority and set your actions accordingly. This means feeding your union with time and commitment. Do it despite all the other things crying out for your attention and you'll see that a loving relationship helps all else flow more smoothly.

- ⚜ Connect in an intimate, loving way with your partner *daily*.

- ⚜ Once per week have a two- to four-hour Tantra date and experiment with the marvelous processes we've described in this book. During that time, allow and encourage your sexuality to be more than physical. Give yourself freely and fully to your lover and the Divine, despite your fears. Share your body and your heart. Tame your mind. Unite your spirits.

- ⚜ Keep pushing your envelope playfully, respectfully, and boldly. Always have faith in your capacity to create together the passionate, intimate life you want.

Appendix A

References and Resources

We highly recommend the books, videos, and CDs listed here. We use them and have been inspired by the wisdom, sensitivity, insight, and sexiness they contain.

The Internet Websites featuring teachers, products, and Tantra/sexuality information are offered as a service to help readers locate sexuality resources. We do not necessarily personally endorse each one listed. All of the URLs presented below were available as of February 2003, but Internet addresses change rapidly. Links to many of these resources are available at our Website: *www.tantra-sex.com*. We try to keep all of those links up to date and as accurate as possible.

Books

You will find links to many of the books listed here at the 4 Freedoms Books For Lovers Website: *www.tantra-sex.com/erotic-books.html*.

Tantra and Sexuality

The Lover Within: Opening To Energy in Sexual Practice, by Julie Henderson. Station Hill-Barrytown Ltd., 1999.

This is the best book for learning to work with energy that we have found. It is simple and thorough. Very highly recommended.

The Multi-Orgasmic Couple: Sexual Secrets Every Couple Should Know, by Mantak Chia (Editor), Maneewan Chia, Douglas Abrams and Rachel Abrams. HarperSanFrancisco, 2000.

This may be the best guide for couples to the art of sacred sexuality available to date—except for our book, of course! Discover how to have multiple whole-body orgasms and how to reach ever more fulfilling levels of intimacy and ecstasy together.

The Multi-Orgasmic Man: Sexual Secrets Every Man Should Know, by Mantak Chia, Douglas Abrams Arava, HarperSanFrancisco, 1997.

The Multi-Orgasmic Man is an excellent step-by-step, how-to manual for achieving sexual ecstasy. Do not let the title fool you; this book is for women as well as men.

Taoist Secrets of Love: Cultivating Male Sexual Energy, by Mantak Chia and Michael Winn. Samuel Weiser, 1984.

Mantak Chia is a master who gives detailed descriptions of the "how-to" of moving sexual energy. The methods he proposes are very disciplined, and so they work best for people who like structure and have lots of patience and self-motivation. This book is also good for individuals not in a relationship, because so much of the work is done on one's own. Because Chia's work derives from the Taoist tradition (as opposed to Tantric), there is more emphasis on the physical and practical than the mystical, emotional aspects of the work. Al says, "If I could read only one book on sacred sexuality, it would be this one."

Healing Love Through The Tao: Cultivating Female Sexual Energy, by Mantak Chia and Maneewan Chia. Healing Tao Books, 1986.

This and the companion volume *Cultivating Male Sexual Energy* were two of the most important books that Pala and Al used in cutting their teeth on sacred sexuality.

Sexual Secrets: The Alchemy of Ecstasy, by Nik Douglas and Penny Slinger. Inner Traditions International Ltd., 1989.

This book provides a comprehensive and easily understandable introduction to the history, philosophy, and practicality of sacred sex. It has many wonderful exercises and meditations and is particularly suited for people who want to know the background of what they are doing, and like to select on their own the activities they will do in their exploration. It overflows with beautifully erotic drawings by Penny Slinger. Our copy is well-thumbed—it ranks in Pala's top three sacred sex books. *Sexual Secrets* was first published in 1979, with a revised edition in 1999, and has sold more than one million copies.

The Art of Sexual Ecstasy: The Path of Sacred Sexuality for Western Lovers, by Margo Anand, Leandra Hussey (Illustrator). Jeremy P. Tarcher, 1991.

This book is a complete sacred sex course in itself. It is particularly suited for couples who want to open up to each other emotionally as well as physically. There are lots of meditations, activities, and exercises. This is one of Pala's favorites.

The Art of Everyday Ecstasy: The Seven Tantric Keys for Bringing Passion, Spirit and Joy Into Every Part of Your Life, by Margo Anand. Broadway Books, 1998.

With personal anecdotes, exercises, meditations, and rituals, Anand shows how to bring ecstatic energy into the body, mind, heart, and spirit—"to embrace every moment in our totality, to respond bodily, feel from the heart, perceive with clarity, and be fully present to others and to life." Anand founded the Sky Dancing Institute, a worldwide center for New Age learning, and has conducted her Love and Ecstasy Trainings for the past 15 years at Esalen, the Omega Institute, and Deepak Chopra's Center for Well Being.

The Art of Sexual Magic: Cultivating Sexual Energy to Transform Your Life, by Margo Anand. Jeremy P. Tarcher, 1995.

Explains how to generate and focus intense sexual energy for realizing personal and spiritual goals.

Sexual Energy Ecstasy: A Practical Guide to Lovemaking Secrets of the East and West, by David Ramsdale, Ellen Ramsdale, Allan Parker (Illustrator). Bantam Doubleday Dell, 1993.

A *Joy of Sex* for the New Age; contains Tantric and Taoist techniques of sacred sexuality.

The Essential Tantra: A Modern Guide to Sacred Sexuality, by Kenneth Ray Stubbs, Kyle Spencer (Illustrator), Richard Stodart (Illustrator). Jeremy P. Tarcher, 2000.

This was the Tantra book featured in the popular movie, *American Pie 2*. It is three books in one: *Tantric Massage, Sensual Ceremony*, and an expanded edition of *Sacred Orgasms*. All three of the original editions are now out of print. The book is well illustrated. Do a search on Amazon.com for "Kenneth Ray Stubbs" for a complete listing of his many books and videos. Much of his work emphasizes sensual/sexual massage.

Erotic Massage: The Tantric Touch of Love, by Kenneth Ray Stubbs, Kyle Specner (Illustrator). Jeremy P. Tarcher, 1999.

Stubbs' clear instructions, poetic language, and playful, reverent sensibility make this an excellent massage book for beginners. It must be—it's sold 400,000 copies. Complement your reading with his popular Tantric Massage Video.

The Tao of Health, Sex and Longevity: A Modern Practical Guide to the Ancient Way, by Daniel P. Reid. Fireside, 1989.

This is an excellent, easy-to-comprehend guide to Taoist practice.

Tantra in Practice, by David Gordon White (Editor). Princeton University Press, 2000.

The book examines 36 texts from China, India, Japan, Nepal, and Tibet, ranging from the 7th century to the present day, representing the full range of Tantric experience—Buddhist, Hindu, Jain, and Islamic. The book includes plays, transcribed interviews, poetry, parodies, inscriptions, instructional texts, scriptures, philosophical conjectures, dreams, and astronomical speculations, each text illustrating one of the diverse traditions and practices of Tantra. David Gordon White is Associate Professor in the Department of Religious Studies at the University of California, Santa Barbara.

The New Male Sexuality, by Bernie Zilbergeld, Ph.D. Bantam Doubleday Dell, 1999.

Useful information and exercises to help couples achieve sexual fulfillment.

Ejaculation Control Manual for Extended Lovemaking, by David Routh and Tom Newhouse. Starside Publishing Company, 1992.

This book gives instructions and exercises to help a man learn how to maintain an erection indefinitely for extended lovemaking.

How to Make Love All Night (And Drive a Woman Wild: Male Multiple Orgasm and Other Secrets for Prolonged Lovemaking), by Barbara Keesling, HarperCollins Publishers, 1995.

A clear, organized, systematic approach to extended lovemaking for couples.

How to Overcome Premature Ejaculation, by Helen Singer Kaplan. Brunner/Mazel Publishers, 1989.

A practical self-help guide for men who want to last longer.

Male Sexual Endurance, by Robert W. Birch. PEC Publishing, 1998.

A practical self-help guide for men who want to last longer.

Acupressure for Lovers: Secrets of Touch for Increasing Intimacy, by Michael Reed Gach. Bantam Books, 1997.

Gach teaches you new and delightful ways to rediscover your lover's body. Please her with your tender touch as you awaken her senses. Open his energy pathways, and help to heal every inch!

Sex for One: The Joy of Selfloving, by Betty Dodson. Three Rivers Press, New York, 1996.

This book, an updated version of one first published in the 1970s, remains the classic guide to embracing masturbation. Through stories of her own personal journey and the journeys of her lovers, friends, and students Betty helps her readers truly feel good about loving themselves.

For Yourself: The Fulfillment of Female Sexuality, by Lonnie Garfield Barbach. New American Library, 1991.

This book carries a woman along step-by-step in the rediscovery of her own sexuality and the pleasure it will bring her.

The G Spot: And Other Recent Discoveries About Human Sexuality, by Alice Kahn Ladas, Beverly Whipple and John D. Perry. Dell Publishers, 1983.

This book, published in 19 languages, offers authoritative information about the G-spot (in women and men), female ejaculation, and importance of the PC muscle, based upon original research.

Safe Encounters: How Women Can Say Yes to Pleasure and No to Unsafe Sex, by Beverly Whipple and G. Ogden. McGraw Hill and Pocketbooks, 1989.

In this book, the authors focus on sensuality, what they call "outercourse" (the many ways of touching other than intercourse without the exchange of body fluids), and how women can enjoy sensual and sexual pleasure.

Sex Matters for Women: A Complete Guide to Taking Care of Your Sexual Self, by Sallie Foley, Sally A. Kope, Dennis P. Sugrue. Guilford Press, 2002.

"This is a 'must read' for women of all ages."—Beverly Whipple.

Pathways to Pleasure: A Woman's Guide to Orgasm, by Robert W. Birch, Cynthia Lief Ruberg. PEC Publishing, 2000.

In the Foreword, Beverly Whipple, Ph.D., RN, co-author of *The G Spot*, writes, "I love the emphasis in this book on the many pathways to pleasure and not on the single goal of orgasm."

Oral Caress: The Loving Guide to Exciting a Woman: A Comprehensive Illustrated Manual on the Joyful Art of Cunnilingus, by Robert W. Birch. PEC Publishing, 1996.

Sex therapist Birch says: "This is my loving book about understanding a woman's sexual response, listening carefully to her needs, attending to her erotic desires, and appreciating the intimate act of providing effective oral stimulation to the most sensitive areas of her body."

Ordinary Women, Extraordinary Sex: Every Woman's Guide to Pleasure and Beyond, by Dr. Sandra R. Scantling, Sue Browder. Plume Books, 1994.

Scantling, a sex therapist, shows how women can tap latent sexual energy to enjoy ever-richer levels of sexual fulfillment. She helps you identify barriers to pleasure and intimacy that stifle your capacity for sexual enjoyment.

The Woman's Book of Orgasm: A Guide to the Ultimate Sexual Pleasure, by Tara Barker (Editor), Citadel Press, 1998.

A complete guide to everything women have ever wanted to know about orgasm.

Becoming Orgasmic: A Sexual and Personal Growth Program for Women, by Julia Heiman, Joseph Lopiccolo. Simon & Schuster, 1988.

Learn to accept yourself, feel comfortable with your body and take pleasure in your sexuality. For women of all ages.

Super Sexual Orgasm: Discover the Ultimate Pleasure Spot: The Cul-De-Sac, by Barbara Keesling. HarperCollins Publishers, 1997.

Through a series of 12 exercises, sex therapist Barbara Keesling offers women techniques for harnessing the power of their sexuality.

50 Ways to Please Your Lover: While You Please Yourself, by Lonnie Garfield Barbach. E P Dutton, 1997.

For men or women, long-standing partners or newly intimate couples, *50 Ways to Please Your Lover* offers the opportunity for new pleasures, renewed enthusiasm, and very pleasant surprises.

For Each Other: Sharing Sexual Intimacy, by Lonnie Garfield Barbach. New American Library, 1984.

Sex therapist Barbach presents a program for dealing with the complex physical and psychological aspects of a relationship that affect sexual satisfaction. "A book to use and refer to over and over again."—Siecus Report.

ESO: How You and Your Lover Can Give Each Other Hours of Extended Sexual Orgasm, by Alan P. Brauer, Donna Brauer. Warner Books, 1988.

Based on their years of research and clinical work, this book explores the mental, emotional, and physical aspects of sexuality.

The New Good Vibrations Guide to Sex: How to Have Safe, Fun Sex, by Anne Semans. Down There Press, 1997.

This book covers the topic of sex toys perhaps better than any other book on the market.

Good Vibrations: The New Complete Guide to Vibrators, by Joani Blank. Down There Press, 2000.

Confounded by the plethora of possibilities? This guide outlines all the different types of vibrators available, as well as their care and use during solo or partner sex.

Sex in History, Reay Tannahill. Scarborough Books, 1982

Tannahill graces her readers with an exhaustively researched, highly entertaining study of sex from the prehistoric world to modern times. A provocative overview of humanity's fascination with sex through the ages, it is—in the author's very accurate own words—"at once a history of sex, a history of relationships between the sexes, and a history of how sex and sexuality have influenced the whole course of human development."

Sex and Spirit, Clifford Bishop. Duncan Baird Publishers, London, England, 1996.

Part of the "Living Wisdom" series of illustrated guides to traditions of body, mind, and spirit, this book explores the powerful connection between sex and the human spirit. Full-color illustrations amplify the thought-provoking analysis of beliefs and practices both ancient and contemporary.

Erotic/Spiritual Poetry

The Enlightened Heart: An Anthology of Sacred Poetry, Stephen Mitchell (Editor). Harper Perennial Library, 1993.

Superb selections from ancient to modern.

The Enlightened Mind: An Anthology of Sacred Prose, Stephen Mitchell (Ed.), Harper Perennial Library, 1991.

Superb selections from ancient to modern.

The Selected Poetry of Rainer Maria Rilke, Stephen Mitchell (Editor). Vintage International, 1989

"Perhaps the most beautiful group of poetic translations this century has produced."—Chicago Tribune.

The Ink Dark Moon: Love Poems by Ono no Komachi and Izumi Shikibu, Women of the Ancient Court of Japan, Translated by Jane Hirshfield with Mariko Aratani. Vintage Books, 1990.

Timeless, haunting images.

Seven Hundred Kisses: A Yellow Silk Book of Erotic Writing, Lily Pond (Editor). HarperSanFrancisco, 1997.

"...everything is known inside the skin."—Thaisa Frank, Animal Skins

Pleasures: Women Write Erotica, Lonnie Barbach, Ph. D. Harper & Row, 1984.

"A sensitive and intelligent selection of exciting, sensual, humorous and gentle stories..."—Atlanta Magazine.

Emily Dickinson: Collected Poems, Barnes & Noble, 1993. Originally published in 1924 as *The Complete Poems of Emily Dickinson*.

Amazing gentleness and beauty.

The Collected Poems of Octavio Paz (1957–1987). Eliot Weinberger (Editor). New Directions, 1987.

Paz is undeniably a poetic genius.

The Collected Works of W. B. Yeats, Vol. I, The Poems, Richard J. Finneran (Editor). Macmillan, 1989.

"A heart that laughter has made sweet."

Erotic Photography

Eros, by Linda Ferrer (Compiler), Jane Lahr (Editor). Stewart, Tabori and Chang, Inc., 1996

Absolutely excellent black and white erotica—187 pages, large format.

Nudes, by B. Martin Pedersen (Publisher and Creative Director). Graphis Publishing Co., 1995

Absolutely excellent combination of black and white and color erotica—224 pages, large format.

Show Me: A Picture Book of Sex for Children and Parents, Will McBride (Photography), Dr. Helga Fleischhauer-Hardt (Text). St. Martin's Press., 1975.

This controversial book is beautifully illustrated with black and white photos designed to introduce children to the world of sexuality. Excellent to help children learn about healthy sexuality.

Meditation and Prayer

Concentration and Meditation: A Manual of Mind Development, Christmas Humphreys. John M. Watkins Publishers, 1953.

Still one of the best manuals available, but long out of print.

Beginning To Pray, Archbishop Anthony Bloom. Paulist Press, 1970.

If you want to pray but do not know how, read this book.

Aphrodisacs/Pheromones/Essential Oils/ Aromatherapy/Food

Love Potions: A Guide to Aphrodisiacs and Sexual Pleasures, by Cynthia Mervis Watson, M.D. Jeremy P. Tarcher, 1993.

Excellent resource for learning about aphrodisiacs. Includes recipes to make your own.

The Alchemy of Love and Lust, by Theresa Crenshaw, M.D. G. Putnam & Sons, 1996.

Identifies the role our hormones play in the different sexual stages, exploring the age-old concept of chemistry between the sexes and how hormones can determine the course of human relationships. Good section on pheromones. Outdated on hormone replacement therapy.

Bittersweet Journey: A Modestly Erotic Novel of Love, Longing, and Chocolate, by Enid Futterman. Viking Penguin, 1998.

A visually stunning book, part novel, part photography book, part erotica, part travel essay, and part cookbook.

Aphrodite: A Memoir of the Senses, by Isabel Allende. Harper Collins, 1999.

A bawdy memoir-cum-cookbook; very sexy.

The Arginine Solution, by Robert Fried, Ph.D., James Thornton, and Woodson C. Merrell, M.D. Warner Books, 2000.

A well-known nutrient, the amino acid arginine helps your body create nitric oxide (NO), a simple molecule recently found to be of astonishing importance to improved health. NO is essential for men to get and maintain erections, and is also essential for both men and women in having orgasms. L-arginine is a natural alternative to Viagra that can boost potency for men and increase orgasmic response in women. It helps keep internal smooth muscles relaxed making it much easier for men to delay involuntary ejaculation. It has been shown to have many other health benefits as well.

Intercourses: An Aphrodisiac Cookbook, by Martha Hopkins and Randall Lockridge, Ben Fink (Photography). Terrace Publishing, 1997.

Aphrodisiac recipes beautifully and erotically illustrated with color photos.

The Better Sex Diet: A medically based low-fat eating plan for increased sexual vitality, by Lynn Fischer. St. Martin's Press, 1999.

Shows that good health is an essential part of good sex. Includes lots of delicious recipes that will enhance sexual vitality naturally!

Personal/Spiritual Growth

The Path of Least Resistance: Learning to Become the Creative Force in Your Own Life, by Robert Fritz. Fawcett Books, 1989.

Fritz explains better than anyone else how to create the results you want in life. Pala and Al have used this method to create many successful outcomes. Al has attended four workshops facilitated by Robert Fritz. Very highly recommended.

Care of the Soul: A Guide for Cultivating Depth and Sacredness in Everyday Life, by Thomas Moore. HarperPerennial Library, 1994.

One of the best primers for soul work ever written. Moore suggests accepting our humanity rather than struggling to transcend it. "Ritual maintains the world's holiness. As in a dream a small object may assume significance, so in a life that is animated by ritual there are no insignificant things."

Sweat Your Prayers: Movement As Spiritual Practice, by Gabrielle Roth. Penquin USA, 1999.

This book elevates dance into a spiritual practice. Roth suggests the soul has five natural rhythms: flowing, staccato, chaos, lyrical, and stillness and shows how to work those rhythms to facilitate doing your inner work. See the music section that follows for two CDs by Gabrielle Roth that are companions to this book: *Endless Wave, Vol. 1* and *Endless Wave, Vol. 2*.

Be Here Now, Ram Dass. Lama Foundation, 1971.

Being in the moment is a core competency of virtually every spiritual practice in the world. Ram Dass popularized the term in his now famous book from the 1970s. He has been a spiritual mentor to Al for the past 30 years. In an interview at a book signing at the Open Secret Bookstore in San Rafael, California on April 21, 1999, Ram Dass was asked, "Are you hopeful about the future?" Ram Dass replied, *"I try to avoid hope. It is just a subtle form of suffering, you know. I am just 'Be Here Now.'"* All of his books are highly recommended. You can find his books and tapes on his Website: *www.ramdasstapes.org.*

Grist For The Mill, Ram Dass with Stephen Levine. Unity Press, 1997.

"In India when we meet and part we often say, 'Namaste,' which means I honor the place in you where the entire universe resides, I honor the place in you of love, of light, of truth, of peace. I honor the place within you where if you are in that place in you and I am in that place in me, there is only one of us."

A Course In Miracles. Foundation For Inner Peace, 1975.

Al has read this cover to cover at least three times. If there were one book I could take with me to be stranded on a desert island, this would be it. My favorite quote: "Nothing real can be threatened. Nothing unreal exists. Herein lies the peace of God."

The Spiral Dance: A Rebirth of the Ancient Religion of the Great Goddess (20th Anniversary Edition), by Starhawk. HarperSan Francisco, 1999.

Goddess worship from the perspective of one of the great Goddesses of our time, and a Wiccan. This book offers lots of ideas for Pagan ritual and ceremony, many of which would seem to be eminently suitable to the practice of sacred sexuality. If your imagination stumbles over the challenge of creating your own sacred ceremonies, this would be a great book to get you kick started.

Music

4 Freedoms Music For Lovers. Links to sensual, sexy, erotic, and romantic music. You can find links to most of the CDs featured here on our Website: *www.tantra-sex.com/erotic-music.html*

Apertio: Tantra Energy Meditations CD. Meditations by Pala Copeland, Music by Jeff Davies, 2000.

Pala leads you through five Tantra energy meditations accompanied by the sensual music of Jeff Davies. The CD has become a bestseller on Amazon.com in the category Tantra.

Endless Wave, Vol. 1. Gabrielle Roth and The Mirrors, 1996.

The music is fabulous, and Gabrielle talks you through the body parts and 5Rhythms™ to help you get out of your head and into your Divine body. We use this CD in our Tantra workshops. Excellent!

Ecstatica I: Hypno Trance Love Dance. Paul and Marilena Silbey, 1994.

Paul and Marilena have energetically recreated the moods from foreplay to orgasmic climax! Excellent for beginning Tantric lovers and for advanced practitioners as well. You may find yourself playing this CD over and over during an evening of extended lovemaking.

Erotic Cinema. Various Artists, 1993.

Seduce your love to the strains of some of the sexiest songs from some of the hottest Hollywood films.

Non-Stop Erotic Cabaret. Soft Cell. Great 1980s pop.

Two of our favorite cuts are "Tainted Love" and "Soft Cell."

MCMXC A.D. Enigma.

Some of the best music ever to set the mood for lovemaking.

Temptation. Holly Cole.

All songs written by Tom Waits and sung by Holly with her moody, seductive interpretations in slow blues.

I'm Your Man. Leonard Cohen.

Undeniably Cohen's best—suits lovemaking marvelously well.

Poetic Champions Compose. Van Morrison.

One of my (Pala's) all-time favorites, by Van or anyone else, *Poetic Champions Compose* never fails to bring a tear to my eye, a lump to my throat, and a warmth to my heart. Van did everything on this album—wrote, sang, played all the instruments. He's most definitely a poetic champion.

Don Juan de Marco, Motion Picture Soundtrack. Various Artists, 1995.
Very romantic, just like the movie. Features Bryan Adams' hit "Did You Ever Really Love a Woman?"; the Spanish version of that cut is the real gem on this album.

When I Look Into Your Eyes and *Love Scenes*. Diana Krall.
These are just two of many albums by Diana Krall. All contain marvelous, sexy, erotic, romantic jazz compositions. Perfect for romantic lovers' time.

Bosa Nova and *The Other Side of Jobim*. Ana Caram.
On these two albums, Ana performs that Brazilian Portugese Latin sound better than anyone. Wonderful music for romance. She almost, but not quite, makes Jobim sound better than Jobim.

Jazz Masters 13. Antonio Carlos Jobim.
It would be difficult to imagine any music more sexy and romantic than that of Jobim.

CBC's After Hours Bluenote Collection Volume II.
This collection selected by Ross Porter, host of the late night CBC jazz program, perfectly sets a mood for erotic romance.

The Best of Chet Baker Plays and *The Best of Chet Baker Sings*, by Chet Baker.
These are two of our favorite jazz albums. Chet's voice is dreamy and seductive while at the same time innocent.

Ultimate Lester Young. Lester Young; selections by Wayne Shorter.
This is Al's all-time favorite jazz album. No one plays saxophone better than Lester. Pala and I listened to this album all night long as we made love on our balcony overlooking the Pacific Ocean in Tobago under the stars on a hot tropical night with the surf pounding in the background.

Videos

Sex Instruction

4 Freedoms Sex Instruction Videos Page: Huge selection of sex instruction videos to buy or rent. You can find links to most of the videos listed here at our Website: *www.tantra-sex.com/erotic-videos.html.*

Blue Door Videos offers a seven-day rental for a low price, including return postage, for all sex-instruction and adult videos. If you decide you would like to purchase the video, your rental fee can apply to the purchase price. *www.bluedoor.com/home.cfm?Affiliate=17*

Ancient Secrets of Sexual Ecstasy for Modern Lovers (1997).

This is still the best Tantra/Taoist erotic arts instructional video available. We use it regularly in our Tantra workshops. Be sure to get the X-rated version for explicit sexual instruction. This video includes sections on extended and full-body orgasm, finding the G-spot (saspandana), and using yoga to control ejaculation. The expert panel includes Robert Frey and Lori Grace, Charles and Caroline Muir and Margo Anand. Available online from tantra.com: *www.tantra.com.*

Massage

With massage videos, try playing them while you massage your lover. Watch a technique, then pause the VCR with your remote and apply it. Reverse the tape as required to review the stroke and try it again until you are confident you know how to do it yourself. Cover your remote control devise with a latex glove so it does not get slathered with oil.

Tantric Massage. Directed by Kenneth Ray Stubbs. 58 minutes.

Easy-to-follow Swedish massage techniques.

Fire on the Mountain: Male Genital Massage (Lingam/Penis Massage Techniques). Directed by Joseph Kramer. Produced by EROSpirit. 45 minutes.

"The difference between a 'hand job' and Taoist Erotic Massage is the difference between banging on a piano or playing Mozart." —Joseph Kramer.

Fire in the Valley: Female Genital Massage (Yoni/Vulva Massage Techniques). Directed by Annie Sprinkle. Produced by EROSpirit. 55 minutes.

"With this massage you can satisfy a woman to her core...every time!"—Annie Sprinkle.

Rosebud Massage: Gay Sex Wisdom (External Anal Massage Techniques). Directed by Joseph Kramer. Produced by EROSpirit. 35 minutes.

Do not imagine that this is only for gay men. This is an excellent aid to helping anyone learn about anal massage.

Internet Resources

Locating Tantra Teachers on the Internet

Al Link and Pala Copeland—4 Freedoms Relationship Tantra.

Tantra weekends for couples monthly near Ottawa, Ontario, Canada. Weeklong Tantra retreats in tropical locations around the planet. People travel from all over the world to attend our workshops because of our emphasis on Tantra in committed relationship.

E-mail: 4freedoms@tantraloving.com

Toll-free from USA and Canada: 1-800-684-5304

Local and long distance: 1-819-689-5308

Fax: 1-819-689-5656

www.tantra-sex.com

Tantra.com

Tantra.com maintains a registry of Tantra Sacred Loving—Spiritual Sex teachers. Click on "Teachers" and/or "Workshops" from the menu bar on the left. Note: Tantra.com only lists teachers and workshops if they have paid to be registered.

www.tantra.com

Tantra Magazine

An excellent online magazine. The Website includes many links to Tantra resources from around the world. They have a large list of links to Tantra teachers, particularly from Europe.

Magazine: *tantramag.com/classes.html*

Tantra Teacher List:

tantramag.com/directory/display.cgi?poz=1&dir=instructors+tantra

Yahoo and MSN search engines

Both of these offer a number of spiritual and sacred sex discussion groups. Both services allow you to join existing groups or to start your own group on any topic imaginable.

Yahoo Discussion Groups: *groups.yahoo.com*

MSN Discussion Groups: *groups.msn.com*

Tantra Websites

4 Freedoms Relationship Tantra with Pala Copeland and Al Link

www.tantra-sex.com

> Toll-free from USA and Canada: 1-800-684-5304
> Local and long distance: 1-819-689-5308
> Fax: 1-819-689-5656
> *www.tantra-sex.com*

> Free Tantra newsletter, rich source of sex-education information, and lots of links to other Websites featuring sexual products, instructional videos, and music for lovers. 4 Freedoms affiliate program is free to join.

Tantra.com

www.tantra.com

> Central registry for Tantra teachers from around the world. Rich source of sex-education information, products, and services.

TantraWorks

www.tantraworks.com

> Links to Tantra information presented by Nik Douglas, author of *Sexual Secrets: The Alchemy of Ecstasy.*

Institute for Ecstatic Living

www.ecstaticliving.com

> Tantra workshops with Steve and Lokita Carter in Cobb, California.

IFC Temple of Divine Love

www.ifc-net.org

> Tantra workshops in the United Kingdom with Sri Param Eswaran.

Kundalini Tantra

www.kundalini-tantra.com

> Lots of Tantra information resources. Free Tantra newsletter.

Making Love—The Art of Tantra

www.love4couples.com/E/home.html

> Tantra workshops with Puja and Raja Richardson in various locations around the world.

Tantra at Tahoe

www.tantraattahoe.com

> Tantra workshops with Jeffre TallTrees and Somraj Pokras in Truckee, California.

Tantra Dance

www.tantradance.com

Tantra massage and sacred dance with Christina Sophia and William Florian, Sebastopol, California.

Tantra in Atlanta

www.tantrainatlanta.com

Tantra workshops in various locations around the world.

Tantra Magic

www.tantramagic.com

Tantra workshops with Swami Maya Pitri bin Tantra in Arvada, Colorado.

The Tantra Center

www.angelfire.com/tn/tantra

Tantra workshops in Australia.

Transcendence—The Tantra Connection

www.martinj.dircon.co.uk

Tantra workshops with Sarita and Geho in Britian.

Ipsalu Tantra

www.tantrikainternational.com

Toll-free in the United States: 1-888-826-8745

Tantra workshops from Tantrika International. Various teachers and locations in the United States.

Oceanic Tantra

www.oceanictantra.com

Tantra workshops with Kutira and Raphael in Kahua, Hawaii.

Skydancing Tantra

www.tantraskydancing.ch/instit.html

Tantra workshops in many countries.

Source School of Tantra

www.sourcetantra.com

Tantra workshops with Charles and Caroline Muir in Wailuku, Hawaii. Free newsletter.

Sacred Space Institute

www.lovewithoutlimits.com

Love Without Limits workshops and retreats with Dr. Deborah Anapol, proponent of polyamory.

Nepal Institute
www.newfrontier.com/nepal
> Tantra workshops with Swami Virato in several states in the U.S. and in Russia. Free newsletter.

Osho's Home Page
osho.org
> Workshops in Pune, India and a range of Osho's products including books and CDs. Osho led a Tantra revival in the East and West over four decades from the 1960s to the 1990s.

Sacred Sex Secrets
www.sacredsexsecrets.com
> Tantra workshops in Vancouver, B. C., Canada with Ishtara.

Human Awareness Institute
www.hai.org
> Workshops on all aspects of relationships, including sexuality, presented in locations around the world.

Gyudmed Tantric University
gyudmed.com
> One of two Tantric universities of the Gelugpa School of Tibetan Buddhism. Founded in 1433 by Je Sherab Sengey, a disciple of Lama Tsongkhapa, founder of the Gelugpa School. This is white (celebate) Tantra. Young monks typically join the monastery at around age 14, and study for the next 15 to 20 years, earning the equivalent of a Tantric Ph.D.

Masturbation Websites
Betty Dodson Online
www.bettydodson.com
> Betty is one of the pioneers promoting liberation masturbation.

Solo
www.solotouch.com/main/main.htm
> Masturbation information for men and women.

Appendix B

List of Exercises and Practices

Chapter Notes

Chapter 1

[1] *The Case for Marriage: Why Married People Are Happier, Healthier and Better Off Financially*. Linda Waite and Maggie Gallagher, Broadway Books, 2000.

[2] "The Inner Life of Americans: Views on Spirituality, Identity, Sexuality, Anxiety and More." *The New York Times Magazine*, National Poll, March 2000.

[3] "Bible Belt Battles High Divorce Rates." *The New York Times*, National Edition, May 21, 2001, by Blaine Harden, *www.nytimes.com/2001/05/21/national/21MARR.html.*

Chapter 2

[1] "Publisher Will Pay Clinton Over $10 Million for Book." David D. Kirkpatrick. *The New York Times*, August 7, 2001. *www.nytimes.com/2001/08/07/business/07BOOK.html?rd=hcmcp?p=03ZkL03Zl147vXf012000mZTwdZTw7*

[2] *Symposium*. Plato. Translation by Benjamin Jowett. 360 BCE.

[3] *The Path of Least Resistance: Learning to Become the Creative Force in Your Own Life*. Robert Fritz. Fawcett Books, 1989.

[4] *Concentration and Meditation: A Manual of Mind Development*. Christmas Humphreys. John M. Watkins, 1953, p. 87.

Chapter 3

[1] *The Enlightened Heart: An Anthology of Sacred Poetry*. Stephen Mitchell (Editor), Harper Perennial Library, 1993, p. 59.

Chapter 4

[1] "Female Genital Mutilation - A Human Rights Information Pack."Amnesty International. *www.amnesty.org/ailib/intcam/femgen/fgm1.htm*.

[2] For fascinating coverage of sex and its relationship to religion throughout the ages we suggest: *Sex in History.* Reay Tannahill, Briarcliff Manor, N.Y.: Scarborough Books, 1982; and *Sex and Spirit.* Clifford Bishop. London, England: Duncan Baird Publishers, 1996.

[3] "Body Pleasure and the Origins of Violence." James W. Prescott. *The Bulletin of Atomic Scientists*, November 1975, pp.10-20.

[4] The American Association of Sex Educators, Counselors and Therapists (AASECT), P.O. Box 5488, Richmond, Virginia, USA 23220-0488, Ph: 804-644-3288, Fax: 804-644-3290, *www.aasect.org*. E-mail: aasect@mediaone.net. AASECT certifies sex educators, sex counselors, and sex therapists in the United States, Mexico, and Canada.

Chapter 5

[1] *The Philokalia, The Complete Text*. St. Nikodimos of the Holy Mountain and St. Makarios of Corinth. Trans. G.E.H. Palmer; Philip Sherrard; and Kallistos Ware. London: Faber and Faber Limited, Vol. 2, 1981, p. 28.

[2] *The Ladder of Divine Ascent*. John Climacus. Trans. Colm Luibheid and Norman Russell. Mahwah, N.J.: Paulist Press, 1982, p. 141.

Chapter 6

[1] *Be Here Now*, Ram Dass. San Cristobel, New Mexico: Lama Foundation, 1974, p. 90.

[2] *The Art of Sexual Ecstasy: The Path of Sacred Sexuality for Western Lovers*. Margo Anand. Los Angeles, Calif.: Jeremy P. Tarcher, Inc., 1989.

[3] *Concentration and Meditation*. Christian Humphries. John M. Watkins Publishers, 1953, p. 72.

[4] *Ordinary Women Extraordinary Sex: Every Woman's Guide To Pleasure and Beyond.* Dr. Sandra Scantling and Sue Browder. Penguin Books-Dutton, 1993. (The authors of this book use the term "absorption" in the same way we use immersion.)

Chapter 7

[1] *Worlds In Collision.* Immanuel Velikovsky. Abacus Edition, 1972, p.105.

[2] "The 9 Systems of Yoga or Phases," Swami Harinanda. *www.real-yoga.com/9.yoga.*

[3] *The Lover Within: Opening to Energy in Sexual Practice.* Julie Henderson, Station Hill-Barrytown Ltd., 1999.

[4] This exercise is on Pala's CD, *Apertio: Tantra Energy Meditations.* Lyrics and voice by Pala Copeland, music by Jeff Davies, 2000.

[5] Quoted in *The Enlightened Heart: An Anthology of Sacred Poetry.* Stephen Mitchell (Editor). Harper Perennial Library, 1993, pp. 24-25.

Chapter 8

[1] Safe Sense Condoms. *www.condoms.net/?SP=SP1558&TO=condoms/index.html*

[2] *The Matrix*, 1999. Directed by Andy and Larry Wachowski.

[3] *Sex for One: The Joy of Selfloving.* Betty Dodson. New York: Three Rivers Press, 1996, p. 3

[4] "Viagra: Is The Stampede Misdirected?" Will Block, *Life Enhancement*, June 1998, p. 31.

Chapter 9

[1] Here are three references with the results of this research on female ejaculation. 1) "Female ejaculation: A case study." Addiego, F., Belzer, E.G., Comolli, J., Moger, W., Perry, J.D., and Whipple, B. *The Journal of Sex Research*, 17, 1981, pp. 13-21. 2) "On female ejaculation." Belzer, E., Whipple, B., and Moger, W. *The Journal of Sex Research,* 20, 1984, pp. 403-406. 3) "Update on the female prostate and the phenomenon of female ejaculation." Zaviacic, M., & Whipple, B. *Journal of Sex Research*, 30(2), 1993, pp. 148-151.

Chapter 10

[1] *The Spiral Dance: A Rebirth of the Ancient Religion of the Great Goddess.* Starhawk, New York: HarperCollins, 1999.

[2] *Sexual Secrets: The Alchemy of Ecstasy.* Nik Douglas and Penny Slinger. Destiny Books, 1979, pp. 248-9.

Chapter 11

[1] Touch Research Institutes. *www.miami.edu/touch-research*

[2] "Do Touch: The benefits of skin on skin go deeper than feeling good." Elizabeth Larson, Utne Reader, Issue #86.

[3] *Acupressure for Lovers: Secrets of Touch for Increasing Intimacy.* Michael Reed Gach, Ph.D. Bantam Books, 1997.

Index

About the Authors

Pala and Al have been practicing Tantra since 1987 and teaching since 1997. Hundreds of couples from all over the world have attended their Tantra weekends because of the emphasis on Tantra in the context of a hot, monogamous relationship. They have been featured in magazines, newspapers, radio, and TV talk shows in Canada and the United States.

They live near Ottawa, Canada and have six children and three grandchildren between them. Pala has also produced Apertio: Tantra Energy Meditations, a best selling CD on *Amazon.com* since publication in 2000.